WOMEN AND EDUCAT

Women and Education, 1800–1980

Jane Martin and Joyce Goodman

First published 2004 by
PALGRAVE MACMILLAN
Houndmills, Basingstoke, Hampshire RG21 6XS and
175 Fifth Avenue, New York, N.Y. 10010
Companies and representatives throughout the world

PALGRAVE MACMILLAN is the global academic imprint of the Palgrave
Macmillan division of St. Martin's Press, LLC and of Palgrave Macmillan Ltd.
Macmillan® is a registered trademark in the United States, United Kingdom
and other countries. Palgrave is a registered trademark in the European
Union and other countries.

ISBN 0–333–94721–5 hardback
ISBN 0–333–94722–3 paperback

This book is printed on paper suitable for recycling and made from fully
managed and sustained forest sources.

A catalogue record for this book is available from the British Library.

Library of Congress Cataloging-in-Publication Data
    Martin, Jane, 1959–
    Women and education, 1800–1980 / Jane Martin and Joyce Goodman.
        p. cm.
    Includes bibliographical references and index.
    ISBN 0–333–94721–5 (cloth)—ISBN 0–333–94722–3 (pbk.)
        1. Women in education—Great Britain—History—19th century.
    2. Women in education—Great Britain—History—20th century. 3. Women
    educators—Great Britain—Biography. I. Goodman, Joyce, 1946–   II. Title.

LC2042.M37 2003
370′.82′0941—dc21   2003051442

10   9   8   7   6   5   4   3   2   1
13 12 11 10 09 08 07 06 05 04

Printed in China

Contents

Acknowledgements

This book began life in the history of education network within the European Educational Research Association. Travelling together to the annual conference in Lahti, Finland, 1999, we pooled ideas and hammered out themes for this joint project. We are grateful to numerous people for many reasons, for example for enjoyable and useful discussions on joint interests and although we can't name everyone thank you. We also want to thank each other!

Most of all, Jane owes a special debt of gratitude to the late Brian Simon and his wife, Joan, for their warm support, advice and encouragement during the research on Shena Simon. They were unfailingly helpful and memorably hospitable at all times. Brian read and commented on Chapter 6 in this book offering sound advice and thoughtful discussion. Jane would also like to thank Christina Hughes for her friendship, warm support and encouragement over the long term. She also read and commented on parts of the book. During the research Jane worked at University College Northampton and London Metropolitan University and would like to thank both institutions for their material support and her colleagues within them for friendship and discussions. Special thanks go to Elizabeth Burn and Chris Richards for useful suggestions on Chapter 4. There is also a debt of gratitude to the staff at the following libraries and archives: Girton College, the London School of Economics, Manchester Central Reference Library, London Metropolitan Archive, Newnham College, the North London Collegiate School, and the TUC Library Collection at London Metropolitan University. Last, but not least, Jane wants to thank her husband, Paul, who has been unstinting in his support.

Joyce wishes to thank King Alfred's College for the support that made much of this research possible, particularly the small scale research grant that facilitated research in the Cheshire Record Office on the Sandlebridge archive and the travel grants that enabled earlier versions of the work on Elizabeth Hamilton and Sarah Austin to be presented at ANZHES in Auckland and Melbourne. A number of people have been particularly encouraging: Kay Morris-Matthews, whose commitment to the history of women's education is inspiring, Marjorie Theobald, who pointed out that Hamilton's complete works had reached Australian libraries, Annemieke van Drenth for sharing her early work in the gendered history of special education, Ruth Watts, whose question about the compatibility of Dendy's hereditarian views with earlier Unitarian thinking framed the argument of one chapter and Bridget Egan, who read and commented in a critically supportive way over a number of years on earlier versions of Hamilton, Austin and Dendy. Thanks are due to librarians and archivists at the Cheshire Record Office, Melbourne University archives and to Liz Fletcher in King Alfred's Library, whose help in tracking down articles and books at busy moments was invaluable. Particular thanks must also be given to the East Cheshire National Health Care Trust for granting permission to view the closed records of the Mary Dendy Hospital, Great Warford, Alderley Edge, Cheshire and to Dr John Dendy for help in the fruitless quest to track down Mary Dendy's diary. While the book was in press, Lily Rusby, Joyce's much loved aunt died. Joyce would like to acknowledge her debt of gratitude to Lily, whose stories were important to the development of her ideas about women's education, employment and family lives.

Introduction: Changing Lives? Women, Educational Reform and Personal Identities, 1800–1980

In 1873, 38-year-old Jane Agnes Chessar was elected to serve on the new single-purpose educational authority called the London School Board. She had already won for herself considerable standing in the metropolis, where she spent most of her adult life, and was returned with the support of some among the leadership of the nineteenth-century women's movement. Her successful election illustrates the tenacity of the social relationships that underlay feminist organizations due to her close connections with the Langham Place group, established in the 1850s and named after its cultural centre in London's West End. Employment in teacher education meant she shared professional concerns with the headmistress, Frances Buss, and with Emily Davies, the founder of Girton College, Cambridge, who were both equally dedicated to the foundation of new educational opportunities for women. Emily Davies was a very close friend of the pioneer doctor, Elizabeth Garrett, another prominent member of the Langham Place Circle. This forum served as a conduit for political patronage in the school board division of Marylebone, where Jane Chessar took over the Garrett seat. Jane was forced to retire from public life on grounds of ill-health but continued to demonstrate a political will and strength of purpose in her approach to education. The circumstances surrounding her death tell their own story. In August 1880, Jane Chessar and Frances Buss travelled to Brussels for an educational congress. Jane was never to return. She died there of cerebral apoplexy less than a month later.

All but written out of history, Jane Chessar was an educated woman who had both a career and a fulfilling personal life. She questioned the dominant discourses of her time by crossing the line between the public and private spheres: turning her back on traditional sources of identity, such as wifehood and motherhood, and

1

defining herself in terms of her profession. Her highly visible location as a member of the London School Board prompted much speculation, focus and interest regarding the impact of the female presence and her story highlights the dilemmas that women face in educational leadership. Female leaders complicate and partly contradict the general connection of authority with masculinity. This association remains relatively intact in the field of educational leadership, where the voices and actions of female leaders are often confined to patrolling the margins, ubiquitous but largely unrecorded. Indeed, you could be forgiven if you failed to question the presumption of male domination over women and unequal power relations that characterize the gendering of educational work in orthodox accounts. All too frequently, it seemed women were only present as 'victims' of educational gender differentiation: the principle of male-as-norm positioned the female pupil as the 'Other'; discourses of masculinity and femininity positioned the waged female worker as teacher, rather than leader.

Beginning in the late 1980s, we have collected data on British women educators, feminists and leaders in the period 1800–1980. We were motivated by the absence of women in orthodox accounts of British education generally, as well as the exemplar of feminist revisionism. To read Carol Dyhouse's *Girls Growing Up in Late Victorian and Edwardian England*, first published in 1981, was inspirational, moving issues of gender from the margins to the centre without losing sight of the interacting dynamics of social class. Dyhouse's primary focus is on *experiences* of growing up, but she also pursues the links between feminism and girls' education through the period studied. In so doing, she discusses the contribution of leading female educationists in the development of state schooling and the new girls' high schools and university colleges for women. This whole process of revision throws doubt upon the orthodoxy that neglects the role women have played as political actors in the establishment of state education. It amply illustrates the exceptional woman who penetrates particular powerful groups of white, male elites. Patricia Hollis's *Ladies Elect. Women in English Local Government, 1865–1914* (1987) has become a classic, and a few other histories focus upon the gender/power relations in educational administration (Turnbull, 1983; Dyhouse, 1987; Hunt, 1991; Martin, 1999; Goodman and Harrop, 2000). While not discounting the centrality and influence of class in this context, feminist scholarship has served to illuminate and explicate gender differentials and inequalities and this is crucial in appraising the possibilities for women to make a difference as educators, feminists and leaders.

Our particular focus in this book is the relationship between aims, visions and actions. However, the danger with any deterministic assumptions of women's potential to constitute and exert a counter-hegemony lies in their essentialist presumption of 'sameness' amongst politically aware women (Blackmore, 1999). Given this, we seek to explore how individual women expanded their opportunities and the problems and dilemmas they faced. In the process, we show ways in which they worked through personal and political tensions, as they negotiated the political and gendered machinations of public life. How did they make sense of their lives, experiences and activities? How did this relate to their educational philosophies? What were (and are) the tensions inherent in women trying to act as change agents? These are the key questions that inform the selection of the lesser-known educators who form the focus of our narrative. Our concern is not with the lives of 'women worthies', nor do we wish to substitute alternative female heroines. In writing this study, our starting point was a joint interest in the culture and social relationships that underlay the struggles to gain greater access for women to the public world of education. We adopt a collective biographical approach in order to appraise the social significance of our subjects' achievements. We do not start from the premise that the women we have identified are of interest because their differences from other women made them exceptional among their sex. Rather, we seek to know not just what they did, but how they managed to do it within the familial and social constraints to which, as women, they were subject. Consequently, we delve into their identities and motives to examine how they negotiated what are generally understood to be the common patterns of womanhood to explore the links between gendered practices and discourses and personal action at particular historical moments.

The chronological structure of this book evolved in response to these considerations. We tell the stories of six women whose participation in the politics of education is little known: Elizabeth Hamilton (1785–1816), Sarah Austin (1793–1867), Jane Agnes Chessar (1835–80), Mary Dendy (1855–1933), Shena D. Simon (1883–1980) and Margaret Cole (1893–1980). Combined, their highly influential activities span almost the whole of the nineteenth and twentieth centuries. In the first instance, the choice of women simply reflects our sense of a major gap presently in the literature on educational policy debates over the last two hundred years, and the role of women within it. We set out, too, with a particular approach to the use of case studies stemming from our interest in exploring the personal, political perspective which is an integral part of feminist analysis. Our selection was motivated by a desire to use individual life stories to simultaneously inform the reader of a number of lesser-known figures and explore the ways particular personalities negotiate the complex interaction between the public/private divide and associated roles. The dilemmas that the women educators in this book faced are seen in relation to wider social and cultural change over two centuries.

One of our primary goals is to re-map understanding of women's participation in changing philosophy, policy and practice in education. In their own particular spheres, the influence of Hamilton, Austin, Chessar, Dendy, Simon and Cole was pervasive and far from inconsequential. All the subjects of this study recognized education as an important feature of social progress and projected their belief that social policy should be designed to reinforce these aspirations. Together, they see education as part of an emancipatory project. Individually, they define it in different ways, in different contexts, with different outcomes. As a consequence, their reconstructed stories demonstrate both sameness and difference. On the one hand, there are the macrostructural factors positioning them within the gender category of 'women' in history. On the other, there is the championing of alternate possibilities for education and their strong sensibility about the mass provision of education and the complexities of the relation between theory and practice. We wanted to explore the culture and the social relationships which underlay their particular educational philosophy or commitment. We wanted to know how Hamilton, Austin, Chessar, Dendy, Simon and Cole created empowering identities and how they became educators, feminists and leaders. We consider how they experienced the girlhood and womanhood of the time. Studying a relatively homogenous group of white, middle-class, female educators enabled us to expand our knowledge of how particular women widened their horizons, their different strategic approaches and effects, as well as their capacity and desire to act as change agents. By locating their lives within the networks of relatives, friends, mentors, or associates we examine the extent to which social conventions could, or could not, be negotiated, or modified, by particular individuals. This raises the possibilities of producing a transformative historical account: one that will seek to show what was typical and what was exceptional about the historical experience of these particular personalities. In so doing, we pose a number of questions. What did they achieve and how? How did they react to the dominant masculine culture of public affairs? Did they rebel against the gendered organizational culture? Did they challenge the *status quo*? If so, to what extent did they rattle the patriarchal cage?

The lives of Hamilton, Austin, Chessar, Dendy, Simon and Cole, their interests, attitudes and actions, their respective roles as educationists, all these have been accessible through sources of various kinds. These include the published writings of Elizabeth Hamilton and Sarah Austin and nineteenth-century published memoirs and correspondences of both women (Benger, 1818; Ross, 1888). In Hamilton's case, with the exception of Rendall (1985) and Russell (1986), subsequent discussion has largely focused on her relationship to feminism, literature, orientalism and national identities (Kelly, 1993; Rendall, 1996). The Hamburgers' (1985) intellectual biography of Sarah Austin tends to subordinate Sarah's ideas to those of her husband, while their account of her 'literary' affair with Count Pückler-Muskau (1991) underplays her intellectual accomplishments. Sarah Richardson's more recent work has begun to redress this balance (Richardson, 2000). Mark Jackson's (2000) scholarly study of Mary Dendy and her work for the Sandlebridge Schools was published at the time of this research. The chief sources for the chapter here on Dendy were McLachlan's (1935) account of the Dendy/Beard family, plus the official records of Sandlebridge and Dendy's career, her evidence to the Royal Commission on the Care and Control of the Feeble-minded (1908) and her published writings. Material in the Melbourne University archives pertaining to the work of Arthur Dendy was also consulted. The diary on which McLachlan drew his account proved illusive to trace, despite the help of Mary Dendy's family. The chapter on Shena Simon makes full use of manuscript material by Joan Simon (1986) and the political papers deposited in the Manchester Central Reference Library. Material on Margaret Cole's life is to be found in her memoirs, her letters, her publications and Betty Vernon's comprehensive biography (1986). Jane Chessar is the only educationist discussed here who left very little first-hand testimony. Her story has been constructed through the official records of the London School Board, correspondence and electoral materials in the collection of papers left by Emily Davies, and by the representations which others made of her in their letters, memoirs and reminiscences, and press reports.

The politics of historical survival imposes possibilities and limitations on the telling of these women's stories and perspectives, but we seek to analyse the tensions facing women in positions of power and authority. We use a case study approach to focus on similarities *and* differences. It is the focus on the playing out of contradictions that make the book cohere as a whole rather than as a collection of individual biographies. We present a group of women who were working within a system that was not of their own making and who placed under tension the seemingly natural association of rationality, masculinity and educational leadership. Consequently, they frequently needed to reconcile the separate components of their lives, motivations and expectations. Each of the chapters in this volume trace the particular tensions this engendered: contradictions surrounding the public/private divide as also the personal/political; the dilemma of the powerful/powerless; notions of care and control; the relation between local/national in politics; the tensions within languages of feminism; and the radical and conservative aspects of women's friendship networks. These, then, provide a framework within which to explore the contradictions played out in the lives of individual women and for identifying patterns among the group as a whole.

Chapter 1 presents an overview of key texts on auto/biography. It provides an insight into why biographical research offers a particularly appropriate vehicle for exploring the lived connections between personal and political worlds, while acknowledging the selective and interpretive nature of the biographer's role. A discussion of network analysis and recent theoretical debate on the concept 'woman', the state, citizenship, national identity and professionalism establishes a framework for exploring the meaning of six female lives in education. The introduction and chapters 1 and 8 were written collaboratively; chapters 4, 6 and 7 by Jane Martin; and chapters 2, 3 and 5 by Joyce Goodman.

1
Individual Lives and Social Histories

There is that marvellous, perpetually renewed and as yet largely untapped aid to the understanding of human motives, which is provided by biography and autobiography.

(Virginia Woolf, 1986, p. 9)

Recent decades have seen a burgeoning literature of feminist autobiography and biography stimulated, in part, by the level of enthusiasm for the recovery of 'ordinary lives' hitherto under-represented. There has also been a shift in the conventions of story-telling and autobiography. However, these are not phenomena of recent times. Some of the new directions in biographical research recall the discourse of the 'new biography' in early twentieth-century Britain. Discussing Virginia Woolf's *Orlando*, published in 1928, Laura Marcus (1994) notes the way in which Woolf expressed the desire to write outside the linguistic conventions of popular narrative forms as a primary means of personal expression. Born in 1882, Woolf was the daughter of a professional writer. Coming from the articulate, professional, liberal, middle class, she inhabited a particular social space associated with intellectual and cultural development. A male family tradition of literary autobiography extended back seven decades. Her great-grandfather wrote his memoirs for the 'use of his children' (Anderson, 2001, p. 92). Helping to assemble the nation's cultural inheritance in *The Dictionary of National Biography* was one of the principal steps on the path to canonization as biographer by his contemporaries, for her father, Sir Leslie Stephen. With this legacy it is perhaps not surprising that she should advocate autobiography as method.

During the 1920s and 1930s Woolf's arguments about women's exclusion from educational and cultural institutions appealed to many feminists, including Shena Simon (J. Simon, 1986; Caine, 1997).

In *Three Guineas* (1938) Woolf wrote about education, exclusion and war. Various claims have been made for *Three Guineas* and *A Room of One's Own* (1929) as her 'true autobiography' (Stanley, 1992, p. 248). Both works are concerned with Woolf's struggles as a woman writer to find a voice – something connected to her personal struggle for self-definition. Awkwardly situated within the family lineage of autobiographical writing, Woolf's problem is to find a place in cultural production and male literary traditions. Within the milieu of London's Bloomsbury in the 1900s, she coined the term the 'new biography' to exemplify a critical stance towards the taken-for-granted assumptions of Victorian biography and by implication the assumptions about biography held by her father. She rejected essentialism (the belief that there are basic characteristics that all people share), realism and the referentiality of 'traditional, conservative "Great Men" approaches to lives, literature and history' (Marcus, 1994, p. 92). In the face of this dilemma, Woolf develops several strategies, both personal and artistic. She tries to problematize and destabilize autobiography as cultural practice and to place ambiguities of gender and genre under scrutiny. In *Orlando* she explores the margins of fact and fiction with her choice of subject based on a living individual – her friend/lover Vita Sackville-West. She subverts the logic of conventional biography to propose alternate time scales and alternate endings since Orlando is alive during the 300 years of text-time. Finally, her hero-turned-heroine transgresses gender borders and boundaries as s/he lives first as a man and then as a woman. Although *Orlando* is a fantasy Marcus observes that it opens up the 'conditions and limits' of the biographical paradigm (1994, p. 131). In so doing, a kind of intellectual spotlight is trained on the boundary between autobiography and biography, closely linked with the oppositions between self and world, private and public, subjectivity and objectivity, and subject/object.

It is the purpose of this chapter to reflect on the place of the personal in academic study and research in the field of education. This reflection starts from support of C. Wright Mills's vision of the 'sociological imagination that enables us to grasp history and biography and the relations between the two within society' (1970, p. 12). Biographical approaches can help us to ask questions about the gaps in the historical record and to explore the experience of 'hidden' individuals and groups. Feminism has encouraged attention to gender in the writing of educational history. Recognition that the personal is political grew out of the Women's Liberation movement in the early 1970s particularly the practice of consciousness-raising to pool the collective experience of women and help them understand their own lives and feelings. In this sense, there exists a history of praxis: not just a concern to describe the world differently, but something to hope and struggle for. Feminist re-conceptualizations of history were crucial to the Women's Liberation movement and the feminist education project included a clear sense of the past. Besides tracing the development of formal rights, formal access and opportunity for girls and women, scholars extended an existing interest in the ways schools reproduced social forms to include gendered patterns as well as class processes. From the mid-1970s, there was an increasing emphasis on the importance of gender as an historical category; and in the last fifteen years or so, there have been attempts to articulate the personal and the theoretical together. Put another way, the notion of what Nancy Miller has called 'the authority of experience' made it possible to see that 'the personal is part of theory's material' (1991, pp. 14, 21). To the extent that one of the original premises of the 1970s feminism was a concern with making women visible, it is perhaps not surprising that the interaction of personal and historical pasts has become a staple of feminist scholarship.

Taking up the story of feminist engagements with biographical research methods and biographical theory, Alison Prentice suggests that 'perhaps only in the lives of single individuals is it possible to glimpse the complexity of motivation and experience that make up human history' (1999, p. 37). Greater consciousness of how people make themselves through the act of writing and of what people do with history, draws out the ways in which feminist scholars, and history as a discipline, have engaged with debates about poststructuralism. Poststructuralism represents a rejection of the fundamental assumptions of modernism, including the idea that there can be an ultimate truth that offers a way of understanding the entire social world. The rejection of grand theories, or 'meta-narratives', also heightened awareness of the pitfalls of generalist history. In feminist theory, the shift from 'woman' to 'women', with increasing attention to difference prompted scholars to question the application of patriarchy as a way of understanding the predicament of women in terms of one all-embracing principle. Greater recognition that the term 'gender' includes men as well as women was accompanied by a concern to infuse the concept with historicity by carefully delineating different time periods (Martin, 1999). This led to much discussion of a number of important themes. In particular, we have seen debates about the discursive constitution of concepts of selfhood and identity alongside the newer interest in performativity (Butler, 1999). For instance, while Kathleen Weiler (1999) does not explicitly locate her work as poststructuralist, she comments that three key concepts have come to shape her own reading and approach to 'telling women's lives': knowledge, language and subjectivity.

The question of what counts as historical knowledge touches on the epistemological limits to history, including the nature of the evidence about the past and the kind of truth claims that can be made about it. Poststructural feminists, such as Denise Riley (1988) and Joan Scott (1992), have proposed the value and importance of a history grounded in close attention to language and the category of experience itself. They both exemplify a style of questioning and rethinking of historical records that is likely to privilege the deconstructive. For them, it is no longer possible to embark on an unproblematic search for the real woman. Instead, they seek the performative qualities of discourse(s) – a set of images, meanings, metaphors, representations, statements and so on – that together produce a particular way of seeing the constructed subject. Riley argues for the 'inherent shakiness of the designation "women" which exists prior to both its revolutionary and conservative deployments' (1988, p. 98). However, Weiler cautions against 'slighting other kinds of evidence and failing to raise questions other than those of the workings of language' (1999, pp. 45–6). Although sensitive to the linguistic turn, like Linda Gordon, she retains a concern with understanding the material past. As Gordon points out, differing approaches to writing history have implications for the meanings of gender:

> Scott's determinist position emphasizes gender as 'difference', marked by the otherness and absolute silencing of women. I use gender to describe a power system in which women are subordinated through relations that are contradictory, ambiguous and conflictual – a subordination maintained against resistance, in which women have not always defined themselves as other, in which women face and take choices and action despite constriction (Gordon, 1990, p. 852).

Weiler shows how reflection on the usefulness of a range of positions helped create a framework for interpreting her fine-grained, empirical study of rural women teachers in California. The written and oral accounts of these schoolteachers illuminate how lives and experiences are shaped by material forces, even though the various ways of categorizing and understanding the self may be mediated through the workings of language. A recognition of the practices of self-invention is captured by the term subjectivity, to imply the constructed quality of memory and experience. It includes the struggle and contest over identity; the process of identification and an unstable shifting subject constructed through dominant conceptions and resistance to those conceptions. For Weiler: 'the construction of gendered subjectivities through discourse, the contradictions of our various ways of categorizing and understanding what happens in our lives and who we are, naming ourselves, becomes the point of entry for historical analysis' (1999, p. 47).

The emphasis on the historical creation of women's public voices is an important methodological premise of feminist research. But what does the emphasis on subjectivity mean for women who have been silenced? How do we find the 'subject in the archive'? It is difficult to escape the implications of this for our approach to notions of 'selves' and 'lives'. Using feminist lenses, we explore the strains of being a woman exercising authority, leading and managing in education at a particular time in a particular culture. The personal, political perspective is an integral part of feminist analysis and Jane Ribbens (1993, p. 83) makes the point that biographical research offers a particularly appropriate vehicle for exploring 'the links between "private" and "public" knowledges and ways of knowing'. Critical reflections allow the possibility of analysing how women learn to act in masculine environments. The value of a biographical approach lies precisely in its potential to expand our understanding of the way in which people deal with their dissonance. In this book, we are interested in the processes of subject formation and identity; and we share a relational understanding of difference in which 'Otherness' is not an oppositional category. Instead, there is an emphasis on specificity, variation and heterogeneity. We interweave the biographical with the theoretical as we focus on the experiences of early women 'pioneers' who crossed the gender line and took on public roles. Finding themselves as outsiders in a masculinized cultural sphere, they may appear to be complicit in, and colluding with, some dominant discourses, while at the same time accommodating and challenging from both within and without. While the concept of knowledge and power residing within discourses is of key importance, Sue Clegg (1997) is right to insist that discourses about women are not identical with their oppression. As she says: 'Social structures endure and act to constrain as well as enable historical action and only a history grounded in a realist ontology can hope to elucidate the mechanisms of oppression' (p. 207). This points to a need for a model that combines a route for unravelling identity with the potential to deal with the dilemma identified by Clegg.

The central issue is the problem of trying to hold together what Heywood and Mac an Ghaill (1997) 'identify as materialist and deconstructionist identity epistemologies' (p. 263). The metaphor of a web, which philosopher Morwenna Griffths (1995) places at the centre of her account of how women are socially produced, is useful in this regard. The metaphor of a web allows for the notion of female agency (as the individual spins her own web), but not in circumstances of her own making. It is used to make the unfamiliar understandable by describing the construction of social identities as if it were analogous to a familiar process. The notion of invisible bonds provides a powerful image of the structural properties of social relations and a means of considering social practice as it relates to gender relations within and between immediate situations and organizing structures. Bob Connell refers to this as *gender projects*, which he defines as:

> Processes of configuring practice through time, which transform their starting-points in gender structures…We find the gender configuring of practice however we slice the social world, whatever unit of analysis we choose. The most familiar is the individual life-course, the basis of the common-sense notions of masculinity and femininity (Connell, 1995, p. 72).

In an earlier discussion of gender and power, Connell (1987) uses the terms gender order and gender regime to demonstrate the links between historically constructed social, cultural and institutional patterns of power relations between men and women and definitions of femininity and masculinity. As such, the complex association between structure and agency in individual lives is contingent upon the way in which the macropolitics of the *gender order* (as a collective core) shape social practice within any given *gender regime* (familial or institutional).

We have found it productive to hold onto this theoretical frame-work when analysing how women negotiate a space for themselves in the public world, given the opportunity. We have concentrated on patterns of connection in small groups and multiple meanings and subjective understandings of self and others in time and place. The collective biographical approach of the book helps to highlight how these operate across generations and across and within the domains of the private and the public. We use the concept of intersubjectivity to encompass ways in which all selves are structured by interactions with others, and to highlight a more general attention to ways in which the self is framed and created by the social. This implies that the narration of a life or self can never be confined to a single, isolated subjecthood.

Auto/biography and Situated Knowledges

Our work is informed by Liz Stanley's writing on biographical research methods and biographical theory. The intertextuality of biography and autobiography has been expressed by Stanley (1992) through the term 'the auto/biographical I'. The term auto/biography indicates that the divisions between biography and autobiography are seen as inextricably intermeshed and so can-not be considered separately. The 'I' denotes the active, inquiring presence of researchers in constructing, rather than 'discovering' knowledge. According to Stanley (1991, p. 214) necessary features of auto/biography include a textual recognition of the importance of the labour process of the researcher/theoretician and 'an insistence that works of auto/biography should be treated as textually-located ideological practices'. It is the burden of Stanley's argument that to produce what she calls 'accountable' knowledge the researcher must make clear his, or her, own 'intellectual biography'. The purpose is to give the reader access to the value commitments, stylistic and political preferences which design and colour 'the findings', the outcomes. As Stanley puts it:

> Here the boundaries of self and other, biography and autobio-graphy, fact and fiction, fantasy and reality, are traversed and shown to be by no means as distinct as is conventionally supposed; and these 'opposites' not only coexist but intermingle in ways that encourage, not merely permit, active readership (Stanley, 1991, p. 206).

Feminist auto/biography challenges the idea that we can split the production of new knowledge from the experience and/or standpoint of the researcher. It refuses the binary between epistemology and ontology, between conceptions of social reality and how to study it. In terms of data collection and analysis, the approach of auto/biography proposes that: 'The writer/speaker, the researcher and author, are certainly not treated as transparent or "dead", but very much alive as agents actively at work in the textual production process' (Auto/Biography Study Group joining leaflet, 1995, quoted in Stanley, 2000, p. 41). The outstanding merit of the auto/biographical mode lies in the capacity to give agency and voice to those who have been neglected by history. Fresh light is thrown on the move to reclaim agency and subjectivity and the interplay of different voices unravels a representation of the past as a complex and elusive terrain.

Yet methodological and conceptual dilemmas present themselves to the would-be feminist biographer/historian. One dilemma is that auto/biographical texts cannot be accepted at face value. This is of immediate interest to those of us involved in the study of female auto/biography as 'act' and as a specific type of narrative. We are faced with complex issues of interpretation that demand some understanding of the macropolitics of gender in given historical periods, since there is an interplay between what is unique in a personal trajectory and what is held in common with the experience of others from comparable social origins. A second dilemma touches on the conceptual distinctions of fact and fiction, fiction and history. The idea that these texts can provide facts has been brought into question. If they cannot be read as an 'accurate narrative of the past', the spotlight moves to the construction and negotiation of accounts (Weiner, 2000). Meaning making practices become important, with the potential to create a space for women's culture and history.

All of this makes biographical research a particularly appropriate frame for historians wishing to disrupt the linear trajectories of progress typical of the earlier accounts of women's experience in education (Burstyn, 1976). Biographical research is responsive to critiques from feminist scholarship and insights from women's and gender history that have disrupted grand narratives of education's past that consistently privileged the ideas and activities of men. Our study is located within the literature concerned to outline a women's educational tradition, exemplified by the collection edited by Mary Hilton and Pam Hirsch (2000). In our narrative, the trope of the 'heroic fairy tale' of pioneer women defying the odds is reconstructed as a reflexive interpretation of women's lives in educational contexts (Goodman and Martin, 2000a). Sari Knopp Biklen (1993) acknowledges her intellectual dilemmas as a feminist researcher of teachers as she reflects on the cultural visibility of women teachers and the criteria against which they were assessed as lacking. The heroic metaphor is an important facet of this judgement. While this may help to affirm the careers of the women she profiles, there are disadvantages as well:

> First, discourses of the heroic are deeply gendered. The hero is entrepreneurial, individualistic, free to travel, works with little sleep. Lines between public and private life blur. Heroes are single-minded. So, the heroic life takes over, and a family life is possible (unless the hero is single) only if someone else can undertake childcare responsibilities. Also, men's and women's activities are labeled 'heroic' for different reasons: men's when they are active and accomplish something, women's when they are able to accept and survive harsh realities. Women can become heroes just by defying the odds (Biklen, 1993, p. 11).

How useful is the heroic metaphor in understanding the small band of women in this book? What is the value of the comparison? Like many women teachers, education expanded their futures. Unlike women teachers, they have suffered from cultural invisibility – their experiences and their histories have been silenced. We aim to create 'noise' around our subjects. So, we widen the interest in auto/biography beyond the textual.

In so doing, we also make auto/biographical practices the object of study. That is, the 'way in which, across a range of social and cultural practices – public and private – individuals are compelled to display self-knowledge through the creation and presentation of stories about the self' (Cosslett *et al.*, 2000, p. 1). Carolyn Steedman (2000) illustrates the long tradition of enforced stories elicited from the poor by the administrative state under settlement and bastardy examinations and by philanthropic societies in return for dole (p. 30). In their account of what had brought them to this circumstance, the poor recounted their lives from a fixed standpoint, told in chronological order. Such stories demonstrate clearly that auto/biography is not a 'straightforward telling of the self' and not the same thing as 'the life lived' (p. 36). The auto/biographical injunction, embedded in and performed through ordinary, routinized social encounters, is: 'a history of expectations, order and instructions, rather than one of urges and desires' (p. 28).

Steedman questions the expropriation of the narratives of the poor by others in different classes and circumstances 'Who tells the story of the Self? Who does it most at one time, in one place? Who uses these stories? How are they used, and to what ends?' (ibid.). Auto/biographical 'moments', occurring in everyday social practices, are part of a process through which 'knowledge about lives is made, exchanged and remade' as organizational as well as interpersonal hierarchies 'trade' in a 'currency of spoken, written and visual lives' (Stanley, 2000, p. 42). Auto/biographical practices are highly political processes saturated by power relations. Eliciting 'stories', then, constitutes practices of authority. Both Steedman and Stanley highlight the need to pay close attention to the social organization in which the speaking and writing and picturing of 'selves' takes place. But Stanley argues that a notion of interiority, regulated and produced through exteriorities, does not necessarily denote a deterministic view of 'made-selves'; for the idea of auto/biographical practices positions 'selves' neither in terms of inner processes, nor in terms of disembodied discursive practices but in the complex 'in-between':

> This analytic tack sees women as agents who are the subjects of their own lives and who are (potentially, actually) performers in organisational encounters by working with, around and through 'women's made-selves' rather than as selves resulting from confessional impulses, which are perhaps 'self-made-women' but have no agentive control in relation to the terms, conditions and methods of this making (Stanley, 2000, p. 57).

Professions, Communities, Citizenship and the State

Steedman has discussed how 'the modern study of biography as a literary and historical form has highlighted its tendency to elevate the life of an exceptional individual above the life of an unexceptional' (1990, p. 10). Steedman's claim highlights ways in which auto/biography and the professional have historically existed in symbiotic relationship. Biographies of 'great men' have valorized the 'professional' in terms of masculinist definitions of professions

(Corbett, 1992). In his *Essays on the Study and Composition of Biography* (1813) James Field Stanfield argued that professional biography should focus on individuals who pursued a regular vocation, had a sense of purpose and were successful in the pursuit of their career: 'or who, at least have evidently proceeded in a systematic way towards accomplishment of a purpose' (Stansfield, 1813, quoted in Marcus, 1994, p. 100). In such accounts, 'the plotting of the life-course becomes inseparable from the life structures specific to bourgeois masculinity' (Marcus, 1994, p. 26). Stansfield's view of a career, as an upward movement through a hierarchy, and in terms of a commitment demonstrated by a lack of interruption (Shakeshaft, 1989), exemplifies Biklen's (1985) argument that historians and auto/biographers have recorded as 'career' and as 'profession' the historical actions of men. As Shakeshaft notes, this androcentric bias has limited our ability to illuminate the professional lives of women. 'For many women, the climb to the top of the mountain is not even desirable – they would much rather gather around the valleys and rivers, "where life is really lived"' (Shakeshaft, 1989, p. 65).

Stansfield's theme of professional accomplishment and ambition also implies a self-assertion and self-display at variance with historically constructed views of femininity (Heilbrun, 1989). Spacks (1980) notes the tendency for prominent women with significant accomplishments to mute their success by depicting themselves as having been called by God or Christ to service. Women's professions often kept a religious air – teaching, for example was represented as a special vocation of the select, spiritually gifted minority (Copelman, 1996) – and young professional women had a strong sense of mission, of being pioneers and furthering opportunities for others (McKinnon, 1997, p. 27). Women's 'spiritual call' authorized an achievement and accomplishment otherwise inexcusable in a female self. The literary genre of spiritual autobiography provided a means in which the auto/biographical 'self' could be linked to identification with an 'other'. For some women the reworked genre of spiritual biography was one way of representing the ambiguities of professional life. For others, it provided a language with which to depict 'conversion' to causes like socialism. But even when identity was grounded through relation to a chosen 'other', women have tended not to represent themselves as entitled to credit for their own accomplishment, whether these have been depicted in spiritual terms or not (Mason, 1980). Heilbrun (1989) notes the difficulties for women well into the twentieth century of admitting into their autobiographical narratives the claim of achievement, the admission of ambition, and the recognition that accomplishment was neither luck, nor the result of the efforts, or generosity, of others (p. 24).

The relation of biographical description to theoretical discussion has tended to portray the rise of the 'learned professions', with their accent on training and certification, as an over-ridingly masculine affair. Nevertheless, the notion of the professional pursuing a regular vocation with a designated purpose did provide space for women to claim professional status. Like their male counterparts, professional women combined a stress on service with notions of expertise, personal independence and autonomy, which they used to argue for participation in the public sphere generally. The term 'profession' 'conferred prestige and suggested moral superiority, intellectual ability, modernity and efficiency' (de Bellaigue, 2001, p. 964). It spoke of training, expertise, qualification and certification. At a point when independence and autonomy were contested categories for women, the success of middle-class women's professions often rested upon the development of formal and informal communities, which offered support, companionship, respectability and important contact (Vicinus, 1985; Copelman, 1996). These same communities effected processes of closure, exclusion and control as part of the processes of professionalization by excluding the unqualified and 'inadequately' socialized (Oram, 1996).

Networking and notions of professional community were central to moves to strengthen collective identity and authority for women educationists (de Bellaigue, 2001). This was the case for early nineteenth-century professionalization strategies around spiritual motherhood or social maternalism, effected by organizations like the Ladies Committee of the British and Foreign School Society (Goodman, 2000a) and female missionary societies (Haggis 1998), as much as for teacher groupings like those around the Home and Colonial Society, the London Schoolmistresses Association, the Manchester Board of Schoolmistresses (de Bellaigue, 2001; Pope and Verbeke, 1972) and the Association of Head Mistresses (AHM). But professional communities could contain their own contradictions. Founded in 1874 as a professional organization for headmistresses working in the new public secondary schools for girls (Price and Glenday, 1974), the AHM depicted two contrasted types of teacher: the 'professionally networked' headmistress; and her 'Other', the 'isolated' headmistress working in her own 'limited' sphere (Goodman, 2002). This drew on longer-standing representations of professionals exchanging valuable experience that had been used to legitimate the need for teachers' professional organizations (Willis, 2001). It built, too, on exchanges of schoolmistresses through the earlier teachers' associations (de Bellaigue, 2001). But this amateur/professional dichotomy was itself ambiguous. Within the rise of professional society, professionals retained their distance from the particular organizations which employed them by claiming that only they had the expertise to apply professional knowledge in specific contexts by virtue of an independent cognitive base within institutions of higher education (Savage *et al.*, 1992). For men teachers, this involved a resistance to any training 'unless they were teaching in elementary schools' (Brehony, 2000, p. 186). Since schoolmasters in the public schools had received a university education, they were not expected to undertake any professional training. Being a professional, therefore, presupposed a distance and marking of boundaries between the 'expert' and the 'amateur', a practice which underpinned the philosophy and the work of the AHM. This was not necessarily to suggest that the lady-proprietors of earlier schools were amateurs. As de Bellaigue (2001) notes – rather it substituted one professional model for another. But the AHM's stress on the importance of professional networking built upon, sustained and masked an 'isolation' deployed in other situations as a strategy of professionalization.

Many early 'professional' women teachers developed an innovative approach based on progressive pedagogy and the home (de Bellaigue, 2001). The 1870s arguments that women were specially qualified to serve the state drew on the notion of the 'communion of labour' that Anna Jameson used in the 1850s to argue for women's incorporation as citizens (Martin, 1999). Jameson (1859) maintained that men's and women's capabilities were different but complementary and that women's distinctive contributions were as important as those of men. She used the language of reciprocal rights and duties and particularly stressed notions of work and social responsibility, arguing that women needed access to employment and the professions and to the administration of all institutions dealing with women and children. She argued that if women and men worked together in a 'communion of labour', each bringing their specific capabilities, they would together transform the character of the nation. Arguments for access to the professions and for involvement as active citizens were mutually constitutive. Jane Rendall illustrates that political notions of 'active citizenship' were reworked by liberal intellectuals from the 1850s onwards by interweaving the abstract notion of equal rights and their attendant responsibilities with notions of altruism, duties, service and the idea of individuals acting together for the public good (Rendall, 1994). Alison Oram (1996) shows how the gendered languages of professionalism constituted through ideas of liberalism, individualism and merit developed by women broadly equated to aspects of middle-class identity. This focus on rights and equality, expressed through gender-neutral ideologies of professionalism came to characterize many of the arguments of women teachers' professional organizations around equal pay and the marriage bar.

The stress of the AHM on its 'valuable exchange of experience' located the Association within a web of relationships in which headmistresses built expertise and together wove the threads that constituted professional identities. This view of professional identity as intersubjective and collective points to communities as shaping forces of individuals and individuals as sites of community building (Corbett, 1992). Griffith's (1995) metaphor of the 'web of identity' is illuminative here. Griffiths argues that people can think of themselves as individuals, as members of small face-to-face groups and as members of large groups. Processes of exclusion and inclusion incorporate individuals as members of some groups by choice, while membership of other groups is not a matter of choice. Plurality is the result of 'the effect of overlap and multiple choices between groups' as the complexity of connections increases with age and the number of ways in which groupings can be made increases (p. 91). The creation of identity, then, is collective but also individualistic as each individual creates her own identity while constrained by circumstance in, and through, the various communities of which, through processes of inclusion and exclusion, she is a member (p. 93). In this argument, personal autonomy (the ability to order one's personal life) is the freedom to make the self in recognition of the way the self is made in (and against) communities (although not determined by them) and out of the material conditions in which it finds itself (p. 142). Public autonomy refers to the conditions under which individuals contribute to the ordering of public life: institutional, laws, customs, culture. Her theoretical stance leads Griffiths to argue that the dichotomizing of public and private as an explanation for the exclusion of women from public life is unsatisfactory. Rather, what is required is a re-conceptualization of what counts as private and public in a reworking of the 'political' which recognizes the importance of public decisions in matters that have been deemed part of the private world of women and family.

Re-conceptualizing the political in terms of the public and the private is also central to Ruth Lister's (1997) discussion of female citizenship. Lister argues that both the rights approach and the obligations approach to citizenship rest on essentialist categorizations of men's and women's qualities and capacities and a set of dichotomies, saturated with gendered implications and associations, in which the citizen is seen as the abstract, disembodied individual. Here, the public–private divide facilitates the relegation of the private sphere and to it the functions and qualities deemed incompatible with the exercise of citizenship in the public. Lister argues that attempts to include women on the same terms as men (equality), or to recast citizenship's premises to accommodate women's particular interests (difference), force women into male citizenship paradigms that stunt and contort women's process of self-development and take feminists to a politically paralysing dead end. Rather, the oppositions that run through citizenship theory – equality/difference, justice/care, universal/particular and many others – should be seen as potentially complementary and interdependent. For Lister, the practical barriers to women's citizenship lie within both public and private spheres and their interrelation. She sees the public and the private as an essentially contested construction, whose positioning and meanings are historically and culturally specific and women's citizenship inhibited, but also promoted, at their intersections. Like Griffiths, Lister argues for the re-articulation of the public and the private and for an acknowledgement of its fluid and political nature, as well as for a broadened definition of the political and of the citizen beyond that pertaining to the general government of a society (p. 25). In her view, the terrain of political citizenship is the public sphere; but a public sphere not divorced from what happens in the private, which shapes the contours of the public and can be the proper object of citizenship struggles (pp. 28–30).

Lister suggests a notion of human agency rooted in its social context. She distinguishes between 'simple agency' and 'citizenship agency', which intertwine and act upon each other:

> To act as a citizen requires first a sense of agency, the belief that one can act; acting as a citizen, especially collectively, in turn fosters that sense of agency. Thus agency is not simply about the capacity to choose and act but it is also about a conscious capacity

which is important to the individual's self-identity. The development of a conscious sense of agency, at both the personal and political level, is crucial to women's breaking of the chains of victimhood and their emergence as full and active citizens (Lister, 1997, p. 38).

Lister draws on Anthony Giddens' distinction between hierarchical power (power over) and generative power (power to) to explain how people can at the same time both be the subordinate objects of hierarchical power relations and subjects who are agents in their own lives, capable of exercising power. In this view of women's citizenship, both the self and autonomy are relational. Individual self-development is located in the context of social relations and engagement in collective activities directed towards collective as well as individual ends.

In terms resonant of Griffiths' and Lister's calls to re-vision the political in terms of the public and the private, Kathryn Gleadle and Sarah Richardson (Gleadle, 2001; Gleadle and Richardson, 2000) survey ways in which historians have begun to unravel the interaction of middle-class and elite women with the community and with current affairs. Gleadle and Richardson adopt 'a broad and inclusive approach to politics' to argue that it is important to recognize that the barriers against women's political activities were not as inflexible as has commonly been assumed. Rather, the boundaries between public and private worlds have historically merged and overlapped. This is demonstrated clearly in constructions of national identities deeply embedded in English culture. As Ian Grosvenor (1999) demonstrates, the word 'home' has long been associated with ideas of nation and belonging and the nation as home. In the early nineteenth century, against the background of threat of incursion by Napoleon, women built on notions of patriotism in which, as guardians of culture in the home and transmitters of culture to a future generation, they had the power to build up or undermine the nation. Later, in Imperial Britain, it was the word 'home' that was the link between nation and empire and during the Second World War, home was the domestic space in which women were to create and sustain the nation.

Gleadle (2001) points particularly to the political nature of much of the voluntary, philanthropic work in which women have historically engaged. Given the nature of the English state, characterized by Pat Thane (1993) as a 'minimal state', women's work in voluntary societies has been crucial to their ability to effect educational, social and political change. Seth Koven and Sonya Michel (1993) demonstrate various ways in which women's political participation has been fostered through their involvement in the 'borderland' between an elaborate voluntary and local government apparatus and an efficient central–state administration. Indeed, Koven (1993) maintains that one of the most striking features of social welfare in Victorian and Edwardian Britain was the powers granted to local agents of authority, who wielded enormous influence over the services and resources available to the poor in their communities well into the twentieth century. In previous works (Martin, 1999; Goodman and Harrop, 2000), we have demonstrated Koven's contention that Victorian middle-class women's voluntary associations linked the private, female world of household and family to the public, male-dominated world of politics in a process through which 'women moved between the supposedly discrete spheres of public and private, revealing the artificiality of bipolar constructions of these categories' (Koven, 1993, p. 96). Through their networking and institution-building (and through the deployment of auto/ biographical practices as practices of authority) they transformed the 'borderland' 'from a place of passage between two discrete realms (state and civil society) into an arena of women's own self-activity and construction' (Koven, 1993, p. 96).

Group Biography and Friendship Networks

Linda Eisenmann (2001) identifies four possible interpretative frameworks for investigating the story of women's educational activism. These are institution-building, networking, religion and money. Using examples from the American experience to show a range of foci that are amenable to the first approach Eisenmann argues that institution-building is the most useful framework. This is because it can help us meet the challenge of recrafting 'the wider history of education to include women's participation' (Eisenmann, 2001, p. 470). In writing about the historical creation of women's public voices we build on Eisenmann's work to consider the utility of networking. That is, 'the conscious use of causes and organizations to connect and advance women's interests' (Eisenmann, 2001, p. 457). Proceeding in this way is clearly useful in the light of Gleadle's arguments about women's philanthropic work, Koven's arguments about the role of women's voluntary organizations in the 'borderlands', and in the light of the importance for women's professional development of teachers' organizations. It has the advantage, too, of fitting with our interest in how narrative research can offer more adequate ways of knowing the social world, of learning about individual personality, and exploring images of self through connection with others.

The metaphor of a 'network' of social relations has its origins in classical German sociology where the connotations of fabrics and textiles were used 'to make the unfamiliar patterns of the social world comprehensible' by relating them to a familiar object or process (Scott, 1988, p. 110). Focusing on agents as the main unit of analysis, the network metaphor concentrates attention on the lived connections between personal and political worlds. In this book, our primary focus is on the intertwining of self and everyday life, self and community, self and 'voice', self and others, to bring into fuller view the activities of a number of women. We are interested in how the women we study acted upon their circumstances to bring about change in the social world and how they worked to bring about change. We explore the social networks built out of social relations on the basis of the principle that, as John Scott and Catherine Griff (1984) make clear: 'agents are significantly connected to others, each of whom has similar connections to further agents. As a result, there exists a definite network of relations between agents' (p. 9). Starting with the biographical detail of individual women, we use insiders' accounts to identify complex positioning, cross-cutting allegiances and cross-cutting commonalities.

It is, therefore, important to produce a theoretical model for exploring these aspects of shifting solidarity, coalition and alliances. Peter Cunningham's (2001) work on progressivism demonstrates the promise of prosopography, or collective biography, as a methodology to bring the agendas of less well-known individuals more clearly into focus. In the British context, an exhortation to embrace prosopography as historical method is associated with the work of Lewis Namier in the 1920s. In *The Houses of Parliament: The House of Commons 1754–1790*, Namier examined 'the personal side of parliamentary politics and the parliamentary groups which flourished and manoeuvred, formed, broke and reformed their alliances under cover of debates and constitutional dogmas' (cited in Cunningham, 2001, p. 435). Thinking forward from personal experience can provide pointers to the analysis of motivating force. There is a framework that can connect individuals, networks and structures. In reclaiming the lost histories of women educator activists, prosopography might usefully be rehabilitated. Our principal concern has been the discovery and analysis of individual experience. So, in this book, we replace the category of 'parliamentary groups' by informal associations, societies and journals; and 'constitutional dogmas' become educational philosophies and educational science. This framework enables us to understand the role of structure and the relationship between individual and collective practice regarding change.

This is no easy task, given the materials available to construct auto/biographical accounts of women's lives. We are conscious, for example, that while relationship and community are central to the depiction of many women's public and professional lives, working with such concepts is not straightforward. Marcus (1988) illustrates ways in which women active in the public sphere as professionals tended to portray their lives steeped in their communities and in terms of 'others' with whom they interact. Creating circles of overlapping communities of female friendship and removing the self from the centre of preoccupation, she suggests, formed another strategy to deal with 'anxiety about exposing female selfhood as egotism at a time when Victorian ideals of women's selflessness were deeply ingrained in their consciousness' (p. 124) – a practice that has a long literary tradition. Spacks (1988) notes the apologies about length frequently found in eighteenth-century letters written by women to each other. (These are reminiscent of the apologies found in the prefaces to educational treatise written by early nineteenth-century women educationalists.) Spacks analyses these insistent recurrences of rituals of politeness as stylized aspects dominated by consciousness of the other in which concern for self must not be allowed to block sensitivity to the imagined needs of the recipient: 'Reporting about others substitutes for narratives of the self, while the ideology of self-subordination implies among other things, suppression of narrative about the self' (p. 181).

Yet, it is in this reciprocity – the relation of writer and reader at the heart of auto/biography as method – that both the challenge and joy of auto/biography lies. Marcus (1988) shows both classicist Jane Harrison and musician Ethel Smythe using an active model of auto/biography written in the expectation of collaboration between reader and writer. Marcus argues that this collaboration forms a reproduction of women's culture as conversation, which does not occur in the male model of individualistic autobiography, in which the reader is not expected to take such an active role. Harrison's major works were written in the vivid colloquial style of women's conversation, punctuated with jokes and asides as well as the personal thrill of intellectual discovery. Her concept of themis – the spirit of community life 'in which individual lives were shaped in pre-classical Greece, informed by the ritual of the life and death of the Year Spirit' – was the subject of her work and part of her philosophy of life (p. 141). As Marcus notes, it is this idea of themis – 'a structure of communal ritual that shapes the individual life to that of the community', and which 'insists on the reader's response and sets the writer in conversation with her own community' – which might be seen as the spirit of women's auto/biographical discourse (p. 141). It is in this spirit of reciprocity – one that forms a 'republic of letters, in which writers hold conversations across time and space' (Sapiro, 1992, p. xxii) – that we have aimed to work in writing this book.

2

Elizabeth Hamilton (1758–1816) and the 'Plan of Pestalozzi'

Elizabeth Hamilton was a late eighteenth- and early nineteenth-century Scottish educationist, who was one of the earliest propagators of Johann Heinrich Pestalozzi's work in Britain. Elizabeth had a fascination with the 'science of the human mind', central to much work of the Scottish Enlightenment philosophers in whose Edinburgh circles she moved. Elizabeth's contemporaries thought she possessed the ability to relate abstract philosophical theory to pedagogical practice and to write about both in ways that were useful for mothers educating their children. Maria Edgeworth noted that Elizabeth had:

> thrown open to all classes of readers, those metaphysical discoveries or observations which had been confined chiefly to the learned. To a sort of knowledge that had been considered rather as a matter of curiosity than of use, she has given real value and actual currency. She has shown how the knowledge of metaphysics can be made serviceable to the art of education. She has shown for instance how the doctrine of the association of ideas may be applied in early education to the formation of the habits of temper, and of the principles of taste and of morals. She has considered how all that metaphysicians know of sensation and abstraction can be applied to the cultivation of the attention, the judgement, and the imagination of children (Edgeworth, 1816).

Between 1796 and 1815, Hamilton used a variety of genres to present her educational ideas to a popular audience and particularly to women. She was quoted and reviewed by nineteenth-century women educationists (Trimmer, 1805) and her texts are to be found in libraries in Australia. She achieved this when, from the stand-point of the history of educational thought, women thinkers were in double jeopardy: 'penalized for their interest in the education of their own sex...and penalized simply for being women' (Roland Martin, 1994, p. 38).

Elizabeth Hamilton was also a practical educationist, chairing meetings of the management committee of the Edinburgh House of Industry. One of her last published works, *Hints Addressed to the Patrons and Directors of Schools* (Hamilton, 1815a) was dedicated to the Edinburgh Education Society. Elizabeth aimed *Hints* at middle-class women active in school management. She outlined the practi-cal application of Pestalozzi's method, as well as both theoretical and practical ideas on education. She argued for a child-centred, active, experiential learning method and presented 'many pertinent remarks on the management of public institutions' (Benger, 1818, i, p. 223), calling, particularly, for the 'vigilant inspection of intelligent managers'. In *Hints*, Hamilton described Pestalozzi's method as both 'extremely simple and extremely obvious' (Benger, 1818, i, p. 224), 'simply attending to the laws of nature' and '*the practice of the presence of God*' (Hamilton, 1815a, pp. 62–4).

In this chapter I construct a social, cultural, political and intellec-tual biography to explore Elizabeth Hamilton's affinity with the ideas of Pestalozzi, and to examine the complexities of her educa-tional theory. I apply aspects of 'critical auto/biography' to counter-act the 'theoretical evacuation of the social subjects producing theory' (Marcus, 1994, p. 283) that relegates aspects of the personal to the margins of texts (Anderson, 2001). I draw on Elaine Chalus' (1997) notion of 'social politics' to view Hamilton not as an individ-ual writer but as located in her networks, through letters, meetings and social activities, and in respect of the 'influence' of others on her writing. Chalus uses 'social politics' to denote the importance of salons, dinners, teas and visiting in the workings of contemporary politics and the centrality of women to these activities. In the chapter, I use 'social politics' in terms of intersubjectivity and inter-textuality. I begin with a brief account of Elizabeth Hamilton's life but I do not seek to provide a chronological *Bildungsroman* trajectory looking forward from the beginning or back from the end to survey her life and writings as a whole. Rather, in an approach that is not entirely chronological, I follow Liz Stanley's intertextual approach, in which sets of 'voices' speak referentially to and about each other (Stanley, 1992, p. 15). In *Hints*, Elizabeth presented herself as popularizer and practitioner. Maria Edgeworth's obituary and Hamilton's biographer, Elizabeth Benger, portrayed her in a similar light, with Benger praising her ability to add 'new value to [philosophers'] knowledge by rendering it practically useful' (Benger, 1818, i, p. 143). To end the chapter, I use insights from auto/biographical theory to unpack the representation of Hamilton as popularizer rather than theorist.

Elizabeth Hamilton was born in 1758 in Belfast. Her mother died shortly after her birth and Elizabeth was brought up by her aunt and uncle Marshall, near Stirling.[1] Some of the roots of Elizabeth's interest in child-centred learning can be traced to her upbringing. She later compared the upper-middle-class home of her aunt and uncle Marshall to the Wolmar household in Rousseau's *La nouvelle Héloïse* (Rousseau, 1761). Her sister attended Manson's 'progressive' school in Belfast. Manson (1762–92) believed that children should be given a choice of actions, rather than forced to act on the commands of the teacher. In a scheme that shared similarities with that of Comenius, he made lessons in reading and spelling more closely related to life. Each morning he divided the children into ranks in a Royal Society on the basis of their performance. He gave them tickets as rewards for spelling, which they could eventually exchange for medals; and for correct answers; in grammar he attributed them with rent that could be exchanged in the Royal Society (Stewart, 1972). In her novel, *The Cottagers of Glenburnie*, Elizabeth portrays the reforming Mrs Mason reorganizing the local school according to Manson's method. The boys are placed in 'three distinct orders; viz., landlord, tenants and under tenants', with the landlord responsible to the master, or superior lord, for the discipline and progress of the class (Hamilton, 1808, pp. 292–3).

From the age of eight until her late teens, Elizabeth attended a boarding school in Stirling, where she received a 'sound' education (without the classics), before becoming her aunt's companion. She turned to writing as an alternative to marriage. Her love of learning was fostered by her brother Charles, an Orientalist, who was given leave by Warren Hastings to return to England from India to translate the Persian code of Islamic law. With Charles, Elizabeth moved in London circles, where she met Dr Gregory and his wife and they remained lifelong friends. Devastated by Charles' death in 1792, Elizabeth fictionalized his career in *Translation of the Letters of a Hindoo Rajah* (1796). She learned early of the difficulties of being a woman of learning. As her aunt's companion, she was forced to continue her studies in secret, having been warned that learning would seem 'unfeminine'. But 'like many other solitary thinkers', she was 'irresistibly impelled to become a writer' (Benger, 1818, i, p. 43). Success with *Letters of a Hindoo Rajah* gave Elizabeth the financial independence she needed to move from her aunt's home into single lodgings, where she studied in the morning and received friends in the evening. She lived for a time in Edinburgh, where she moved in the circles of Scottish Enlightenment philosophers. From 1804, a Civil List pension provided her with further financial security.

Precisely how Elizabeth came to her knowledge of Pestalozzi's methods is not entirely certain. Influenced by Rousseau's *Émile* (1762) and his *Social Contract* (1762), from 1774 onwards Pestalozzi developed his educational work with the poor successively at Neuhof, Stans and Yverdon (Silber, 1960; Heafford, 1967). He also wrote a series of educational texts and letters on education, of which the best known are *Leonard and Gertrude* (Pestalozzi, 1781) and *How Gertrude Teaches her Children* (Pestalozzi, 1805). With the cessation of the Napoleonic wars, a number of English educationists – Andrew Bell, Henry Brougham, James Pierrepoint Greaves, Richard Lovell and Maria Edgeworth, Charles and Elizabeth Mayo, and James Kay – visited Pestalozzi at Yverdon. When Hamilton was writing *Hints*, however, knowledge of Pestalozzi's work in England was growing, but was still sporadic as a result of the Napleonic wars (Silber, 1960). Russell (1986) suggests that it was likely that Elizabeth heard about Pestalozzi's ideas from her friend Maria Edgeworth. Maria and her father, Richard Lovell Edgeworth, travelled together in Belgium and France during 1802 and 1803 and heard Pestalozzi lecture in Paris, where he was representing his native canton of Zurich in a deputation to Napoleon on legislation. While in Paris, Pestalozzi worked hard to disseminate his teaching method (Silber, 1960) and among those who attended his lectures were Maria and her father (Colvin, 1979). Partly as a result of escalations in the war, and partly because of their worries about the health of Maria's brother, Henry Edgeworth, Maria and her father returned home in 1803 via Edinburgh, where Henry was boarding with the family of Dugald Stewart, whose lectures at the University of Edinburgh he was attending. Stewart (1753–1828) was a distinguished Scottish Enlightenment philosopher who had studied at the universities of Edinburgh and Glasgow. From 1775, he occupied the Edinburgh chair of mathematics before becoming professor of moral philosophy in 1798 (Brodie, 1998). While the Edgeworths were in Edinburgh, Stewart introduced Elizabeth and Maria (Benger, 1818; Hare, 1894; Brodie, 1997; Rendall, 2002).

Hamilton's discussion of Pestalozzi's work in *Hints* in 1815 was timely. Some French expositions of Pestalozzi's work were available in England. Daniel Alexandre Chavannes' *Exposé de la Méthode Elémentaire de M.Pestalozzi* (1805); Marc-Antoine Jullien's *Précis sur l'Institut d'Éducation d'Yverdon* (1810) and his larger work *Esprit de la Méthode d'Éducation de M.Pestalozzi* (1812). Jullien's works were read in many European countries (Silber, 1960). In 1813, two years before *Hints* was published, the Unitarian William Turner read John Bruce's paper on Pestalozzi to the Newcastle Literary and Philosophical Society (Watts, 1998a). A widely read and reviewed source on Pestalozzi published in translation England in the same year as Turner read his paper was Germaine de Staël's *De l'Allemagne* (1810, trans. 1813). This included a description of Pestalozzi's work based on Germaine's first-hand observation at Yverdon. De Staël (1766–1817) was drawn to many of Rousseau's ideas (Deane, 1988, p. 28) but like many women she disapproved of his views on education (Hilton, 2001). In *De l'Allemagne*, she praised Pestalozzi's method over the education proposed by Rousseau (de Staël, 1813). When it was published in France, *De'l'Allemagne* was suppressed by Napoleon on the grounds that it was hostile to France and de Staël was exiled. After the Peace of Amiens (1802), when France was seen to threaten the existence of England, those like de Staël, who had demonstrated internal opposition to Napoleon, were strongly supported in England (Deane, 1998). De Staël had literary and social contacts among British women that stretched back to the early 1790s (Burney, 2001; Pange, 1980). When she visited England in 1813, she was received at court by the Prince Regent, the Queen, the Duchess of York and the Duke of Gloucester (Herold, 1959). She was widely 'introduced' in society and spent a 'brilliant fortnight' at Bowood, the cultural centre of the Earl of Lansdowne, where to her regret, Maria Edgeworth narrowly missed meeting her (Hare, 1894). Soon after de Staël arrived in England, the publisher Murray bought the rights of *De l'Allemagne* for fifteen hundred guineas (Herold, 1959). News of the fall of Leipzig to Napoleon's army reached London the day *De l'Allemagne* went on sale. Two thousand five hundred copies were printed and it sold out in three days (Isbell, 1994). There is no direct evidence that Hamilton met Germaine de Staël. But during her visit, de Staël was shown around by Lady Davy, an acquaintance of both Maria Edgeworth and Elizabeth's Edinburgh friend, Eliza Fletcher. In 1814, Elizabeth Benger, Hamilton's future biographer (whom she met through Dr Gregory), published *Remarks on Madame de Staël's Germany* (Aiken, 1827). De Staël's was a first-hand account of Pestalozzi's application of his method. Hamilton's *Hints* was a discussion of the application of Pestalozzi's method to the education of the poor with a more philosophical bent.

Pestalozzi's 'method' was both 'empirical' – based on the observation of children – and deeply philosophical. His method was most comprehensively expounded in the series of fourteen letters that constituted *How Gertrude Teaches her Children*. Pestalozzi built on Rousseau's notion that education must harmonize with nature (Heafford, 1967). He aimed to find a 'psychological' method of instruction, compatible with discoverable laws of human nature.[2] He did not see the new-born child simply as a *tabula rasa* on which sense-impressions 'wrote'. Rather, he thought a fundamental power of the human mind underlay all mental activity and made all knowledge possible. This he termed 'Anschauung'.[3] To enable individuals to reach the highest possible degree of knowledge, 'Anschauung' had to be 'turned into an art', cultivated, educated, made conscious. 'Art' for the teacher, or parent, constituted 'the conscious acting according to principles'. For the pupil it was 'his methodically cultivated powers' (Silber, 1960, pp. 138–9). 'Art' assisted nature, helping it follow its course. It imitated nature, drew out what lay within the child and guided the child towards independence and the best realization of him or herself. Pestalozzi thought it necessary to discover the laws according to which the human mind operated and to formulate specific principles to guide the child's education in accordance with these laws ('psychological' laws, or the 'laws of human nature'). Pestalozzi hoped that by ordering knowledge and experiences in line with nature, he would find teaching methods that would prove universally applicable. At the same time, the individual needs of children could be taken into account by careful sequencing from the simple to the more complex, matched to the child's stage of development. Fundamental here was close observation of the child to gain insight into the way children's minds developed, in order for the teacher to 'stimulate' and direct the 'awakening' faculties of each child:

> I saw that... the constituents of instruction must be separated according to the degree of the growing power of the child; and

that in all matters of instruction, it is necessary to determine, with the greatest accuracy, which of these constituents is fit for each age of the child, in order on the one hand, not to hold him back if he is ready, and on the other hand, not to load him and confuse him with anything for which he is not quite ready (Pestalozzi, 1805, p. 26).

Central to Pestalozzi's 'method' was self-activity. This under-pinned Pestalozzi's trenchant critique of the rote learning used widely in the education of the poor. In order to cultivate the child's powers of perceiving, judging and reasoning, the child was to arrive at his, or her, own solutions and the curriculum was to be concerned with the active process of search (Silber, 1960). Pestalozzi attempted to reduce education to its most simple elements: form, number and language. He then based his educational method on the three-fold principle of observing objects: counting, measuring and naming (Heafford, 1967; Hilton, 2001). Pestalozzi summed up his method in the following terms:

I have fixed the highest, supreme principle of instruction in the recognition of *sense-impression as the absolute foundation of all knowledge*. Apart from the *special teaching* I have sought to discover the *nature of teaching itself*; and the *prototype*, by which Nature herself has determined the instruction of our race … I have reduced all instruction to three elementary means; and have sought for special methods which should render the results of all instruction in these three branches absolutely certain (Pestalozzi, 1805, p. 39).

Pestalozzi took a holistic view of education that encompassed intellectual, physical and moral education. His stress on the centrality of moral education meant that the child's early education was of paramount importance. Because moral education began from the moment of birth, education was not just a matter of the head but of the senses and of the heart; for it was the realization of the divine in human nature (Silber, 1960).

Elizabeth Hamilton shared many of Pestalozzi's concerns. At thirteen she had met Dr Moyse, a lecturer on experimental philosophy, who had fostered her early interest in experimental philosophy through correspondence and by giving direction to her studies (Russell, 1988). Hamilton's *Letters on Education* demonstrated her interest in an education that was both intellectual and moral and, like Pestalozzi's, concerned with the heart as well as the intellect.

The education of the heart was central to her two-stage educational theory and her two-fold aim of education: 'the cultivation of the various principles of nature, both speculative and active', and the monitoring of 'the impressions and associations which the mind receives in early life in order to engage its prepossessions on the side of truth' (Hamilton, 1810, ii, pp. 10, 20–1, 28–9, 274, 311). She used associationist philosophy and psychology based on sense-impressions,[4] to build a theory of the education of the intellect on the education of the heart. She argued that when taken together, the education of the heart and the education of the intellect, brought 'all the powers and faculties of our nature to the highest perfection of which they are capable' (ibid., ii, p. 2). She put forward the view that there was an innate moral sense but that this and other senses could be influenced by external stimuli, with the result that education could either strengthen or weaken 'nature'. She maintained that early associations which affected the heart were rendered permanent and had consequences for the later development of the intellect. This enabled her to reverse a contemporary viewpoint, which she regarded as masculine, that early education was a 'blank' and that education began with the development of the intellect. In her later publication, *A Series of Popular Essays: Illustrative of Principles Connected with the Improvement of Understanding* (Hamilton, 1813), she discussed the relation between the understanding, the imagination and the heart; outlined the utility of the study of the mind and its relation to educational reform; stressed that attention was the key to intellectual development; and related this to imagination and taste (Kelly, 1993).

Edinburgh Circles

The publication of *Letters on Education* in 1801 brought Hamilton 'the acquaintance and correspondence of many celebrated individuals' (Benger, 1818, i, p. 162). Most pleasing to Hamilton was the approbation of Dugald Stewart. Elizabeth wrote: 'it would be a poor affectation to say, that I was not flattered by such praise from a character so distinguished' (Benger, 1818, i, p. 163). Stewart published biographies of Adam Smith, William Robertson and Thomas Reid. The latter developed many of the distinctive doctrines of the Scottish school of common-sense philosophy, of which Stewart,

himself, was a proponent (Brodie, 1998; Rendall, 1978).[5] The fundamental building block of Hamilton's educational theory – the
centrality of the education of the heart to the education of the
intellect – followed closely the aim of Scottish Enlightenment
philosophers of the common-sense school to build a 'science of the
human mind' based on the writings of John Locke (Hutcheson,
1772). Building on the writings of Francis Hutcheson, the common-
sense school argued that each individual had an innate moral sense.
Although common-sense philosophers employed the theory of the
association of ideas, they departed from Locke in that, like
Pestalozzi, they did not believe that ideas were formed solely by
external stimuli (McCosh, 1975; Rendall, 1978, 1985; Russell, 1986).
Stewart maintained that explanations of the development of the
mind through the association of ideas needed to be combined with
arguments about the way in which people had an innate capacity
to receive and to order eternal stimuli (Bryson, 1945). For Stewart,
intuition, and hence the heart as well as the head, played an important part in the process of moral development (Stewart, 1792). This
emphasis on the heart and intuition was a common theme in the
common-sense school of philosophy. Henry Kames, for instance,
wrote that 'the culture of the heart' was important to education and
that education should train both the intellect and the emotions
(Russell, 1986, p. 25).

By 1803, Elizabeth and her sister had travelled through Wales, the
lakes of Westmorland and Scotland, and had spent time with their
friends Eleanor Butler and Sarah Ponsonby, the romantically
involved 'Ladies of Langollen'. Elizabeth wrote: 'the few days we
spent with them passed in that sort of enthusiastic delight so seldom
experienced when the days of youthful ardour are gone' (Benger,
1818, i, p. 166). Urged by the Stewarts to spend the winter months in
Edinburgh, Elizabeth noted with pleasure: 'I shall derive from it the
advantage of literary conversation, in a very chosen circle of society;
and expect much improvement, even from the casual hints and
observations of such a man as Mr. S' (ibid., ii, p. 31). During their
travels, Elizabeth busied herself by working on her conjectural and
philosophical history, *Memoirs of Agrippina* (Hamilton, 1804). In
this, she was encouraged by Stewart, who had coined the term 'conjectural history' for the practice of speculating from evidence based
on similar societies on the likely course of events (Rendall, 1992;
Brodie, 1997). Her decision to take up residence in Edinburgh was

swayed by her desire 'to have it in my power coolly to decide upon the propriety of the plan [*Agrippina*] I have adopted' (Benger, 1818, ii, p. 38). She submitted two-thirds of the first volume of *Agrippina* to Stewart for his perusal, noting: if 'his opinion is against it I shall without scruple consign it to oblivion' (ibid., ii, p. 38).

The Edinburgh society in which Elizabeth came to reside formed a lively intellectual *milieux*, though whether it constituted a 'salon' culture is open to debate.[6] Dinner parties and hot suppers had been replaced by large evening parties, where card-playing had given way to music or conversation. The 'company' often gathered around nine and parted at twelve o'clock. Tea and coffee were handed around at nine and guests sat down to some light cold refreshments later on in the evening; but people came to talk and listen rather than to eat (Fletcher, 1876). Elizabeth found Edinburgh society 'in many respects superior' to the society she had previously met:

> Seldom indeed are so many people of eminent talent to be met with in one friendly circle. Few days have passed in which we have not seen some persons of distinguished abilities and of the numerous parties to which we have been invited have found none that could be termed flat, stale or unprofitable (Benger, 1818, ii, p. 39).

Elizabeth, herself, attracted visitors of repute. Her daily routine started with study in the morning until two; she then 'descended to the drawing room', to meet 'some intimate friend'; from seven until ten in the evening she read, following her aunt Marshall's practice of reading aloud 'for the benefit of the whole party'. On Mondays, she admitted visitors all morning:

> Such was the esteem of her character and such the relish for her society, that this private levée was attended by the most brilliant persons in Edinburgh and commonly protracted till a late hour (ibid., i, p. 190).

The political importance of women's engagement with early nineteenth-century salons, dinners, teas and visiting should not be underestimated (Gleadle, 2001a,b). But despite their role in Edinburgh's intellectual milieu, women were debarred from the city's male literary and philosophical clubs and from Edinburgh University. Maria Edgeworth noted Sir James Mackintosh's report that Stewart's lectures 'breathed the love of virtue into whole generations of pupils'. But, commented Maria:

> I have not heard him lecture; no woman can go to the public lectures here, and I don't choose to go in men's or boy's clothes ... Mrs Stewart has been for years wishing in vain for the pleasure of hearing one of her husband's lectures (Hare, 1894, i, p. 146).

Rather than in the 'masculine' University, it was with the 'feminine' philanthropic House of Industry that Elizabeth was engaged. Nonetheless, women's involvement in early nineteenth-century philanthropic and educational programmes and with institutions to 'rescue' and 'reclaim the fallen' can also be read as a form of interventionist politics (Gleadle, 2001a,b). Elizabeth's friend, Eliza Fletcher, commented: 'For ladies to take any share, especially a leading share, in the arrangement of a public institution was considered so novel and extraordinary a proceeding as ought not to be countenanced' (Fletcher, 1876, pp. 76–7). This was particularly the case for women holding 'democratic' principles, like Eliza. Through her soirées Elizabeth did much to clear the reputation of her friend, whose sympathies for the French Revolution had led to rumours that she carried a small guillotine and used it to behead poultry or 'rats and mice and such small deer', in order to be an expert when 'French principles' and practice should prevail (ibid., p. 70).

A Female Romanticism?

Elizabeth Hamilton and Eliza Fletcher were introduced to each other by the Scots Romantic poet, Hector Macneill, to whom Elizabeth dedicated her most popular work, *Glenburnie*. This was a story of contemporary Scotland in the style of Hannah More's *Cheap Repository Tracts*. It followed the reforming work of Mrs Mason in the poverty-ridden village of Glenburnie. Alongside the 'domestic realism' Elizabeth used to depict the dirt and disorder of the unreformed village of Glenburnie,[7] the novel included evocative descriptions of Scottish countryside, through which she paid Romantic homage to nature:

> The rocks which seemed to guard the entrance of the Glen, were abrupt and savage, and approached so near each other, that one could suppose them to have been riven asunder to give a

passage to the clear stream which flowed between them. As they advanced, the hills receded on either side, making room for meadows and corn fields through which the rapid burn pursued its way in many a fantastic maze (Hamilton, 1808, p. 192).

Mary Hilton (2001) has discussed how scholars have found it difficult to construct a female Romanticism: 'given that Romanticism's most defining characteristics in the nineteenth century were enmeshed with the idea of the man of genius, a notion which yielded renewed cultural authority to men' (p. 471). Kelly notes that it was the domesticity of a sentimental, socially nurturing and ameliorative kind that was considered proper for women writers, rather than the Romantic and the sublime, which were generally regarded as unsuitable for women, or beyond their experience, the province, rather of men such as Samuel Taylor Coleridge and George, Lord Byron (Kelly, 1993). Germaine de Staël's *De l'Allemagne* had a Romantic agenda, which Isbell claims formed part of her invention of a form of European Romanticism (Isbell, 1994). De Staël counted among her personal friends the German Romantics Johann Christoph Schiller, Johann Wolfgang Goethe, and Friedrich and August Wilhelm Schlegel. August Wilhelm Schlegel particularly encouraged her interest in the ideas of Romanticism. Jean-Charles Sismondi and George, Lord Byron, were visitors to the Castle of Coppet, Germaine de Staël's exile base between 1804–10 (Herold, 1959). De Staël's inclusion in *De l'Allemagne* of her eye witness account of Pestalozzi's work calls for further study of the links between women's work in education and a female Romanticism.

Hilton argues that British women of the liberal intelligentsia re-appropriated certain features of Romantic thought, principally through the poetry of Wordsworth, with its strong Platonic doctrine of *anamnesis* (pre-existence), emanating from Cambridge in the early years of the nineteenth century (and expressed in his *Immortality Ode*). The response of Hamilton's friend, Eliza Fletcher, on reading Wordsworth's *Lyrical Ballads* for the first time, demonstrates the impact Wordsworthian Romanticism could have on women:

[It] was like a new era in my existence. They were in my waking thoughts day and night. They had to me all the vivid effects of the finest pictures, with the enchantment of the sweetest music, and they did much to tranquillise and strengthen my heart and mind, which bodily indisposition had somewhat weakened (Fletcher, 1876, p. 79).

In his *Prelude*, Wordsworth demonstrates his view of the deadening effect of a purely intellectual education – one that ignored the 'vital feelings of delight' (Curtis and Boultwood, 1953, pp. 305–6). He came to regard the education of the feelings as important, if not more so, than the education of the intellect.

Elizabeth Hamilton's stress on the education of the heart as well as of the intellect shares aspects with this Wordsworthian agenda. In *Glenburnie*, Hamilton invoked aesthetic categories of landscape description: the sublime, the beautiful and the picturesque. Alan Liu claims that the evolution of picturesque art towards subjectless images of landscape before which the spectator reposed, constituted a Protestant method of rehearsing culture (Keane, 2000):

> Picturesque arrest was evacuated liturgy. Fixed in a ritual posture of religiosity… the picturesque tourist stood in worship… Where once there rested the image of the Mother of God, now there reposed Mother Nature (Liu, 1989, quoted in Keane, 2000, p. 37).

According to Liu, the picturesque landscape can be read in terms of a panopticon through which the Whig state supervised, regulated and encouraged the productivity of its subjects. In this formulation, the picturesque tourist was imaginative overseer, surveying the landscape with an eye for detail (ibid., p. 37) (much in the way Elizabeth suggested in *Hints* that the school manager should observe the pupils). Elizabeth's Romantic homage to nature in *Glenburnie* may well have been closely allied with her 'domestic realism'; for her descriptions of the countryside surrounding Glenburnie demonstrate a clear Whig trajectory within an Anglo-British frame.

National Identities and Professionalizing Motherhood

Colin Kidd (1993) argues that in the late eighteenth and early nineteenth century, Anglo-Britishness built on the idea that Scottish society had historically been more backward than England, that union with England had brought liberation from anachronistic feudal institutions, and that liberty was a by-product of the modernity that accompanied Anglicization:

> England represented modernity rather than a dominant core, and the peripheries were seen less as threatened pluralisms than as areas of backwardness, fortunate enough to be undergoing assimilation and accelerated progress (Kidd, 1993, p. 210).

In *Glenburnie*, Elizabeth's Anglo-British project took two inter-related paths: through her depiction of the cottagers as backward and her use of the Scots language. In contrast to her Romantic invocation of an unsullied 'nature' she deploys domestic realism to depict Glenburnie's countryside in ways that suggest the Scots' backwardness:

> The meadows and corn-field, indeed, seemed very evidently to have been encroachments made by stealth on the sylvan reign; for none had their outlines marked with the mathematical precision in which the modern improver so much delights. Not a straight line was to be seen in Glenburnie (Hamilton, 1808, p. 93).

She describes the dwellings and the villagers in terms of a domestic 'backwardness' she was keen to improve. The cure for the villagers' 'backwardness' begins with the reforming Mrs Mason's return to Scotland, which Kelly (1993) reads as an allegory of the transference of more 'forward' English cultural practices to Scotland.

In *Glenburnie*, Hamilton made use of the Scottish language in ways that resonated with the poetry of her friend, Hector Macneill. Kelly argues that Macneill 'assimilated the popular dialect verse tradition of Robert Burns (but eliminated Burn's licentiousness and immorality and especially his pro-Revolutionary sentiments) in order to reform the lower class, while creating a national Scottish identity within that of Britain' (p. 279). Hamilton distributes the written form of spoken Scots almost entirely to lower or lower-middle-class characters and recurrent phrases – 'Ilka place has just its ain gait' and 'I canna be fashed wi it' – to characters in need of 'reformation'. The third person narrator and the reforming Mrs Mason, in contrast, both use Standard English and can handle the Scots language (Kelly, 1993). Kelly claims that writings like *Glenburnie*, in which local and regional identities were celebrated ('invented') only to be subsumed into a larger national identity and interest, were defined 'not so much from within the "nation" as by external, global and historical, Revolutionary and post-Revolutionary struggles against France and America' (p. 184). As such, *Glenburnie* formed part of the project through which a new nationalism, supposedly inspired by Revolutionary ideas, was harnessed to the kind of cultural, social, political and economic modernization that would strengthen Britain's resistance to French imperialism (ibid.).

With the advance of Napoleon, the spread of French influence was regarded by many as threatening the stability of Britain. Initial enthusiasm for the French Revolution and for the plight of the French Catholic clergy, exiled from France by the revolutionary government in August 1792, waned with the shock at the executions of the French king and queen (Deane, 1988). In 1795, Eliza Fletcher wrote of the backlash in Scotland to events in France:

> The country did become exceedingly alarmed … and the subsequent atrocities committed in France by an unprincipled faction, – the worst enemies of liberty, – produced such a horror (amongst) the higher orders especially in Scotland, that every man was considered a rebel in his heart who did not take a decided part in supporting Tory measures of government (Fletcher, 1876, p. 66).

Eliza's husband's law practice was detrimentally affected and in 1814, she conveyed to a friend her sadness at the subsequent course of events in France.

The French Revolution and the rumblings of the Napoleonic wars lent support for those educators who, like Elizabeth Hamilton, stressed domestic virtue as the backbone of national interest and prosperity at a time of crisis. Women educators, like Hannah More, invoked a patriotism that exemplified the belief in the dual potential of women for national good or evil. More was adamant that by exerting themselves, 'with a patriotism at once firm and feminine', women had an important role to play as guardians of the national interest. 'In this moment of alarm and peril', she called them to 'come forward, and contribute their full and fair proportion towards the saving of their country' (More, 1838, pp. 13–14). Elizabeth Hamilton, too, put forward the view that domestic virtue constructed national identity and brought national prosperity or decline and maintained that women held the power to undermine or build up the nation. In *Glenburnie*, she demonstrated that national re-generation began with the woman within the individual family; for even when reform has its origins in Mrs Mason's exertions with the girls in the schoolroom, it was transmitted back into individual families and from there outwards to the rest of society.

Pestalozzi's novel, *Leonard and Gertrude*, carried a similar message and in similar form. Based on German village life, *Leonard and Gertrude* opens with the misery brought by unscrupulous officials, shows the punishment of the villains, the causes of their moral degradation and demonstrates the means of reform: a better education for the children and a new attitude in the home that lies at the heart of good administration in the village and spreads beyond it to the country as a whole. Pestalozzi connects Gertrude, the mother in the family, and the nation. From her cottage, her qualities as the mother of her children affect the well-being of the community and the nation (Silber, 1960).[8]

For Pestalozzi, the child's relationship with the mother is fundamental because moral education develops from an awareness of the inner world through the heart (Heafford, 1967) before moving from cultivation of the emotions to the exercise of judgement (Silber, 1960). Pestalozzi traces the progression of the child from the satisfaction of physical needs to feelings of trust, love and gratitude for the mother, feelings that will be extended to other human beings (Heafford, 1967). The mother takes the place of God during the child's infancy; for the child can only become aware of God and God's love for humanity by experiencing the human virtues of love, faith, trust and obedience first hand (Heafford, 1967; Pestalozzi, 1805). The untrained mother following Nature without help or guidance, intending only to quiet and occupy the child, follows Nature in her 'pure simplicity', without knowing what Nature did through her. Nature, indeed did much. But, argued Pestalozzi, if the 'high course of Nature' were connected through training with the 'helping Art' – 'the conscious acting according to principles' – it would be possible for the mother 'made conscious' to go on with what she did instinctively for the infant wisely and freely with the growing child (Pestalozzi, 1805).

For Elizabeth Hamilton, too, mothers were central and held the 'master-key' to the minds of children and to the development of character (Hamilton, 1810). Because she believed that association shaped both intellectual powers and moral character, the role of the mother as preceptress in early education proceeded on universal principles in all societies – although the way mothers educated their children differently in different countries had different outcomes for national character (Hamilton, 1810, i, p. 9). Elizabeth's domesticated preceptress, engaged in the education of the heart, was guided by religion as to which associations she should foster in her children (Hamilton, 1810, i, pp. 28, 40, 42). But, like Pestalozzi's mother, she was to be helped – she needed educating, herself, in order to effectively plan the early education of her children:

> [I]t will not seem hyperbolical to assert, that if mothers were uni-
> versally qualified for the proper performance of these important
> duties, it would do more towards the progressive improvement of
> the human race, than all the discoveries of science and researches
> of philosophy! (Hamilton, 1810, i, pp. 20–1)

A 'Safe' Path?

Elizabeth Benger wrote that Hamilton had shown that she had
'studied the history of the human mind' and had 'made herself
acquainted with all that has been written on this subject by the best
moral and metaphysical writers' (Benger, 1818, i, p. 244). She had
recommended 'to her own sex, the study of metaphysics as far as it
relates to education' (ibid.). Alexander Tytler, a former professor of
history at Edinburgh University, described Elizabeth Hamilton
as: 'One of the ablest of … writers who have treated the subject
of education according to philosophical principles' (Tytler, 1807,
pp. 207–8). Hamilton offered women a professionalized model of
motherhood, based on an understanding of how the mind operated,
closely allied to observation of children. Elizabeth Benger claimed
that in outlining metaphysical theory for women to enable them to
educate their children along rational lines, and in her call for mothers to be given the requisite education to enable them to educate
their children, Elizabeth Hamilton:

> did much in awakening the attention of parents, of mothers
> especially, to future enquiry; she has done so much by directing
> their enquiries rightly – much by exciting them to reflect upon
> their own minds and to observe what passes in the minds of their
> children: she has opened a new field of investigation to women –
> a field fitted to their domestic habits, – to their duties as mothers,
> and to their business as preceptors of youth, to whom it belongs
> to give the minds of the children those first impressions and
> ideas which remain the longest, and which influence them
> often the most powerfully through the whole course of life
> (Benger, i, p. 226).

She offered a similarly professionalized role to women managing
the education of the poor, based on the managers' role in observing

the actions of the teacher with the children and watching the children's progress. Both were underpinned by an epistemological framework of the 'science of the mind' that she had developed largely by self-study and by 'social intercourse' and correspondence within the networks of men and women interested in education and philosophy in which she moved. She placed early education and mothers central to the task of national regeneration, contributing to an Anglo-British political project.

Yet, Gary Kelly's summary of the critical reviews of Elizabeth Hamilton's work demonstrates just how difficult a task this was. Reviewers of *Letters on Education*, for example, variously deplored its 'unfeminine' philosophical character, its ignorance of real children; the fact that women did not possess the strength of judgement and force of mind to enable them to handle the more abstracted intellectual functions; and portrayed Hamilton as a 'metaphysician of the School of Hartley associated with Revolutionary metaphysicians pursuing interests ill becoming the elegance of the female mind' (Kelly, 1993, p. 296).

With her stress on the importance of mothers and the domestic to both education and the nation, and in her role as writer, Hamilton has an ambiguous relation to the construct 'woman' of her day. Gary Kelly traces how, in her early works, Elizabeth positioned herself within the post revolutionary critique of feminism. This stance is evident in *Memoirs of a Hindoo Rajah* and more explicitly in *Memoirs of Modern Philosophers*, published in 1800, which included a satire on modern philosophy and particularly female philosophers. But despite her open critique, from 1800 onwards Elizabeth's writing moved towards revolutionary feminism. In much of her work, she feminized masculine discourses, including philosophy, history and theology. Kelly notes that beginning with *Letters on Education* in 1800, Hamilton 'offered herself as a model for the new intellectual-domestic woman' (Kelly, 1993, p. 265). She both stressed that there was 'no distinction in sex' when it came to matters of intellect and represented 'domestic woman' 'as professionalized custodian of the "national" conscience, culture, and destiny' (ibid., p. 21). But even as she focused on 'domestic affections', Elizabeth Hamilton transgressed the limits of 'domestic woman'.

Hamilton walked a tightrope as a woman 'metaphysician' who critiqued women 'modern philosophers', 'metaphysical speculators' and 'utopian feminists' – to whom she partly attributed the *'portentous crisis'* of the age (Kelly, 1993, p. 266). Paradoxically, she advanced her critique through the 'philosophical devices' and 'masculine' genres deployed by those she critiqued. Aware of the difficulties of the path she trod, she kept her name off the title page of early editions of *Memoirs of Modern Philosophers* (Kelly, 1993). Concerned that her feminization of Enlightenment epistemology and moral philosophy was too abstract and philosophical, she quickly rewrote *Letters on Education* to 'render the subject perfectly clear and intelligible to readers of every description' (Hamilton, 1802, Advertisement). Such tensions led to periods of stress, when she doubted her abilities. But this also stimulated her philosophical interest in subjectivity, Enlightenment epistemology and moral philosophy through self-examination (Kelly, 1993).

Elizabeth Benger claimed that Elizabeth Hamilton did:

> not aim at making women expert in the wordy war; nor does she teach them to astonish the unlearned by their acquaintance with the various vocabulary of metaphysical system-makers: such jugglers tricks she despised; but she has not, on the other hand, been deceived, or overawed, by those who would represent the study of the human mind as one that tends to no practical purpose, and that is unfit and unsafe for her sex. Had Mrs Hamilton set ladies on metaphysics merely to show their paces, she would have made herself and them ridiculous and troublesome but she has shown how they may, by slow and certain steps, advance to a useful object. The dark intricate, and dangerous labyrinth, she has converted into a clear, straight, practicable road, – a road not only practical but pleasant and not only pleasant, but what is of far more consequence to women, safe (Benger, i, pp. 227–8).

Auto/biographical theory alerts us, here, to the possibilities of this 'safe path' being one mode of auto/biographical representation for a woman metaphysician at a time when women metaphysicians, historians and theologians were by no means the norm. It is difficult to know how far such representations have coloured Hamilton's reception. There is the issue, too, of how far Hamilton's adoption of domestic woman caused her to be overshadowed as feminist historiography has focused on the 'revolutionary feminism' of those like Wollstonecraft and the 'Romantic feminism of the Revolutionary aftermath' (Kelly, 1993, p. 143). And how far has Elizabeth Hamilton suffered a 'double jeopardy' from the previous marginalization of Scottish historiography and then the marginalization of women within Scottish historiography as it developed (Russell, 1986)?

The literary politics of gender have positioned Elizabeth Hamilton differently from male theorists and led to her invisibility in the history of educational ideas. This has been supported by her ambiguous location as 'practical theorist' (as woman, neither adequate as theorist or practitioner according to some of her reviewers) across a theory/practice divide in which theory has been valued more highly than practice.

Writing after her visit to Pestalozzi, Germaine de Staël noted that Pestalozzi had pushed further than any other the theory and practice of gradation in the art of instruction. But, she pointed out: 'the method of P, like everything else that is truly good, is not entirely a new discovery but an enlightened and persevering application of truths already known' (de Staël, 1810, p. 372). Pestalozzi, himself, did not claim that his theories were entirely new:

> It is in no way my intention to stress any one of my points of view because it is new; I hold fast to my system because I believe it consistent with human nature, and I am convinced that educational theory in all aspects in which it is fully developed, corresponds to that which is true in my system. I am convinced that every good educationist was more or less on the scent of my most important ideas (quoted in Heafford, 1967, p. 42).

In many respects, this statement comes close to descriptions of Elizabeth Hamilton's writings. Elizabeth Benger noted that it was Elizabeth Hamilton's aim not to state and explain new truths, but to suggest for those already known a prompt and practical application. 'She prescribes not rules, but enforces principles, immutable in their nature, in their operation universal' (Benger, 1818, i, p. 143).

Elizabeth Hamilton's life and writings illustrate how, for a woman educational theorist, the relation to the 'new' has been dangerous. For early nineteenth-century women to develop 'new' theory was to risk the 'unwomanly' stance of the 'modern philosopher' and the 'dangerous' relation to citizenship and nation that Hamilton, herself, at times decried. On the other hand, for an educational theorist to be depicted as producing theory that was simply popularizing the known was to risk oblivion. Yet, even a popularizing relation to the 'new' contained gendered undercurrents. Heafford concludes that even if Pestalozzi's ideas, considered singly, were not all original, the impact of his ideas was undeniable: 'For Pestalozzi not only had positive ideas but also ... the personality and perseverance to force them on the attention of an age which hovered between revolution and conservatism' (Heafford, 1967, p. 42). Elizabeth Hamilton shared much in common with Pestalozzi: an interest in the 'science' of the mind and its development; a view of education in which aspects of affect, morality and reason were viewed holistically; a stress on the importance of early education; an active experiential pedagogy; and a trenchant critique of rote learning – all of which were reflected in her advice to managers in *Hints* (Hamilton, 1815a). But in contrast to Pestalozzi, for a woman educationist like Elizabeth Hamilton, who earned her living by her pen, to force ideas to the attention of an age hovering between revolution and conservatism was a far more risky and uncertain business. A largely gender-blind history of educational ideas testifies to this tale.

3

Sarah Austin (1793–1867): 'Voices of Authority' and National Education

In the England of the 1830s, popular education was largely financed through philanthropic, voluntary activity and state involvement in working-class education was a controversial political question (Barkin, 1983; Brewer, 1972; Green, 1990; Kay-Shuttleworth, 1862; Maynes, 1985; Wyse, 1839). In the face of growing working-class agitation in the 1830s and 1840s, there was interest in continental systems of education and particularly Prussian education (Johnson, 1977). In Prussia, schooling was compulsory (1763); a Ministry of Education was established (1808); communities were required to maintain schools and employ teachers certified through a state examination (1826); there were systematic pedagogical methods (often organized according to Pestalozzian principles of graded learning and inspection); and there was 'policing' of the curriculum (although the latter was not compulsorily mandated) (Miller, 1998). Some English experts envisaged a complete state system of education requiring legislation, comprising a Ministry of Public Instruction with powers over the curriculum, and responsibility for the training, certification, selection and conditions of service of schoolteachers. The attendance of pupils was to be compulsory and school rates levied statutorily; and a structure of local administration was to be set in place. Others preferred municipal solutions under enabling legislation (Johnson, 1977).

Until comparatively recently, the story of English campaigns for a national system of popular education in the 1830s and 1840s has been an overridingly male affair. Women's absence from these accounts suggests a historiography based on models of expertise and political action and a related historical methodology that are exclusionary. Elaine Chalus argues that unconstructed notions of women's place in society, combined with the customary political constraints which prevented women from voting and holding places or seats in Parliament, have fostered a belief that women's political involvement was limited and anomalous and ultimately secondary to men's: 'At best they were thought to have been political actors at one remove, operating indirectly or behind the scenes in their manipulation of men and situations' (Chalus, 1998, p. 210). Kathryn Gleadle and Sarah Richardson argue that while women did not have the same opportunities as their male contemporaries, barriers against women's political activities in early and mid-nineteenth-century England were not as inflexible as has commonly been assumed (Gleadle and Richardson, 2000). Chalus (1998) identifies four interrelated roles for (eighteenth century) women's political participation: confidante, adviser, agent and partner, the latter demonstrating a degree of independence that was both direct and public. Through such activities, women built their own intellectual and political communities, which extended across the Atlantic and Europe and took them into the political arena of international relations.

In this chapter I use biography to interpolate Sarah Austin more clearly into the mid-nineteenth-century story of national education and its development. Sarah was a writer, translator and Visitor of the innovative Westminster infant school, and a passionate advocate of national education for the children of working people. Through translation she familiarized a mid-1830s and 1840s English audience with the works of continental writers and educationists, stating her own views in the introductions and annotations to her work. Her life story and her multiplicity of roles as writer, translator, wife, mother, teacher and holder of an intellectual *salon*, illustrate the complexities of her conception of the public role of women, particularly where the development of national educational was concerned. Despite her own serious education within Unitarian circles, and her 'advanced' views on state activity in popular education, her perceptions of the educational needs of girls and women published later in life were more conservative. Sarah was comparatively well-known in her day. She was granted a Civil List pension in 1849, which she accepted 'with pride and satisfaction as proof that her work had been thought useful' (Ross, 1888, p. 232). When her granddaughter, Janet Ross, visited Dresden in the 1850s, she realized that her grandmother was a well-known woman; and in the 1860s, Sarah was still remembered in Malta for her part in the reform of primary schools (Ross, 1912, pp. 33, 89). Yet, she has all but fallen from view in histories of education.

I begin by briefly outlining the key events in Sarah's life. I explore some of her political strategies in the light of the broadened view of political action suggested by Chalus. I examine how some of her political strategies enabled her to play a part in national debate on state education for the working classes. Gleadle and Richardson (2000) note that broadening the concept of the 'political' to incorporate the activities of women calls for 'a reappraisal of the genres which might serve to reconstitute women's political engagement'. Gleadle (2001) argues that in exploiting many sites of political expression, women made use of poetry, novels, letters and travel writing, alongside the conventional political genres of the pamphlet and political disquisition and contributed to radical political culture through correspondence networks and radical salons. Mansell (2001) also demonstrates the political nature of women's memoirs, history-writing and correspondence. In the light of Richardson's (2000) argument that women contributed to literary and political debate through translation of religious and political works, I examine Sarah's contribution to debate on national education through her work as a translator and through engagement in the various networks of which she was a part. I end by discussing her views on the education of working women and its relation to her stance on national education.

Early Life and Political Strategies

Sarah Taylor was born into the Norwich Taylor, Martineau, Reeves family network, a distant cousin to her better-known relative, Harriet Martineau.[1] The Taylors were deeply involved in the movement for the abolition of dissenters' civil disabilities. Sarah's father, John, composed political songs and contributed to the *Cabinet*, a radical journal published at Norwich in 1795, which printed arguments from Godwin's *Political Justice* and Wollstonecraft's *Vindication of the Rights of Woman*. Her eldest brother, Richard, promoted dissenters' interests in the City of London Council. Her mother, Susannah Taylor, known as the 'Madame Roland' of Norwich, celebrated the fall of the Bastille by dancing around a tree of liberty (Hamburger and Hamburger, 1985). Like other Unitarian women, Sarah received an education in advance of her day (Watts, 1998a). Susannah Taylor thought 'solid knowledge' a guard against 'tedium and vapidness' and a resource against poverty and believed the character of girls depended as much upon their reading as the company they kept (Ross, 1888). Sarah studied Latin, French, German (comparatively unusual in the early years of the century for men as well as women), Italian, history, literature, mathematics, philosophy and political economy. Her mother balanced this intellectual education with domestic and emotional training (Hamburger and Hamburger, 1985).To further her education, Sarah spent time in the intellectual circles surrounding Anna Barbauld (Ross, 1888; Watts, 1998b). Sarah married John Austin in 1819. To prepare for an intellectual companionship with her future husband, she undertook an 'apprenticeship', reading the same books as John: Alison, Tacitus, Stewart, Malthus, Smith Condorcet, Bentham, Beccaria, Macchiavelli, Blackstone, Smith, Bacon, Butler, Sallust, Goethe, Hume, Cicero, Mill and Helvetius, some in their German, French and Italian editions (Ross, 1888).

John Austin was called to the bar in 1818 but his frequent bouts of nervous debility militated against court appearances and he quit in 1825, preferring instead to study the principles of law theoretically. In 1826, he was made Professor of Jurisprudence at the new University of London, due to open in 1828. To enable John to prepare for this post, the Austins spent a period in Bonn, taking with them their daughter Lucie, born in 1821.[2] John lectured at London University between 1828 and 1833. He was grave, despondent, sensitive and nervous: a perfectionist, who 'recast and polished a phrase until he could no longer find fault … [he] distrusted himself and was deficient in readiness and self reliance' (Ross, 1888, p. 35). He performed poorly as a lecturer and with no students in attendance, in 1833 he sent in his resignation. He served on the Criminal Law Commission from 1833 but came into conflict with his colleagues and gave up this post in 1836. In all, he was employed only for seven years and the family was frequently in financial straits. To eke out their money and for the sake of John's health, they spent extended periods living abroad. In 1835 they moved temporarily to Hastings before migrating to Boulogne. In 1836, John was appointed Commissioner in Malta, where he and Sarah lived until 1838, when they returned to England. From 1841 they spent seven years abroad: Germany until 1843 (Carlsbad, Dresden and Berlin), followed by France until 1848. When revolution broke out, they returned to England and settled in Weybridge (Hamburger and Hamburger, 1985).

In contrast to John's despondence, Sarah was vivacious and attractive (for several years conducting a clandestine amorous correspondence with Count Pückler-Muskau, an author she translated).

She was fond of society, 'with an almost superabundance of energy and animal spirits' (Ross, 1888, p. 35; Hamburger and Hamburger 1985, pp. 90–4). She turned their London and Paris homes into the resort of 'men of letters and scholars' (Robson and Stillinger, 1981, p. 186). '[A]s remarkable an assemblage of persons as ever met in a London drawing-room', was the *Times'* description of Sarah's London *salon* (Ross, 1912). Barthélemy St. Hilaire noted of her Paris *salon*:

> As she was poor, intellect alone was the attraction and ornament of the house, and all that was most eminent among the foreigners who passed through Paris eagerly sought to be received in her humble apartment. There also the most illustrious Frenchmen of both the Conservative and the Liberal parties met together and ... the most diverse opinions were discussed without acerbity, and to the profit of all ... The salon of Mrs Austin was a centre where France, England, Germany and Italy met and learned to known and appreciate each other. Mrs Austin spoke all four languages (Ross, 1888, p. vi).

Sarah corresponded with influential men and women to whom she proffered advice. She noted that she and William Ewart Gladstone got on 'extremely well together. He was with me for two hours for I am regarded as quite an authority about public instruction and am friends with all who take the subject to heart' (S.A. to Victor Cousin, February 1839, quoted in Ross, 1888, p. 130). She lobbied her friends and acquaintances on causes on which she felt strongly, particularly education. In 1853, she wrote to Gladstone:

> There is a point to which I extremely wish to call your attention ... in consequence of some very curious facts collected and communicated to me by one of the Government Inspectors – Mr Norris. I believe you will find that there exists a great demand, as well as most unexpected resources, for a new and most valuable class of schools ... Now dear Mr Gladstone, give us a scheme for excellent burgher schools, to which the people shall 'pay a good price,' and have in return as much as their money can procure. This matter has been on my mind a year, and if I had been able, I should have written something about it; but if you will take it up, I shall be happy about it (S.A. to Gladstone, 22 January 1853, quoted in Ross, 1888, p. 296).

She worked to persuade, writing that she had converted the MP William Molesworth 'not to Radicalism, but the reverse – to the opinion that the people must be instructed, guided – in short governed' (S.A. to V. Cousin, 2 April 1833, quoted in Ross, 1888, p. 73). And she worked to conciliate, telling Gladstone:

> All I *can* do (and that belongs to my sex) is this. To try to persuade some who think differently from you, and who fancy that you are parted from each other by walls of adamant and not by slender and partial partitions, to give an attentive, respectful and *grateful* ear to your projects, and to see whether it is really demanded by the cause of rational education to reject so much zeal, charity, and knowledge (S.A. to W.E. Gladstone, 18 February 1839, quoted in Ross, 1888, p. 128).

She acted as intermediary, circulating books, pamphlets and ideas about education through her international networks. At the request of Gladstone, she forwarded papers on education to Victor Cousin. Cousin (1792–1868) rose to be lecturer in philosophy at the University of Paris, a member of the Académie Française and the Académie of Political and Ethical Sciences, Inspector-General of Education, a peer of France, Director of the École Normale and Minister of Public Education (Brewer, 1971; Ross, 1912). Sarah and Cousin met while Sarah was living in Bonn and they remained life-long friends and correspondents.

In the face of dire financial straits, Sarah put her knowledge of languages, perfected by periods abroad, to good use and drew on the international networks in which she moved during periods abroad. From the 1820s, she took up paid translation work. She began with anonymous translation, technical and scientific translation and historical and critical commentary, before moving to translate major scholarly works and to write reviews and articles of a literary and educational nature. She became a recognized translator of German works at a point when knowledge of German ideas and literature in Britain was still comparatively limited (Hamburger and Hamburger, 1985). The *Athenaeum* described Sarah as a 'translator of the first class', the *Times*, a brilliant translator, with a virile, masculine intellect and a maturity of judgement. Her translation of Goethe was praised for her unusual grasp of the language and her ability to translate 'metaphysical reasonings, political declamation, and social dialogue – into correct, nervous, vernacular English' (*Athenaeum*, 17 August 1867; Ross, 1912, p. 5; Hamburger and Hamburger, 1985, p. 71).

She acted as John's literary editor, both during his life and after his death. In Malta, her role of partner was more public. Sarah became 'first-lady' and 'consider[ed] herself an equal member of the Commission', regarding her time 'the property of the public' (quoted in Hamburger and Hamburger, 1985, p. 97). She opened her home to convalescents on the outbreak of cholera in 1837; wrote to Cousin and to Nassau Senior for advice about managing schools; worked to establish ten new elementary schools; and raised funds for Maltese institutions by soliciting commissions for Maltese handicrafts from the Queen, Lady Lansdowne and others (Ross, 1888). The *Malta Government Gazette* referred to Sarah as 'La Signora Commissionaria', while the *Harlequin* lampooned her by representing her on horse-back at a carnival: 'with a piece of string she drew after her an enormous jackass, alias donkey; which same donkey was loaded with an immense book inscribed with *political economy*' (quoted in Hamburger and Hamburger, 1985, pp. 105, 118). On their return to England, when Brougham subjected John Austin's work to an attack in the House of Commons (and John took to his bed), Sarah went to Lord Glenelg to discuss the social and religious state of Malta. She wrote to Dr Sciortino in Malta: 'I had to do strange things for a woman, contro il nostro decoro (against our decorum) certainly; but a woman fighting for her husband is always in the right' (S.A. to Dr Sciortino, 10 May 1839, quoted in Ross, 1888, pp. 147–8).

Networking was central to the development and dissemination of Sarah's political views on education. Early in their married life, the Austins moved to Queen's Square, at the heart of the circles of the utilitarian philosophical radicals. They lived next door to James Mill and opposite Jeremy Bentham. Lucie played in Bentham's garden, reputedly avoiding the tapes which marked out on the flower-beds the ground-plan of his panopticon (Waterford, 1937). The young John Stuart Mill, thirteen when the Austins moved next door, read Roman Law with John Austin and learnt German with Sarah, who became like his second mother. The philosophical radicals aimed to overhaul the machinery of state, Parliament, the Church, the judici-ary, old-established corporations, Oxford and Cambridge and the endowed grammar schools. They believed that this could only be achieved if the workers understood that their interests and those of industrial capitalists coincided. This was to be achieved through the extension of suffrage and by 'enlightening' the people through uni-versal education; for if workers were turbulent it was because no appeal had been made to their reason (Simon, 1974a). Brian Simon notes the double-edged nature of their approach. First, they attempted to transform the state's institutions to allow for the political and economic expression of capitalist interest by moulding the people's outlook into willing co-operation within newly developing forms of social relations. Second, classes were seen to need different degrees of education. Since the labouring poor did not have the necessary time for the acquisition of intelligence, there were degrees of intelligence reserved for those who did not have to labour.

Joseph and Lotte Hamburger (1985) have analysed the change in the Austins' stance towards utilitarianism and the role of national education during their stay in Bonn between 1826 and 1888. Benthamite radicals considered that legislators should be elected by democratic suffrage and that they should be responsive to the people's wishes. John, however, came to distinguish between jurisprudence, concerned with the law as it existed and other sciences such as political economy, legislation and politics, which he saw as ethically oriented and concerned with discovering the principles promoting general happiness. He thought there was a valid intellectual foundation to the ethically oriented sciences and that it was possible to establish a utilitarian scientific knowledge of ethics, through which ethical choices in legislation could be made scientifically. As this knowledge of scientific ethics would be the preserve of the few, 'political authority was to be exercised by an intellectual elite, to whom the populus would need to defer on the basis of *authority*, testimony, or trust'. Trust in authority was not, however, to be 'blind' but based on understanding. The populace was to 'clearly apprehend the *leading principles* of political and economic sciences' and as a result be 'docile to the voice of reason' (p. 37). For this, universal education was necessary.

The Gendered Politics of 'Voice'

The chance meeting in Bonn with Victor Cousin, who was collecting evidence for a report on Prussian education for the French Minister of Education, proved influential for Sarah. Cousin's report became the basis of the 1833 French education law and the national system of elementary education developed in France. Sarah was deeply moved by his *Report*, which she circulated; and she lobbied to make more widely known:

I have met Barnes, the omnipotent editor of the Times and have preached to him: ditto the editor of the Examiner ... I have written an urgent letter to Edward Strutt, MP for Derby. Bickersteth, Empson and Romilly, all the men of any note that I know… Strutt…has my copy…after him it goes to Empson; then to Sir W. Molesworth, the young member for Cornwall (S.A. to V. Cousin, 2 April 1833, quoted in Ross, 1888, p. 72).

John Roebuck referred to Cousin's *Report* in the House of Commons in July 1833 during an impassioned plea for a national system of education (*Hansard*, XX, pp. 139–66). When it was first published in French in 1833, it was reviewed in British journals (*Edinburgh Review*, LVII, 1833, pp. 505–24; *Foreign Quarterly Review*, XII, 1833, pp. 273–301). Sarah took the initiative in finding a publisher for an English translation, writing to Cousin that she intended to bring out a cheap translation: 'so that the people may see what is being done elsewhere' (S.A. to V. Cousin, 5 March, 1833, quoted in Ross, 1888, p. 72). She prepared carefully, corresponding with Sir William Hamilton about books on popular education for her annotations (Ross, 1888).

Sarah's translation of Cousin's *Report* was published in 1834. Cousin included a general description of the organization of public education in Prussia, an analysis of the administrative hierarchy and a discussion of the responsibilities of parents and of the duty of local government to provide and pay for primary education. He outlined the different levels of education, examined the training, appointment, promotion and salaries of teachers, the finance, control and supervision of schools and the content of the curriculum, as well as providing statistical information. In addition, he included an examination of the Prussian normal schools and details of the Berlin schools for the poor. The second part was based on his collection of more than one hundred official documents, including syllabuses, abstracts of laws, degrees, programmes of study, sample examinations, yearly reports, statistics and so on. In her desire to make a case for a national system of popular education, Sarah omitted the part of the report which dealt with secondary education and outlined in the Preface her own passionately held views. She argued for a state funded but locally controlled national education system, with the capacity to develop the minds and character of the pupils. She wanted primary education to be compulsory, with a national curriculum, inspection and accountability, all of which were to be supported by changes in pedagogy and teacher training, with pensions for teachers to raise the status of the teaching profession.

Her translation was both timely and well received. James Kay (future Secretary to the Committee of Council on Education) noted:

> The translation of the reports of M.Cousin on the state of primary instruction in Prussia … has made the English public universally acquainted with the inquiry which M.Cousin executed by direction of the French Government (Kay-Shuttleworth, 1862, p. 221).

Thomas Wyse MP commended 'Mrs Austin's excellent translation' in a paper on Prussian education (Wyse, 1839, p. 375) and Leonard Horner, Inspector under the Poor Laws, commented:

> There cannot be a doubt that the publication of … reports of the primary schools in Prussia through the medium of the admirable translation of Mrs Austin has been of the greatest service to the practical working of a most ingeniously contrived and most effective system (Horner, 1838).

The *Leeds Mercury* rejoiced that Englishmen now had the description of the Prussian system before them and believed that 'it will soon begin to be duly appreciated and that some attempt worthy of a free and enlightened people and a liberal legislature will be made to naturalise among us' (quoted in Cousin, ed. Knight, 1930, p. 119). The *Athenaeum* said that in translating the report, Sarah deserved the gratitude of the country, not merely because of the ability and fidelity with which she had performed the undertaking but also because she had drawn 'the attention of her countrymen to their most important interests':

> She wrote fervidly and with compelling logic on behalf of compulsory school attendance legislation, which was an important feature of education in Prussia, although she was fully aware of the deep and prevalent belief in England at the time 'that the prime excellence of a government is to let alone'. Compulsory school attendance would be an infringement of liberty, it was believed. But Mrs Austin appealed for the children. Is exemption from compulsion to attend school salutary or pernicious, she asked. Shall the whole future lives of the children be sacrificed to the present interest of the persons who have the disposal of them? She argued that the government should secure to the children

'for life the blessings of physical, moral and intellectual health' (ibid., pp. 120–1).

Robert Southey wrote that he had read the translation with great interest (Ross, 1888) and the translation was welcomed by radical educationists William Fox and the South Place circle (Watts, 1998a). Favourable reviews were carried by a range of journals in England and America, where there was a similar interest in state support for schooling (*North American Review*, XL, 1835, p. 513). The part dealing with the administrative organization of education in Prussia was reprinted in New York in 1835 and influenced provision in Michigan and Massachusetts (Brewer, 1971; Cousin, ed. Knight, 1930). By 1837, parts of Cousin's report, with J. Orville Taylor's preface to the American edition and Sarah's introduction had been published in Canada, with a plan for the organization of educational inspection and draft legislation (Curtis, 1992; Orville Taylor, 1836).

In 1835, Sarah published a review of translated French documents in *Cochrane's Foreign Quarterly*. Here, she examined the implementation in France of the Prussian system of education and drew on evidence from Italy, America and Holland to make suggestions for education policy in England. When *Cochrane's Foreign Quarterly* failed to reach a third number (and with the public largely unaware of its existence), she was persuaded to reprint the review as a book, which came out in 1839, entitled *On National Education*. In compiling *On National Education*, she interwove the voices of translation, summary and comment and relegated the translation to the status of quotations to support her views, characteristically noting in the preface that she had 'doubts of the value of everything it contains except the quotations' (Austin, 1839, p. xi). This, too, was a polemic plea for state provided primary education, with a national curriculum, inspection and accountability, supported by changes in pedagogy and in teacher training, in which translated French documents were manipulated to address the contentious issues of state intervention and the role of the church in education, the form and content of popular education and teacher training.

Sarah's translations were undertaken for financial gain but as these two educational texts illustrate, her choice of topic and text and her own prefaces and appended notes provided a vehicle through which she disseminated her political views. But public exposure was something Sarah feared, particular when this was related to political polemic. No longer publishing anonymously, as in *Cochrane's Foreign Quarterly*, caused Sarah concern. Like many nineteenth-century women, her ambivalence about her public political voice is demonstrated in her comment to Gladstone on the translation of Cousin's *Report*: 'On the subject of the education of the people, I did indeed once venture on a few words, but only under cover of a great name' (S.A. to W.E. Gladstone, 27 May 1839, quoted in Ross, 1888, i, p. 133). Friends like Thomas Carlyle thought that she had the ability to produce original work – but she told Barthélemy St. Hilaire that she feared by publishing anything of her own to expose herself to criticism and that 'she always considered it improper in a woman to provoke a possible polemic, which generally ends in manner disagreeable to herself' (Ross, 1888, i, p. ix). Fearful that *On National Education* was going to put her in the full glare of publicity, prior to publication she sent Gladstone proof copies for comment, telling him:

> But now, seeing the violence and bitterness with which the subject is ... handled by the Press, I take fright. I have always shrunk from appearing before the public in my own person or behalf, as the author or champion of any opinions whatever. ... I never felt that I had the least pretension to instruct the world ... I ... would bear martyrdom if it would do any good; but I am, after all, a woman; and I cannot bear, without a good reason the coarse and disgusting hands of the daily press to be laid upon me. I feel ... I may and must express opinions which may be misstated and distorted ... and my courage is tottering (S.A. to W.E. Gladstone, 27 May 1839, quoted in Ross, 1888, i, p. 133).

In her translation/writing, like Cousin, Sarah employed a quiet mode of agitation, aimed primarily at a middle-class public. Typical tactics in this approach were slow accretion of the 'facts' of educational 'destitution' and a mass of propaganda, much of it in the form of official reports spelling out the consequences (Johnson, 1977). In 1808, the French philosopher, César Auguste Basset, argued that in collecting information about foreign education systems it was necessary to 'judge men and things in accordance with real and established facts, and not in terms of written systems of speculative plans' (Brinkman, 1960, p. 7). This formed part of the development of education as a 'positive science'. In 1817, Marc-Antoine Jullien noted:

> Education, as other sciences, is based on facts and observations, which should be ranged in analytical tables, easily compared, in

order to deduce principles and definite rules. Education should become a positive science instead of being ruled by narrow and limited opinions, by whims and arbitrary decisions of administrators, to be turned away from the direct line which it should follow, either by the prejudice of a blind routine or by the spirit of some system and innovation (quoted in Hans, 1949, p. 1).

Like Cousin, Sarah located her writing within the developing science of education. Although finding the official documents for *On National Education* 'repulsively dry', Sarah was keen to 'let the facts speak'. Echoing, Basset, she aimed 'to stop rumours and to give authentic details' and noted: 'The materials for our article are ... of an official and historical, rather than of a speculative, nature' (Austin, 1835, pp. 260, 275, 300; 1839, pp. viii, 12). She stressed it was the business of the state 'to collect information and opinions from all sources; to diffuse them again through every part of the empire, and to impress upon the whole one uniform and national impulse and direction' (Austin, 1835, pp. 269, 298). She presented much of her critique of education systems through the metaphor of the machine (the mechanism) – used by 1830s social analysts to represent a system in which all working parts were subordinated to the productivity of the whole (Poovey, 1995):

> We entirely agree ... that beautiful as is the mechanism of the Prussian system, it does not accomplish half what it might and ought; and though the *how* is admirably provided for; the *what* of education ... is defective. But we confidently believe that, could we but obtain this mechanism, we should outstrip all other countries in the application of it (Austin, 1835, pp. 300–1).

Sarah represented the health, welfare and prosperity of the nation through the metaphor of the social body, claiming 'it is not the *vox populi*, but the *salus populi*, which is *suprema lex*' (p. 301). Sarah described the Prussian system of education as 'a system living and working', which 'can only be appreciated when studied connectedly and in detail' (Austin preface to Cousin, 1834, p. vii). The constraints put on people by state legislation, 'secure to them for life the blessings of physical, moral and intellectual health' (p. ix). The Prussian system of education was the 'parent', the French education system Prussia's 'first-born offspring' (Austin, 1835 p. 260). Using the analogy of the dead body, she remarked, 'what we have been pleased to call education' is 'meagre, unfruitful and lifeless' (p. 287). Employing sexual metaphors of the body, she quoted Milton's allusion to the 'pregnant soil' of the nation (p. 260) and François Guizot's fear that the 'great work would remain sterile' (p. 293).

Social analysts used the metaphor of the social body to treat one segment of the population as a special problem, while pointing towards the interests which (theoretically) united all parts of society. This was a gendered metaphor, for social analysts depicted the health of the social body undermined by 'abnormal' social relations (Poovey, 1995). Poovey argues that the metaphor of the social body fostered the growth of statistical representation. Sarah was friends with Babbage, who pressed the British Advancement for the Advancement of Science to establish a statistical section (which it did in 1833). In the 1830s, statisticians tended to juxtapose numerical representations alongside historical or explanatory narratives (Poovey, 1994). As translator, Sarah had dealt with statistical tables in Cousin's *Report* and in Malta had subsequently aimed 'to get something in the way of a statistical table to represent educational provision' (S.A. to Mrs Senior, 7 March 1838, quoted in Ross, 1888, p. 120). But *On National Education* was to be a small and cheap edition for a popular audience and in line with an oft-repeated mid-century charge – that statistics were boring if not unreadable (Poovey, 1994, p. 406) – Sarah dispensed with statistical tables to save space and in consideration of her 'popular' audience.

Where women were concerned, the growth of statistics, and 'fact' gathering were contradictory. The disembodied nature of abstraction was at variance with definitions of women as a relational being, although the metaphor of the social body, grounded in 'nature' did open up a space for women's intervention (Poovey, 1995). 'Fact' gathering could prove problematic for women when concerned with institutions of the state and semi-official bureaucracies of foreign education systems. As early as 1808, Basset argued for the appointment of a university official to travel in order to make observations about education and instruction in general. This official was to be a scholar with literary ability and an administrator familiar with all aspects of liberal and popular education. Cousin exemplified this model. In his *Report* he notes that after mastering the laws and regulations of a foreign system he verified them by accurate and detailed inspection. He carried a letter of introduction from the Minister of Public Instruction in France to Baron von Altenstein, the Minister of Public Instruction in Berlin, who granted him an interview and assigned to him 'one of his confidential councillors to give … not only every possible information but whatever documents, whether printed or manuscript, [he] might desire'. Cousin reported, 'Nothing that I had the least desire to know was concealed from me' (Cousin, ed. Knight, 1930, p. 118).

As a (married) woman, Sarah's civic disabilities precluded her travelling as an official of the state, although, as her role in Malta and immediately after demonstrates, she was quite prepared to flout conventional womanly behaviour should the need arise. Travel enabled women like Sarah and her friend Mary Berry to compare what they saw of educational systems at work in other countries with their own ideals (Dolan, 2001), but they did not do so with the same official support as men. Unlike Cousin, Sarah had to draw on her own networks and initiative. On her return from Malta, she visited Italian infant schools. In the style of Cousin she wrote 'At Milan my first care was to find out some one who could give me information about the state of education in Lombardy' (Ross, 1888, i, pp. 123–4). To supplement her own accounts, she drew on eyewitness accounts from her acquaintances (Austin, 1835, p. 299). This 'difference' played out at the level of audience, with Victor Cousin's text being presented to the French Minister of Education, while Sarah's was for a popular audience.

The Politics and Pedagogy of Universal Popular Education

Underpinning Sarah's calls for a national system of education were fears of the upsurge of working-class radicalism in the 1830s and 1840s. This engaged philosophical radicals and whigs alike. Roebuck argued in his 1833 Education Bill that popular education was about making England safe for democracy and a necessity if working people were to 'understand their social condition' right, so that there would be no more discontents, no more rick-burning, no more combinations and 'futile schemes of reform' (quoted in Green, 1990, p. 251). Kay urged that 'good secular education' was necessary to prevent anarchy because it would enable the working people 'to understand the true causes which determine their physical condition and regulate the distribution of wealth among the several classes of society' (quoted in Hamilton, 1989, p. 100). In this vein, Sarah wrote in her preface to Cousin's *Report*:

> Society is no longer a calm current, but a tossing sea. Reverence for tradition, for authority, is gone. In such a state of things, who

can deny the absolute necessity for national education? (Austin, preface to Cousin, 1834, pp. viii, ix).

Although she advocated universal popular education, Sarah thought it misplaced to instil in the minds of the people that education was the way to advancement; that knowledge was power; and that to better oneself one needed learning. She argued that universal primary education was the one guarantee of social order and stable government (Austin, 1835, p. 295):

> Whenever education shall have done its work – whenever the people shall be sufficiently enlightened to see all that the business of legislation demands – then, and not before, will they cease to struggle for a power they will see it is impossible they could wield; then and not before, will the grand conflict that now agitates the world cease – cease, not by the destruction or the subjection of a party, but by the steadfast and enlightened will of convinced men (p. 301).

Sarah proposed an education that was moral and religious and based on reason. Like her husband John, she thought it should 'embrace all the most important parts of ethical science; a science consummately important to man as *man*, without distinction of country, or rank, or occupation (p. 238). It was to touch the 'nature of man' (p. 287) and engage the intellect by the consideration of principles. For this, the minds of the children were to be put in constant contact with the mind of the master – an intelligent, zealous and kind-hearted man who would call them around him daily, talk to them of what he wished them to learn and to be and hear their thoughts (Austin, 1839, p. 161). In this, she mirrored Cousin, who spoke of the 'high calling' and vocation of the teacher, whose duties were 'closely allied to religion' (Cousin, ed. Knight, 1930, p. 170). The teacher was to know the individual character and qualities of each pupil and to lead [pupils] to 'simple and lucid principles' by 'enlightened observation and their own experience' (Cousin, ed. Knight, 1930, p. 171).

This view of the teacher's role had its roots in German Pietism, which celebrated 'inwardness' and stressed the role of education in shaping personality (Green, 1990). Pietists built their education system around the individual power of a Christian father–teacher and his ability to imbue his charges with self-discipline. 'Out of the depths of their innermost soul, the children should strive to please their fatherly schoolmaster and beyond him, their worldly rulers and ultimately the patriarchal God in his Heaven' (Miller, 1998, p. 152). Pietist schools, founded in Prussia in the late seventeeth century, established the German reputation for the most advanced pedagogical techniques. A key innovation was the simultaneous method of classroom teaching, which was thought to bring the mind of each child 'at all times under the influence of the master' and in touch with his 'moralising and formative influence' (Hamilton, 1989, p. 103); to enable 'a more adequate explanation of the principals underlying the lesson'; and to facilitate 'the exercise of understanding rather than memory' (Jones and Williamson, 1979, p. 88). Other innovations included: ability grouping for students; the practices of student hand-raising and roll call; standardized text books; the concept of 'free-time' (the cultivation of self-disciplined work), and methodical teacher training (Miller, 1998; Green, 1990). The appeal of Pietist pedagogy lay in 'its simultaneous promotion of submission and autonomy' (Green, 1990, p. 118), which made it attractive to absolutist states like those of Prussia and in tune with the Austins' view of the need for an educational system able to foster the attachment of a people to their government.

This high reputation for advanced pedagogical techniques continued in the next century when German schools were ahead of all others in the application of new methods particularly those of Johann Heinrich Pestalozzi (Green, 1990; Barkin, 1983). In her 1841 *Fragments from German Prose Writers*, Sarah included an extract from Johann Gottlieb Fichte's *Addresses to the German Nation* to the effect that Pestalozzi's pedagogical principles had the power to raise the masses (Austin, 1841, p. 145). Here, she described Pestalozzi as 'the most original and efficient of the leaders in the great movement ... in favour of the moral and mental culture of the people', 'a man of genius', who 'threw out a vast quantity of the most prolific suggestions, on which all succeeding labourers in the same field have continued to work – and must continue, since they are founded on the nature of the human mind'. Sarah had contacts with English advocates of Pestalozzi and proponents of the English infant school movement. At the request of James Mill she became a frequent visitor at the Westminster Infant School, where she met James Buchanan. A Swedenborgian, Buchanan disseminated the ideas of David Stow, the Scottish infant school pioneer (McCann and Young, 1982, p. 20). Sarah thought Buchanan made infant schools what they ought to be: 'nurseries for the body and soul, and not exhibitions of learned babes' (S.A. to Brougham, 21 February 1851, quoted in McCann and Young, 1982, p. 41). The London private school to which Sarah sent Lucie in 1831 was run by Dr Edward Biber, a German refugee and publicist for infant schools and supporter of Pestalozzi. With James Pierpoint Greaves (who helped produce the English edition of Pestlozzi's *Letters on Education*), Biber founded an infant school in Shoreditch (p. 169).

Sarah thought that making 'men and Christians, beings led by reason and conscience', could not be left either to philanthropy or market forces (Austin, 1835, p. 287). This would result in the poorest areas being the most educationally deprived. Education had to be 'fit for all' and an 'organised system' and was, therefore, the duty of the state (p. 279). She thought education had to be supplied to create demand (p. 287). In this respect, Law was the educator of the nation (p. 284): 'all government is coercion. It is the end alone that is to decide whether that coercion be just and wise' (Austin, 1839, p. 140). She commended the French government for forcing education upon the people – for they had consulted their interests rather than their inclinations (Austin, 1835, p. 298). Her texts abound with allusions to the need for the people to be made aware of their best interests in order to foster the safety of the country.

The Politics and Pedagogy of Education for Working-class Women and Girls

During the 1830s and 1840s, Sarah's views on the education of working women resonated with her analysis of national education. She thought the separation of girls and boys one of the 'very suspicious refinements of later times' (Austin, 1835, p. 291). Because of the general low educational achievements of school mistresses she also thought girls were better educated when taught by a man (Austin, 1839, p. 159). She commended 'the good sense' and 'pure and healthy doctrine' of Cousin, who urged in his *Report* that both boys and girls should receive the same curriculum, save for the omission in the girls' curriculum of geometry and the addition of needlework.

By 1839, Sarah's notes in *On National Education* show a more conservative strain:

The education of women is good as that of men is good, if it conduces to make them cheerful, efficient labourers in the field of usefulness allotted to them by heaven; if it trains them to self-control, self-denial and to a constant predominance of the reason of kindly and pious affections (p. 145).

Although she still advocated girls being taught the intellectual part of their education by men, here she laid more stress on the acquisition of domestic skills. This shift is discernible after her visit to Norwood, James Kay's model school for the training of teachers, set up according to Dutch and Prussian examples (Selleck, 1994). Sarah praised Kay's espousal of co-education – 'a pure and healthy system' (Austin, 1839, p. 158) – but notes his opinion that factory girls were lamentably ignorant of household management and that the withdrawal of the majority of married women from work outside their own homes (except in cases of absolute necessity) was indispensable if the domestic training of girls was to improve (Kay-Shuttleworth, 1862). Sarah mirrors Kay in her view that the situation of working-class women in the large manufacturing towns had worsened since the introduction of manufacturing 'which congregates young women in large masses *away from home and home occupations* and prevents them acquiring housewifely management and skills' (Austin, 1839, p. 144).

Sarah's views on working women's education became increasingly conservative. In her *Two Letters on Girls' Schools*, published in 1857 after she had left France (Austin, 1857, p. 23), she compared English working-class women detrimentally to their continental counterparts:

> It is impossible to conceive the waste and improvidence which reigns in the lowest English households. The women buy improvidently, cook improvidently, and dress improvidently. The consequences are, want, debt, disorder, and all that can make a man's home comfortless and irritating, take from him all hope of improvement in his condition, all regard for so useless a partner and drive him to the alehouse (p. 25).

Through the metaphor of the social body, Sarah expressed her fears of the effects of 'the fatal subversion of domestic life' and the 'universal discontent' to which she believed this had led (p. 35):

> I am convinced that the perplexities and grievances of mistresses, the inefficiency and recklessness and corruption of servants, and

the miserable deficiencies of working men's wives are only symptoms of a general disorder of our social body (no member of which has a distinct life); and that, in order to arrive at a radical cure of any one of these evils, we must go into a complete examination of their mutual relation and common source (ibid.).

She portrayed as a 'social monster' the existence of a village in which a thousand women and girls were employed in a factory, while there was no corresponding occupation for men. She represented the disturbance to social life that she thought came from such 'disorder' as a 'torrent sweeping away domestic life among the humbler classes of England' (p. 14). This image of the torrent was the same metaphor through which she had earlier described the danger to the country from an 'unenlightened' populus. Her critique of working-women's shortcomings stands in stark contrast to aspects of her own early upbringing within Unitarian circles, her partnership in some of her husband's endeavours and her own espousal of the bread-winning role within her family. Yet, her critique can also be located in her own need for domestic skills, thrift and economy if her family was to survive (Hamburger and Hamburger, 1985). Despite her amorous correspondence with Pückler-Muskau, she continually stressed the social disorder that would result from loss of the sanctity of marriage.

The Hamburgers argue that Sarah's attitudes to women changed as a result of the French Revolution and because the stirring of the feminist movement posed a threat to the self-image through which she managed her husband's unfulfilled potential (p. 154). Sarah, herself, looked back to her experience of France in 1848 as a turning point in the development of her political opinions (p. 169). Her views on women's roles can be gleaned from her biographical practices and critique of the biographical practices of others. Though she promoted German literature, when discussing the biographies of German authors like Johanna Schopenhaur, she noted that Romanticism's disclosures of 'what Germans call the inward life [were] destructive of the reserve which it is neither safe nor graceful for a woman to lay aside' (Austin, 1841, p. 341). In such critique, she drew on fears of women cutting across the boundaries of the public and the private and also on mid-century charges of vanity and egotism that were regularly levelled against practitioners of autobiography (Marcus, 1994). Her hagiographical memoirs of the lives of women like the Duchess of Orleans, the widow of the heir to the

French throne, who fled France with her children in 1848 and became Lucie's neighbour at Claremont, and Mme Recamier, whom Sarah met at the Abbaye aux Bois and who was exiled from France because of her friendship with Germaine de Staël, illustrate her increasing traditionalism where women's roles were concerned (Hamburger and Hamburger, 1985, p. 157). Such views were bolstered by men in her networks, like François Guizot and Auguste Comte, who frequented Sarah's Paris salon and whose Sunday gatherings Sarah attended (Ross, 1888, p. 194). Sarah held to her belief in intellectual equality for women but saw the struggle for women's emancipation and rights as part of the more general conflicts 'stirring society in all its depths' (Austin, 1854, p. 270). She noted that her views, especially regarding women were diametrically opposed to those of her relative Harriet Martineau (Hamburger and Hamburger, 1985).

By 1857, Sarah was openly admitting to changed opinions on the education of girls. She argued that the more 'intellectual education offered girls in the national schools was detrimental to the aspirations of parents and children alike' (Austin, 1857, p. 10). She traced the 'depreciation of the manual skill … essential to every working woman' back to the training given to female teachers. In large institutions 'in a sort of collegiate manner', far from 'all participation in the business and cares of the household', student teachers' views of excellence came to be 'associated with the studies which engross their minds'. This, in turn, reacted on the minds and characters of their pupils and 'powerfully contributed to give a non-domestic tendency to … modern education' (p. 7).

Sarah re-worked the philosophical radicals' view of different intelligences being developed by different classes, to argue that an education consisting solely of book learning 'would never develop the intellect of working-class girls *in the direction and manner* in which it is important that it should be developed' (p. 4). She still held to the view that education was to be geared to the 'cultivation and development of the intellectual faculties and the moral perceptions' but now it was to do so 'in a way that had a bearing on life' (p. 5). She claimed that the conduct of a household 'with order and economy' made large demands on 'the reason and on the faculties of observation' and left these faculties strengthened for their application to intellectual ends. Furthermore, '[t]he conduct of a household with grace and dignity' made large demands on 'the sense of fitness, harmony and beauty; and ripens the sense for exercise on purely aesthetical objects' (p. 28):

> The assumption that the intelligence is more exercised and forti-
> fied by learning by rote a vast number of so-called facts, names,
> dates, scraps of science, or propositions unintelligible to the
> learner, than by the exercise of the accurate observation and rapid
> induction required in household operations, is an entirely false
> one, and has a very mischievous tendency to exult the showy
> above the useful, and the superficial above the solid. What we are
> calling out for is, careful, intelligent, conscientious labour (p. 6).

To this end, working-class girls were to be given a basic diet of reading, writing and casting accounts 'the three great and powerful
instruments by which further knowledge may be acquired' and
which in the hands of clever girls were 'vehicles for awakening
thoughts and inculcating habits which would have a steady reference to the conditions of her future life' (p. 5).

Sarah found her ideal working-class girls' education at the small
day industrial school for girls from the shopkeeping and artisan
class established at Norwich by her distant relative Francis
Martineau, cousin of the more famous Harriet. Here, in two adjoin-
ing houses knocked into one, was 'every variety of pantry, cupboard
and place of stowage: rooms large and small, wash-houses,
playground, – in short, *a place for everything*' (p. 16). Sarah noted that
the instruction given was 'precisely the thing wanted … and the
want of which is manifesting itself in the most calamitous forms
throughout our social fabric' (p. 15). The charge was 6d and the
school under Government inspection. The curriculum included
scripture, reading, writing, arithmetic, grammar, geography, part-
singing, outline drawing, English history, 'elementary instruction
upon natural objects', general knowledge, plain needlework
(including cutting-out, making and mending clothes) and household education. The playground was large enough 'to afford recreation and healthy refreshment' and the children brought their
dinners, which were 'served with due attention to comfort and
order' (pp. 17, 18). In Fanny Martineau's view, the 'superiority' of
her school lay in the (trained) mistress 'so capable of teaching the
higher branches of knowledge, and yet so anxious to give an interest to all home and useful duties' and the housekeeper. She was a
former servant to Amelia Opie and 'one of those paragons of neat-
ness, those finished artists in the great and complicated business of

cleaning' (p. 19). After her visit, Sarah praised the object lessons, the arithmetic, the writing and the girls' domestic skills:

> I saw one at her work, washing the earthen vessels, wiping, *not smearing*, them and arranging them dry and bright, on pantry shelves of spotless whiteness. It was with peculiar satisfaction that I soon afterwards saw the same girl come into the school and teach a class of younger girls arithmetic. This, thought I, is the real type and expression of the life and duty of woman.... There is nothing higher than this; – the comfort, order and good government of the house, and the instruction of the young. To fit herself to fulfil these paramount duties of her sex, a woman must acquire qualities intellectual and moral, second to none possessed by man or woman (p. 20).

The Gendered Politics of Historical Memory

In many respects, Sarah and her better known 'feminist' cousin, Harriet Martineau held similar views when it came to the education of working-class women and girls. As Gaby Weiner demonstrates, Harriet's approach to female education was at the same time traditional and advanced: 'Martineau firmly located the ideal place for woman in the home and frequently described their "natural" occupations as wives and mothers' (Weiner, 1991, pp. 58–9). With this in view, Harriet advocated a form of female education which, like that espoused by Sarah, would both extend working-class women's thought processes and advance their domestic skills.

In her *Daily News* leaders, Harriet Martineau followed much the same path as Sarah in her calls for popular education. Harriet advocated state finance to support a national system of education for the working class, opposed the monitorial system, supported industrial training, a relevant curriculum, the 3Rs, industrial and manual training and oral work, the teaching of common things and household skills, and called for infant schools to be less didactic (Weiner, 1991). Harriet recognized a similar potential for class war in the Chartist movement and the 1848 revolution as did Sarah. Along with Charles Knight, Harriet launched the *Voice of the People* to combat class theories of society with a nationalist analysis that underlined the role of the propertied classes in preserving popular sovereignty (Finn, 1993, pp. 79–80).

On other issues, particularly feminist issues, Sarah and Harriet disagreed and an antipathy can be identified between them. Sarah was quick to note where her views on the extension of the female role and the 'rights' of women differed from those of Harriet and was deprecating of Harriet's motivations for turning down her Civil List pension. Harriet, for her part, included Sarah in a list of women whose 'gross and palpable vanities ... made women blush and men smile' (Martineau, 1877, p. 352). While the two women shared views on working-class education, Harriet's 'advanced' views on middle-class women's education have gained her a place in the history of changing ideas about women, with the result that she figures in histories of women's education; although her views on working-class women's education sit rather awkwardly within current feminist educational historiography. Despite the similarity of Harriet's and Sarah's stances on the education of the working class and that of working women, the traditionalism of Sarah's views on women in her old age may well have caused her to have been passed over – a reactionary in a feminist trope of 'progress'. This, in turn, may have bolstered her absence in a historiography of education underpinned by masculinist frames of political action and expertise. For a woman who lobbied politicians on the causes she held dear, and whose voice reached to the United States and Canada, this is undeserved.

4

Jane Chessar (1835–80): From 'Surplus' Woman to Professional Educator

When Jane Chessar started work in the 1850s, ideals of domesticity positioned women in the home. Notably the single woman from the middle-class home who was labelled redundant amid anxieties that emigration had upset the sex ratio and left an excess of 'surplus' women. Social commentators touched a chord when they damned those who sought to challenge their culture and class by necessity and choice – even though they could not all be made to fit into the mid-Victorian myth. Moving through education and feminism, Jane successfully reworked the negative connotations of redundancy. Circumscribed by the context in which she was living and working, she reinvoked maternalism to create empowering identities and self-representations both within and against the dominant male narratives in teacher education and local government politics. Yet, the substance of her story has been virtually forgotten today and it is difficult to assemble the circumstances of her life and personality. I use biographical approaches to reveal how she sought a role outside the home. They provide a framework for revealing the effect on her life of having access to education as a developing form of employment and the consequences for her emergent subjectivity including the negotiation of identity. My purpose is to capture the qualities of agency, movement and change and to use the individual biography to reveal common experiences, to look at the structure–agency relation, the personal and the public, the self and significant society.

In her brief biographical account of two key figures in Victorian education, Dorothea Beale and Frances Buss, Carol Dyhouse writes 'education was (and is) one of the few areas of public life where women *have* achieved a measure of status and authority' (Dyhouse, 1987, p. 23). Beale, Buss and Chessar had much in common. Teaching offered them a recognized and acceptable form of work and a means to support themselves as single women. Chessar is important for two reasons in particular. First, she pioneered collective working, networking and the pursuit of alternate strategies in order to get women's voices and demands into the relatively autonomous but still embryonic educational bureaucracy. Second, she was one of the first women in the UK to be elected to a position of political responsibility. An account of her atypical life as a local politician and educator draws her out of obscurity and provides an opportunity for thinking about a series of dialectical tensions: between such dualisms as public and private, patriarchy and matriarchy, power and marginality. This study provides evidence that Chessar did transgress boundaries and barriers as a woman who moved into leadership. To what extent she was seen as 'troubling', 'trouble' or 'troubled' remains to be seen (Blackmore, 1999).

The chapter begins with a brief account of Jane's early life and social background for clues to her 'revolt against redundancy' (Vicinus, 1985). In telling her story I examine her social and professional identity as a female educator, her contribution to local government politics, as well as her personal and political collaboration with Mary Richardson. What she lived out in her teaching career will serve to elucidate crucial facets of the historical construction of gender/power/knowledge relations in educational work. The focus on the increased politicization that sprang from a wider commitment to a developing feminist culture makes it possible to construct a clear picture of webs of friendships and shared values, as well as party politics. Such dynamics provide a framework for considering her service on the London School Board. No other state in Europe or America offered women a comparable public role at such an early period and I will argue that the activities of Jane Chessar had significant implications for communities of practice rooted in a larger tradition of female activism.

Early Life and Social Background

The account of the early years of family life in the Chessar household is fragmentary and anecdotal. Very little is known other than what can be gleaned from her obituaries, written by friends. She was born in 1835 in Edinburgh. Her father is recorded as a 'man of intellectual ability' suggesting that she came from a middle-class home.

The education she received was designed to fit her for the genteel labour market and her father's relatively early death at the age of 44 probably made Jane conscious of her economic vulnerability (*Englishwoman's Review*, 15 October 1880). One of three daughters, with family support she received an organized programme of study in co-educational private schools and classes. Jane hoped to earn her living by teaching or governessing and underwent full-time training at the Home and Colonial College, London, founded in 1836.

Those who held power within the Home and Colonial Infant School Society were composed overwhelmingly of early Victorian bankers, lawyers, parliamentarians and peers who should be classed as 'evangelicals' (McCann and Young, 1982, p. 180). Its basic objectives made it clear that this was an out-and-out Evangelical organization:

> First, 'the improvement and extension of the Infant School system on Christian principles', in the colonies and other countries as well as Britain; second, the training of persons of 'character and piety' who were 'apt to teach'; third, to afford existing teachers the means of improvement (cited in McCann and Young, 1982, p. 190).

Male clerical authority was dominant in the earliest period of teacher education in England. Early developments were in the control of the voluntary denominational societies but those associated with the Church of England were by far the most numerous (Heward, 1993). Government funds became available in 1833 and the need to keep down the cost of teacher education to the Society was to impel revision of its heavily evangelical public image. Because of the expense involved in the provision of initial teacher training it became necessary to widen the support base by moving from a position of religious isolation to acceptance by the Established Church and the new forms of government bureaucracy. In 1841 the rules were changed to be ' "the improvement and general extension of the Infant-school system, on the Christian principles, *as such principles are set forth and embodied in the doctrinal articles of the Church of England*" ' (cited in McCann and Young, 1982, p. 194). So, when Jane arrived at the training college in 1850, the religious and moral tone was orthodox Anglican. The length of the course was 24 weeks with 56 hours' tuition. Academic work (mainly in their subject specialism) occupied 36 hours, professional instruction occupied nine and three quarter hours, with ten and a quarter hours spent on practice in the model school in front of an audience of fellow-students. One of the two practice schools in the Gray's Inn Road was for students

who intended to work in state-supported infant schools; the other
for nursery governesses and kindergarten teachers in private estab-
lishments. In 1846 the Society had taken the initiative in offering a
hostel for trainee educators and it seems likely that Jane joined the
private teachers' department (Lawrence, 1952, pp. 40–1).

The Home and Colonial Infant School Society was significant for
its pioneering of progressive pedagogical methods associated with
Samuel Wilderspin in Britain and Johannes Pestalozzi in Europe.
Because Wilderspin wanted the schools to remain non-denominational
in their approach to religious teaching, however, the conventional
historiography has eradicated his contribution to the central training institute at the level of ideas (McCann and Young, 1982). Here
I wish to focus on particular aspects of progressive thought that
were shared and adapted by women. The first was on the subject of
their vital educative role. Pestalozzi promoted the influence of
women and ideas. His belief that the clue to educational progress
was to be found in appropriating maternal practice left a significant
legacy. Talk of a woman's educational mission that involved identification with the child and stressed the necessity of education and
training provided a space for professional discourse that lent his
ideas a very specific appeal to a particular audience in Britain.
Hilton and Hirsch (2000, p. 12) note that Pestalozzi had developed a
pedagogy 'based on the observed behaviour of the interactions
between a "good" mother and her child, which gave cultural
authority to ideas already extant in women's educational work' (see
Chapter 2). Second, the remaking of teaching as a 'pedagogy of the
feminine' (Walkerdine, 1994) was furthered through another area of
progressive ideology – Friedrich Froebel's idea of the kindergarten.
Going beyond Pestalozzi, Froebel argued 'it was the task of the
mother in the home, as it was the teacher in the school, to provide
the right environment for the young child – the "child's garden"'
(Smart, 1994, p. 10). Firmly set within middle-class society, by mid-
century Froebelian ideas appealed to those concerned about the
poor quality of the education and career opportunities for girls and
young ladies. Apart from the figurative use of the 'garden' as a
proper setting for child development (Steedman, 1990), supporters
promoted the theme of play and the use of specific educational
apparatus (known collectively as the 'gifts' and the 'occupations').
In this way, a community of interests provided women involved in
the publicity machine of the Froebelian movement with a *raison
d'être* (Brehony, 2000). A number took up social service allured by a
compelling vision in which women were active as educators and

reformers in the home, school and locality. Women teachers were 'the mother made conscious' (Steedman, 1985) and prominent Froebelians could take on the structures of professionalism to contest powerful representations of 'redundancy' and remove the threat of being considered 'deviant'.

With this loophole, leading women educationists of the Victorian age could construct a professional model. Central to this effort was the belief in the different natures of men and women at the heart of older philosophical arguments about the moral and regenerative contribution of women to society. Women writers in feminist journals like the *Englishwoman's Review* commonly argued that just as the family and household required the active co-operation of feminine with masculine brains and hands, so the voices of women should be heard in the wider sphere beyond. From this it follows that maternalist discourses lay at the heart of early claims for women's authority in the political spaces of society and expanded a wide range of women's movements and movements of women. Indeed, the dualism of public and private, patriarchy and matriarchy became stretched in various directions as a weapon for social change. Many articles on female education and employment for women appeared whose proposals were grounded in logical argument based on notions of sexual difference, service and liberal equality. The ethic of self-sacrifice was constantly evident in this concern about the rights of women; and the ideology of social maternalism reinforced belief in women's motherly influence, which was redefined as a source of strength. Reformers were clear that teaching offered the best combination of public service and motherhood, so early claims for single women's employment in teaching can be understood adequately only within a broader context of a specifically female variant of contemporary cultural and social criticism. At a time of expanding career opportunities for single middle-class women, teaching offered a career that appeared to rectify the most glaring irregularity in these women's private lives – their apparent rejection of marriage and motherhood. While the wider society exaggerated the differences between women and men, the message of Pestalozzi and Froebel provided a moral rationale for middle-class women entering the teaching profession. What were on offer were new opportunities and a lifestyle choice. Contingent upon the conventions of the time, social maternalism became an important rhetorical strategy sanctioning women's right to respectable economic independence.

Jane did very well in college, participating in numerous activities and excelling academically. She found a mentor in another unmarried teacher, Elizabeth Mayo, the first woman in England to be appointed to a post in teacher training and the author of several teaching texts. Here we see the relationships between knowledge and power and the rise of the professions and the ways in which legitimacy is conveyed. Elizabeth was the younger sister of the influential reformer Charles Mayo and her vision of what education should be was strongly marked by his example. Born in London, the Mayos came from an upper-middle-class, professional background. An ordained cleric with a distinguished academic record at Oxford, Charles became interested in Pestalozzi's writings and then, in 1819, joined the teaching staff of his model school at Yverdun. In the 1820s, Charles founded schools on Pestalozzian lines in England, first at Epsom and then at Cheam, where Elizabeth ran the infant section. From the later 1830s, they were becoming the most widely known Evangelical writers on infant education. The leading feature of their approach was demonstrated clearly in teaching manuals such as their 1837 publication *Practical Remarks on Infant Education*. What is transparent in *Practical Remarks* is the extent to which the Mayo's concept of 'education according to nature' was influenced by their view of the ideal society:

> It is very important also to accustom them [the children] to consider what is their right position in society. Teach them that the different grades of rank are established by the Lord, and that each has its appointed work, as each member of our body has its appointed office (cited in Clarke, 1985, p. 81).

Charles explicitly advocated men as teachers and Cheam School was run on the lines of a mid-Victorian family, with the assumption that his natural superior ability allowed him greater authority over the children. However, at this historical moment there was a change in the gender of the ideal infants' teacher arising out of simple economics (women were cheaper to employ than men) and the discursive construction of the 'pedagogy of the feminine'.

Through her study of the infant school literature, Karen Clarke describes a value shift defined by popular constructs about gender roles in the family. According to Clarke:

> The explanation for this has to be sought in the development of the definition of the public sphere as male and the private as

female, with the responsibility of women for early education, which this came to imply during the 1820s and 1830s. The infant school occupied an ambiguous position in relation to these two spheres, being a public substitute for an area of private responsibility. The resolution of the ambiguity was that the practice of infant education became a relatively obscure part of the public sphere occupied by women, while men retained their interest in it at the level of theory and training (Clarke, 1985, p. 84).

The boundaries between the spheres of men's and women's work were, therefore, predicated upon the separate natures of men and women and their consequently distinctive roles in separate social spheres. Men's authority was predicated upon technical expertise, while the conflation of teaching and maternal care provided educated working women, like Mayo and Chessar, with a political world view and an educational rationale. Their career profiles show how individual women interpret and act upon discourses about femininity in selective and subversive ways. By the late-1830s Mayo was a public figure located in a wide-ranging educational network of crucial importance to her as she moved into positions of authority. Close to the establishment of the Home and Colonial Training College from the start, in 1843 Mayo was appointed to a leadership position and expected to manage and organize this foremost teacher training institution. There she commanded respect as she successfully fought to establish teaching as an honourable choice for girls. In time she reworked the dominant narratives surrounding the gendering of educational work to position herself as an 'expert' (through her writing voice) and 'trainer' through her practical work in the new institutional setting.

In Search of Status

On completion of her teacher training course, Jane was appointed as a resident lecturer, a position that she held until her retirement in 1867. This was a significant change to her original plan to accept a job offer of governess in the Home for Daughters of Church of England Missionaries. It reflected her strong academic performance in the final examinations and her aptitude for the teaching profession. Her obituary in the *Educational Times*, written by an old pupil, records that she exerted considerable power and authority over the students during their training college experience:

> Much of the success that placed the Home and Colonial in the front rank of Training Colleges was due, in those days, to her skill as a teacher, and to the great moral influence that she gained over her pupils. Perhaps this power was never more clearly seen than during the first few days of each College year. The students, all new comers, were with few exceptions pupil-teachers from various parts of England. Though well-meaning and sensible on the whole, some were decidedly rough in manner, and many possessed an exaggerated idea of their own abilities. But, before the end of a week, a marked change had taken place. By the power of her presence, by her scorn of pretentiousness, and by the high standard of manners and attainments set before them, the boldest and most conceited were subdued. Then came the all-powerful interest of the lessons, the sense of the justice of her rule, and the charm of a manner always graceful but which became more gay and kindly as her pupils became more thoroughly loyal (*Educational Times*, 1 October 1880).

Jane was a successful teacher, specializing in the academic subjects of human physiology and physical geography. Her teaching duties were combined with writing for the college magazine and she went on to earn a reputation as an accomplished journalist.

Like many other women who came to feminism in the 1850s and 1860s, she was to attend, and participate in, meetings of the Ladies' Sanitary Association founded in 1857. Jane became involved in 1861 when she organized a group of ten trainee teachers from the Home and Colonial to attend a thirteen-lecture course on physiology applied to health and education. The innovatory course was given on Saturday afternoons by John Marshall, lecturer at the nonsectarian University College, London (later the University of London) in Gower Street. Jane maintained her affiliation with the Association and later with the National Health Society (NHS, founded in 1873) by becoming a physiology instructor and giving NHS-sponsored lectures for ladies on the development and physical training of children. By the 1870s, she was a leader writer for the *Queen* and when ill-health forced early retirement she combined education and literary work: lecturing for the NHS; successfully preparing girls for the Cambridge Local Examinations (the equivalent of the later 'O' levels); and teaching special classes at the North

London Collegiate School. Former students bear witness to her personal and professional qualities. She was described as rather stout and plain of face and costume by one of her pupils, the eldest daughter of John Marshall. Jeanette Marshall nicknamed her 'Chessics' and wrote of her with affection. Jane encouraged the quest for knowledge, supported debating groups and involved Jeannette in meetings of the Royal Geographical Society (Shonfield, 1987, pp. 15–16). Another former student, the American Eliza Minturn, must have remembered her with especial fondness. A year after Minturn entered Girton in 1875 she founded the still extant J.A. Chessar Classical Scholarship – a mark of admiration for a favourite teacher (Girton College Register, 1875).

The motivation and commitment of Jane Chessar were strong. She aspired to build a reputation in a number of working spaces in the educational world. In this, the Home and Colonial Infant School Society was an important site for early English supporters of Froebel's propositions. A key moment was the appointment of Heinrich Hoffman, a pupil of Froebel, as head of the college kindergarten department in 1857 (Lawrence, 1952, p. 40). Three years earlier Hoffman had been among the prominent educationists to give public lectures at the first national education exhibition ever held in Britain and then stayed to convey what was understood as kindergarten theory and practice from Germany. Thus, from the outset, Jane was able to pioneer educational networks in a movement composed overwhelmingly of women (Brehony, 2000). Prominent among these was Mary Sim who became known as a foremost exponent of Frobelianism. Jane and Mary had a number of things in common. First, each journeyed from Scotland to train at the Home and Colonial College in the 1850s and second both were of frail health. As a trainee teacher, Mary was so stimulated by Froebelian principles that she went to Germany and on her return to England started kindergartens in private schools in Greenwich and Lewisham. In 1875, she was appointed kindergarten mistress at Southampton Girls' College. This drew Chessar and Sim together again. When the Froebel Society set up examinable courses in 1876, Chessar was one of the first examiners and Sim sent three of the successful candidates (Lawrence, 1952, p. 39). Trained by one of Froebel's students, Fanny Franks secured a first-class qualification in this examination and immediately established a kindergarten in London. Trying to improve her own practices in the classroom and in her school Fanny also went to the ill-fated Brussels conference.

Later in her career, she became principal of Camden House Training School for Kindergarten teachers; and lecturer, examiner and Vice-President of the Froebel Society until her death in 1920 (Liebschner, 1991, p. 28). The arena of influence was extended somewhat by Jane's role as a founder member in the Froebel Society. Contacted by Beata Doreck, Jane attended the first meeting in November 1874, along with Maria Grey and her sister Emily Shirreff, and other young women interested in publicizing Froebel's German kinder-garten system for a British audience. The Society held monthly meetings, organized lectures and established journals and, in 1879, a training college. At the same time she joined the governing body of Cheltenham Ladies' College, the earliest proprietary girls' school in England, under the direction of Dorothea Beale. By the late 1870s, Beale had founded a private kindergarten and started one of the first teachers' colleges and it is indicative of her respected position that Jane was elected to serve as the teachers' representative. It is a strong possibility that she heard of Jane Roadknight, who trained at the Home and Colonial in the 1870s, through progressive educational networks. By the 1890s, the work of Roadknight led to changes in the state-regulated system of infant teaching as she transformed Froebelian ideas into practical reality in the urban environment of Nottingham (Bloomfield, 2000). The Froebel movement served as a means of claiming public, intellectual authority for Chessar, Franks, Roadknight and Sim. It provided them with the tools and space to promote women's autonomy, voice, recognition and connection to community.

Among the early Froebelians, Emily and Maria Shirreff were inde-fatigable advocates of women's educational reform. In the 1870s they established the Women's Education Union to improve female education and employment opportunities. This initiative catalysed the Girls' Public Day School Company, that set up 'improved' schools for girls; and the Teachers' Training and Registration Society founded in 1876 (Levine, 1987). Like Jane, these organizations wished to professionalize teaching and her association with these endeavours is important. Personal contacts opened up a whole range of significant professional and social connections that were to exercise a profound influence not only in the progression of her career but also her move into politics and local-education administration. On the one hand, Elizabeth Mayo offered an early role model on which to pattern her behaviour. On the other, Frances Buss had wider links to the nineteenth-century movement to reform women's lives and their education, as well as the 'liberal intelligentsia' and party political networks. Finally, the working lives of Buss, Chessar and Mayo show that they were all engaged in a profession-alizing project to gain acceptance in a male-dominated world.

At the age of fourteen Frances Buss became a teacher at her mother's school. Both she and Dorothea Beale were early graduates of Queen's College, London, founded in 1848 to train teachers and grant certificates of proficiency. Queen's emerged from the Governesses' Benevolent Institution (GBI), which aimed to improve the position of indigent middle-class women who turned to teach-ing. The GBI was directed by the Revd David Laing (vicar of Holy Trinity, St Pancras) and the Revd Frederick Denison Maurice (pro-fessor of English at the Anglican King's College), both of whom became part of Frances Buss's male network. Looking back in 1889 Frances wrote to Dorothea:

> Queen's College opened a new life to me, I mean intellectually. To come in contact with the minds of such men was indeed delight-ful, and it was a new experience for me and to most of the women who were fortunate to become students (Raikes, 1910, p. 25).

After winning a diploma from Queen's, Frances went on to complete her professional training at the Home and Colonial, where the first meeting with Jane probably took place. 'There, in consequence of this kind of demand, a class for secondary teachers was established, and the mistresses at the Frances Mary Buss schools in the early days were expected to attend and qualify there' (Burstall, 1938, p. 68). Founder of the eminent North London Collegiate School that offered an academic education at a moderate cost, Frances went on to open a second school; the Camden School, and played a leading part in founding the Association of Head Mistresses, which met for the first time in Frances Buss's house in 1874. Frances kept mixed company and belonged to mixed organizations of some kind or another as well. From the beginning, she realized the strategic advantages to be gained from male patronage – particularly the support of those of high social status or some intellectual distinction. David Laing was the school's first superintendent but she was also networked with other men, notably the Pestalozzian William Hodgson, working within the wider movement for education reform.

It is of no small significance that William Hodgson was a found-ing member of the College of Preceptors an occupational association formed by a group of private school teachers in June 1846. In these early years the Preceptors wanted to structure teaching along the lines of a middle-class profession and to secure middle-class status for themselves. For both of these purposes they used the vocabulary of professionalization that promised exclusivity. To support this interpretation, the way in which they sought to control entry into the profession has been cited. For instance, validation procedures would be regulated by the creation of a national register of teachers and a General Teaching Council, emulating the sort of professional auton- omy that existed for doctors and lawyers in mid-Victorian Britain. Other examples are the Preceptors' efforts to define expertise as the assimilation of an established body of knowledge, techniques and skills and provide for the testing of competence by a system of examinations in the theory and practice of education. The Preceptors' foremost aim was to:

> raise the character of middle-class education, by advancing and raising the attainments, ability and fitness of teachers in private schools, and by improving the methods used and the quality of the instruction given to the children of the middle classes (Willis, 1999, p. 95).

In 1847, the Preceptors sponsored a women's side to their organi- zation. A Ladies' Department was set up and arrangements were put in place for eligible female candidates to be elected by a ballot of Council. There were two classes of female membership. The first 'consisted of the principals of ladies' schools and private teachers in modern languages and literature' who were not required to sit an examination. 'The second class included assistant governesses who either had passed an examination in one or more subjects specified by a Committee of Management or were able to produce satisfactory certificates of employment as governesses for seven years' (Willis, 1999, p. 95). Active female educational practitioners of Chessar's ilk welcomed this injection of professional politics. The quest for meri- tocracy, administrative efficiency and social justice served their purpose, while the association with Hodgson was especially close. He was interested in a range of social and educational projects, including the North London Collegiate and played a key role in the introduction of political economy and physiology into the curriculum (taught by Jane). In the National Association for the Promotion of Social Science he proved a reliable and trusted ally of women reform- ers like Frances Buss and Emily Davies, who called for training as similar as possible to that of boys. At the 1864 annual meeting he read a paper on the admission of girls to the local examinations (designed as an external test and standard administered by Cambridge and Oxford Universities to middle-class boys' schools) as a route to eventual participation by women in University Examinations. It is possible to see the long-term implications of his views:

To rest women's claim to the most liberal culture on her right, real or supposed, to share with man the so-called professions implies a complete misunderstanding of the ground on which man's claim is really based. It is not because he is to be a barrister, or a surgeon, or a merchant, but because he is to be a man, with faculties and aspirations, moral and intellectual, and with social duties requiring enlightenment and guidance for their due discharge that the boy demands, and ought to receive a liberal culture. So precisely it is with woman (*Educational Times*, October 1864).

As a Council member, William Hodgson was a major figure in the College of Preceptors when Frances Buss joined in 1869. She rapidly became the first female member elected to the Council, joining William on the education and examination committees. Contemporary Council members included Mr Coghlan (head of the Home and Colonial Infant School Society's school in Gray's Inn Road), Joseph Payne and the Froebelian Beata Doreck. Buss and Doreck were the prime movers in the foundation of the first chair in education in England, held by Payne, and created by the Preceptors in 1872. Like Hodgson, Payne supported the campaign to improve formal education for girls, notably as a member of the Women's Education Union. Fittingly, when Doreck died in office, Jane Chessar was elected in her place. The other new Council members were Dr John Hall Gladstone and Professor Meiklejohn. Gladstone represented Chelsea on the London School Board from 1870 to 1891, while Meiklejohn strengthened the Scottish interest. Chessar, Hodgson and Meiklejohn were all natives of Edinburgh. As Council members, Buss and Chessar tried to formulate an appropriate work ethic that included women by invoking the powerful claims of merit, skill and self-regulation as hallmarks of professional endeavour. Consequently, Chessar had the distinction of becoming the first female visiting examiner in connection with the College's examination of schools.

In one way or another, the key actors in the professional networks sketched here were linked to the wider intellectual and political networks of their time. For such as Maria Grey and Emily Shirreff, it was through wealth and status and the associated social connections. Others, such as Charles and Elizabeth Mayo, grew up in a professional family where religious belief was especially strong and associated with a sense of duty and social obligation. They never doubted for a moment that elites, men and women like themselves, were the rightful arbiters of a particular philosophy, morality and culture. To this extent at least, the sharing of a common culture among women whom Gareth Stedman Jones (1992) has described as 'urban gentry', was an important resource that facilitated learning how to work the existing political machinery. They all thought women had a part to play in school governance and for some of the 'bolder and more adventurous women' (Strachey, 1988, p. 209) this spilled over into local politics. Civic policies and administration were complicated by a tangle of authorities and agencies but the Municipal Franchise Act of 1869 was the first of a number of measures that were to affect women's democratic participation. When the Education Act of 1870 gave women the right to serve as representatives on the thousands of school boards being set up, able women with leadership qualities took that opportunity. The new franchise allowed women with the necessary property qualifications to vote, while multiple voting and the possibility of giving all your votes to one candidate favoured the representation of electoral minorities (Hollis, 1987; Martin, 1999; Goodman, 2000b; Martin, 2000b). In London, Emily Davies, Elizabeth Garrett and Maria Grey all had the confidence to run for political office.

Unlike Elizabeth, Emily and Maria, most women (and men) lacked the resources and motivation to assume these roles. Family connections, friendship, social networks and circumstance, as well as the distinctive personalities of the women involved, provide an explanation for why some did. For instance, the leader of the Langham Place Circle of the 1850s and 1860s, Barbara Leigh Smith Bodichon, introduced Emily and Elizabeth into the English women's movement. Their common interests in university extension and women's education served as an obvious introduction to politics; and Garrett, like Bodichon, belonged to a cousin-based feminist network (Caine, 1990). These two enjoyed an unusual amount of financial independence for women of their time and Garrett incurred no hardship in donating £100 to meet her election expenses.

On 29 November 1870, she and Davies were elected to the London School Board, topping the poll in Marylebone and Greenwich respectively, although Grey was unsuccessful in Chelsea. London was the centre and symbol of imperial and national power and the letters MSBL (member of the School Board for London) after your name made being a member more attractive. At a time when women had no direct say in state policies and practices, they had gained access to what Felicity Hunt (1991, p. 11) terms organizational policy: 'a middle level of decision-making which intervenes between government policy and actual school practice'. Working in uncharted territory, they were responsible for setting the aims and content of elementary education; ensuring school attendance; and planning the provision of sites and buildings, staff and equipment. Davies was chosen to serve on the special committee set up to define an appropriate curriculum and Chessar was one of thirteen practising teachers who appeared before this committee as witnesses. She no longer had a post in teacher training and her appearance was a tribute to her efforts in reforming teacher training and as teacher and proselytizer of the kindergarten.

Jane was favourably inclined towards co-education. She had actual classroom experience of mixed schooling and, for her, co-education was desirable because 'it stimulated the two sexes to rival or surpass each other' (*Minutes of Evidence*, April 1871). The London Board did not apply the principle throughout the whole range of the school years, however. It was not felt to be appropriate for children aged ten and above. In her account of the Home and Colonial Infant School Society's school in Gray's Inn Road, Jane tried to give advice on the way in which the day's work in an infant school should actually be conducted. She made clear the large amount of Scriptural instruction in the curriculum; and argued for object lessons derived from Pestalozzian methods proselytized chiefly through the published work of Elizabeth Mayo. The utilization, by teachers, of natural objects in question and answer gallery lessons was designed to emphasize the careful build-up of sense impressions by means of the concepts of number, form and language. A geography lesson plan published in *The Educational Paper of the Home and Colonial Society* unites associationism with Elizabeth Mayo's theological schema:

Place the children before a map of Switzerland, and interest them in making out its physical features – for example, its chains of high mountains, with their offsets in all directions traversing the country; its valleys, lakes, rivers, glaciers, &c. Then call out their relative powers in discovering how one physical character is the consequence of another; as what causes the lakes, whence rivers, originate, why pine forests are suited to the mountain regions; then let them dwell upon the goodness of God, who in His merciful providence supplies the vast reservoirs of the mountain districts from whence He 'sendeth the springs into the valleys, which run among the hills' (*Educational Paper*, July 1862, p. 86).

In applying these principles to state-regulated schooling, however, the Pestalozzian object lesson was more often misused than well used. Policy-makers at the local, regional and national level were enthusiastic but in the schooling of the urban poor what was realized frequently became repetition and rote learning.

Jane carried forward at the Home and Colonial the value system, described by Mayo. She outlined its methods, which included manual exercises, marching and songs, and exercise in the playground. Stressing the moral function of the infant school, she represented herself as a professional in early childhood education applied to the urban poor. In her opinion, children should start school at the age of two or three 'as they acquired a wonderful number of ideas, and it was considered better that they should learn in a regular, instead of a desultory way' (*Minutes of Evidence*, April 1871). The language of protection and advocacy also linked her conception of herself and her work:

> The habits of order and instruction acquired were of immense advantage to the children, enabling them to act together. Some of them would fall asleep during the afternoon, provision for which was made in the form of basket and cushion. In fact, many of them were better off at school than at home, and the mothers were glad to get rid of them (*Minutes of Evidence*, April 1871).

In her evidence, Jane combines a model of education in terms of training and disciplining the urban poor as workers and citizens, with an endorsement of kindergarten theory and practice in infant schools. Large classes were a major obstacle to a child-centred approach so she advocated a mixture of small group work and gallery lessons of 50 to 60 children taken by trained teachers. As an exponent of educational theories that regarded children as flowers to be cultivated, she expressed concern at female absenteeism and opposed the punitive control of children in Victorian schools. Instead, she supported the use of methods of public shaming to correct behaviour. What was asked from the teacher was an empathy with poor children. The objective was to keep the relationship between adult and child free from fear. Jane did not want a sex-differentiated curriculum and dismissed the teaching of practical cookery as an irrelevance best learned at home. She concluded that education was a 'good' influence, since she had a pathological view of the working-class home.

Educational Administration

In 1873, when the local political machine controlled by Elizabeth Garrett and her allies were looking for a successor, Frances Buss suggested Jane. This provided a clear example of recruitment by patronage, political co-operation and good friendship that were closely allied. For Jane, the fusion of professional politics and feminist aspirations was a mutually reinforcing bond. This gave her the strength of purpose to attempt election even though she did not take the initiative herself.

One of the most striking features of early London feminist circles was the dovetailing of the social, the political and the intellectual. These specific networks struggled to challenge the male totality of public affairs. In her biography of Frances Buss, written in 1938, Sara Burstall (second headmistress of Manchester High School) shows the sort of women Buss wanted the North London Collegiate to produce:

> What is active to-day is her influence in encouraging other women to do their duty as citizens. This influence was exercised through such channels as lessons in economics and civics in the schools, the opportunities given to the members of the staff, as, e.g., in the early days of the Assistants Mistresses' Association, and the share taken by her and her circle in the early election of women to the School Board and on Boards of Guardians. I well remember when I was in the sixth form helping to canvass for the return of Jane Agnes Chessar to the London School Board, my parents warmly approving (Burstall, 1938, p. 73).

Still Jane tried to pull out after Elizabeth Garrett made a point of persuading her sister, Alice Cowell, to accept the invitation to stand for Marylebone alongside her. Despite the best efforts of her supporting committee a public speech was an ordeal for Jane whereas Alice handled the situation with considerable aplomb. In this situation Elizabeth Garrett, as retiring member, quickly grew impatient of Buss's protégé. There were flashes of personal dislike and within days Elizabeth began to highlight Jane's shortcomings in correspondence with Emily. Initially it was her deficiency on the political platform, with 'no humour to hand', that invoked criticism (E. Garrett to E. Davies, 14 October 1873). Attitudes hardened as the campaign progressed: 'It is lucky there is so much her friends can say for her' (E. Garrett to E. Davies, 9 November 1873). Impatient of her less confident colleague, Elizabeth seemed insensitive to Jane's personal inhibitions. This was not an auspicious start to the campaign. Jane was not in good health and had already confided feelings of exhaustion, lack of sleep and worry to Emily (J. Chessar to E. Davies, 14 October 1873).

In the early 1870s, for women to participate in the masculine world of politics was widely thought to be rather shocking and militant. After one public meeting in February 1871, the suffragist Kate Amberley wrote to Helen Taylor, 'people expressed surprise to me afterwards to see that a woman could lecture and still look like a lady!' (cited in Strachey, 1988, p. 121). At a large meeting during the 1870 election campaign, Maria Grey rose to address the crowd:

> She said she was much indebted to them for their cheers, for she needed some encouragement in standing in the unaccustomed position of addressing a large audience. Some, she thought, might blame a woman for taking part in public affairs, but she hoped that such objections applied to the manner, and that she should be able to show that she could conduct her candidature in a womanly way. She thought that without women the School Board would be incomplete, for the men would represent the fathers, and the women were needed to represent the mothers (*Victoria Magazine*, 1870, 16, p. 182).

Frances Buss doubted Marylebone would return two female candidates and Jane exploited her judgement to argue that one should resign and 'I think it should be me'. Elizabeth disagreed but this did not mean she softened her outlook. Ultimately, the reluctant candidate was returned on a platform that appealed directly to London women besides stressing her experience of education.

Conscious that Davies and Garrett had become a token presence (in their last year they managed 34 and 28 Board attendance's respectively, compared to an average of 90), Chessar ended her manifesto with a pledge. 'Should you do me the honour to elect me' she told the electors of Marylebone, 'I shall feel it my duty to give the necessary time and attention to the work with which I may be entrusted' (ED/LSB 58). She and Alice served on the Board together.

Australian and New Zealand scholarship use the term 'femocrat' to refer to feminists appointed to work in women's affairs and women's units in the state apparatuses and bureaucracies (Blackmore, 1999). Next, I use the femocrat phenomenon to consider the question of feminist strategies in relation to Jane's engagement with the bureaucracy of local government at a policy-making level. Since equal rights or liberal feminism was critical to her political candidature, it is arguable that she entered the London Board as a self-identified feminist. Did she become an effective leader?

Held in public, weekly Board meetings were organized like a mini-Parliament, beginning at 3 p.m. and usually continuing until 6.30 p.m., although it was often much later. Their main purpose was to hear the recommendations set out in reports from the various committees and to make policy decisions based on these recommendations. Members had a right to propose alternative motions of policy, and debate them, before an open vote was taken with each individual answering 'yes' or 'no' at the division. Working inside a system not of her own making, Jane served on the high status school management committee, where she advocated policies that built upon and developed her political and professional activities prior to her election. Within the Board she argued from a liberal feminist point of view that girls and women should have access to the same educational provision as boys and men. She intervened in debates on school gender training to express the opinion that lessons on practical cookery were equally suitable for boys; and she successfully opposed a proposal that boys winning scholarships for secondary education should receive a higher level of support:

> In an apparently able argument which was imperfectly heard by the reporters, Miss Chessar proceeded to give the reasons why girls should have equal privileges with boys in the matter of scholarships. She knew that it was sometimes contended that boys were superior to girls, but she did not admit the argument, although she admitted ... that the boys generally enjoyed more

privileges than the girls. She saw no reason why the scholarships should be unequally divided, and although in the present instance the difference was a small matter £2 or £3 she contended that the principle was an important one, and she was desirous that it should be accepted because other scholarships would probably be presented to the Board, and she desired that the proposal should not be accepted as a precedent (*School Board Chronicle*, 16 May 1874).

Looking at the teaching profession through a feminist professional model, she campaigned to improve pay and conditions for women teachers and reform initial teacher training. First of all, she supported efforts for equal pay. Second, she advocated the development of pupil–teacher centres to offer pupil teachers more systematic and organized courses of academic and professional instruction:

> She was convinced that if an arrangement could be made by which the pupil teachers of the different schools near to each other could be massed together, and taught together, in classes of a reasonable size, better results would be obtained. No teacher could undertake to teach all the subjects really well, yet every teacher had one or two subjects which he cared most about. If they could utilise this power, and get all the pupil teachers together in the same stage, the result would be a great improvement, and a great deal more justice would be done to teaching of the teacher therefore, with regard to massing the pupil teachers together, she was entirely in favour of the new scheme (*School Board Chronicle*, 19 June 1875).

Here she was prescient and ahead of her time. Nationally, Jane's vision did not become a reality until the 1880s and 1890s but it is noteworthy that the London Board was among the leading authorities. Four years after her death, the fifth Board launched a pilot scheme along the lines she envisaged, albeit with one exception – the classes were single sex and not mixed.

Faced with networks of powerful, experienced and knowledgeable men who largely reflected and attempted to introduce middle-class, conservative and patriarchal values into London schools, Jane made strenuous efforts to exercise political power. For instance, the vice-chairman, the old Harrovian Sir Edmund Hay Currie, and the Revd John Rodgers, vicar of St Thomas,

Charterhouse, chair of the school management committee, offered support for the line she was taking. Idolized by the teachers, Rodgers was chair of governors of one of London's best voluntary schools (Gautrey, n.d., p. 47) and Board minutes illustrate that he made good use of Jane's specialist knowledge of women teachers and school management. Yet, as the Preceptor Dr Gladstone illustrates, a feminist critique did not sink naturally into the consciousness of some men. Giving his reasons for supporting a proposal that older girls could be taught cookery Gladstone reminded members that:

> The poet had said that woman was a ministering angel, but she was very much more of an angel when she knew how to cook new things, and he should desire that there should be some facility for acquiring a knowledge of cookery in this respect (*School Board Chronicle*, 6 June 1874).

The criticisms of the women members were mocked and they failed to prevent a narrowing of working-class girls' educational opportunities. Jane was a successful professional but this did not mean that all the men deferred to her judgement, even when it was based on fifteen years experience in initial teacher education.

Once elected, Jane adopted a variety of different strategies to negotiate the discourses of gender and power in her municipal role. This is evident in her use of egalitarian rationales, where liberal notions of equality played a key role. She wanted women to meet men as equals in the professional labour market and criticized the discrepancy between men's and women's salaries. Her claim for higher pay pointed to a shortage of trained teachers; teacher supply; opportunities in private schools; and remunerative alternative professions luring educated girls away from teaching (*School Board Chronicle*, 29 June 1874; 11 July 1874; 17 July 1875). At the same time, notions of sexual difference were evident in the way she conformed. For example, she declined the annual invitation to attend the Lord Mayor's banquet since it was an all-male event. Like Emily Davies and Elizabeth Garrett, Jane adopted a traditionally 'feminine' style to influence and persuade her male colleagues. Indeed, an extract from her obituary in the *Englishwoman's Review* begins to show the conditions on which women were acceptable to men in public life: 'She spoke well on questions which she thoroughly understood; but she never interrupted debate by useless talking' (15 October 1880, pp. 435–6). The selection of female candidates for the 1879 election, however, points us to the dangers of stereotyping 'school board women' as a wholly homogeneous social grouping (Martin, 2000a). In her manuscript autobiography, Florence Fenwick Miller (first elected in 1876) left a detailed account of a campaign meeting attended by herself, Elizabeth Garrett, Elizabeth Surr, Helen Taylor and Alice Westlake (among others). She describes a clash over strategies for dealing with the male political establishment that runs counter to earlier representations of past and present women board members working to accommodate one another (Turnbull, 1983; Hollis, 1987; Martin, 1993). In any event, Elizabeth and Alice (Jane's successor as member for Marylebone) counselled against female candidates, explaining how difficult and costly an election was. They appear to have acted out of concern at the more strident political behaviour of the other school board women who were too independently feminist for their taste and espoused more radical politics. Certainly, there were manoeuvrings over the selection of a female candidate in Florence's Hackney seat. In an attempt to split her vote, Sir Charles Reed (Board chair and divisional colleague) proposed that the local Liberal Party field Jane Chessar on the party ticket. Nothing came of it.

In private, distance from family networks meant her primary commitment in emotional and practical terms was to another woman, Mary Richardson. Her friendship with Frances Buss provided close mutual support but she and Mary shared living arrangements at 6, Frederick Place, Gray's Inn Road. Jane opened up the world of politics and reform for Mary, who became involved in efforts to provide recreation, culture and community for single women. Together they sponsored swimming clubs for London's women teachers and a debating society, as well as joining the Somerville Club. At the 1879 triennial election, Southwark Liberals chose the circumspect Mary over the more dynamic feminist, Helen Taylor (who served from 1876 to 1885). At her retirement, Jane accompanied Helen on school visits and to divisional committees but relations had soured in the intervening years. The reason for this is unclear, although the schism involved Mary's friend and colleague, Eliza Orme, the first woman solicitor. A scholarship student, in 1873 Helen Taylor had given £100 so Eliza might start legal training. Three years later, Mary crisply informed her 'after the events of the last two months I do not choose that she should longer remain indebted to you, for what I can with no inconvenience send back to you for her' (M. Richardson to H. Taylor, 4 December 1876). The cheque was returned immediately, for Miss Richardson was 'almost a perfect stranger to her' (H. Taylor to M. Richardson, 5 December 1876), a situation that altered when Jane persuaded her to stand for election. Years later, Mary recalled the debt she owed the friend who taught her everything she knew of committees, debates and public speaking:

> I was elected, and remained upon the Board for six years. It was in many ways an interesting period to me, and, no doubt I learned a great deal. But it was not altogether a pleasant position in which I found myself. Those were the days when women on the School Board were quite a novelty. Several of the ladies held much more advanced views than I did, and, – well! I found it was always my mission to put on the drag (Bateson, 1895, p. 104).

Her discomfort is clear. Mary, like Jane, had to make her own resolution of the conflicting discourses of masculinity and femininity, gender and power. They understood well the importance of promoting feminine respectability in order to hold public office without damage to their public reputation. The question then arises as to whether the term homoerotic, first used by Vicinus (1985) to describe close friendship between women in residential educational communities in England during this period, can be applied to the friendship of Jane and Mary. The answer remains elusive at the present time, precisely because of the difficulty of investigating in full their life stories.

A hardworking, able and ambitious woman, Jane Chessar pioneered a new occupation, new living conditions and new, more public values. Courageously, she chose to challenge the *status quo* by entering male-dominated spheres of politics and educational administration. There is evidence that she became well respected and served as a role model for the British suffrage movement. In the face of charges about the debilitating effects on the femininity of the average woman, the contribution made by women like Jane had beneficial long-term consequences – 'altering assumptions and diminishing the novelty in the idea of a parliamentary vote for women' (Pugh, 2000, p. 78). As to whether she was a femocrat, Hester Eisenstein (1991) identifies four types of intervention by feminists working in or through the state bureaucracy: bureaucratic-individual, bureaucratic-structural, legal reform and political participation. The data shows how Jane adopted different techniques at different times and in different places. At times she played an important part in promoting women-friendly policies and drawing women into political life. At other times, she quickly conformed to existing norms to be accepted. The contradictions, conflicts and dilemmas for femocratic feminisms surfaced during a campaign for women to be appointed as inspectors under the London School Board. In 1881, the radical activist, Helen Taylor, unsuccessfully proposed affirmative action whereas the liberal feminist Edith Simcox (first elected in 1879) called for open competition and equal employment opportunities:

> She hoped the Board would be able to agree to her amendment. If a thoroughly efficient female candidate could be found it would surely be desirable to appoint her to the inspectorship. The new inspector should be on the same footing as the others, as persons placed over particular departments were apt to exaggerate the importance of those departments. A second class female candidate might perhaps be appointed in preference to a first class male; but to show that a first class female inspector might be obtained, she had only to mention the name of Miss Chessar (*School Board Chronicle*, 5 February 1881).

Although the motion was carried, the achievement of Edith Simcox must be judged against the fact that the place was filled by a man. Acceptance of the equal opportunities response to female exclusion from the inspectorate was presented as a gain for feminism. Yet, the outcome shows the limitations of these claims as a political tactic. From within the use of Enlightenment thinking, the word 'equality' is interpreted in terms of moral and rational worth and not in terms of material difference. The implication is that once each individual enjoys the same political and legal rights they can compete equally with each other. As Helen Taylor recognized, however, to assume that each and every individual can compete on a 'level playing field' is simplistic in its ignorance of group-based, material inequalities. Meritocracies encourage the belief that people get what they deserve and deserve what they get; and Jane's success maintained the possibility of female inclusion in educational leadership. Unlike Helen Taylor, who could record few successes in the causes she adopted, she was not seen as 'troubling', 'trouble' and 'troubled'. This allowed her to step outside the training college into positions of authority and responsibility in local government. But the 'problem' of feminism's use of the language of liberal democracy based on the premise of individual rights is still with us. Drawing on research findings in respect of equal opportunities, and some contemporary training policies of the European Social Fund, it has been argued that what happens is that the 'success of a few maintains the crucial belief in the possibility of opportunity and success for the many' (Brine, 1995, p. 21).

Jane adopted a bureaucratic-individual pathway to challenge discriminatory and unjust practices. She did not create new practices. Rather, she used her public voice to advance the interests of women from within local government. Victory on the scholarship issue, for instance, made it possible to fast track selected girls and boys in equal numbers as the route to social and economic advancement. A kind of tokenistic success, that lent credibility to inequalities and injustices within the system. In effect, Jane's own climb up the hierarchical ladder, centred on the assistance of mentors, as well as male and female networks, also evidences this. Part of her success was due to biographical moment and a willingness to package herself as a 'womanly' woman. She did achieve an honourable independence and her story illustrates the possibilities that occur when women do transgress boundaries and barriers in their efforts to lead freer, more atypical lives. At the same time, and for other women, the price of Jane's independence may have been the reinforcement of sexual stereotyping. By fostering a modern ideal of women's sphere, which preserved the primacy of domesticity, she was clearly working within the parameters of middle-class respectability. That ideal, in the end, was the most significant limitation.

5

Mary Dendy (1855–1933) and Pedagogies of Care[1]

Visiting board schools as a member of the Manchester School Board from 1896, Mary Dendy was struck by the 'outcast' children in the school playgrounds and those unable to make use of the education on offer. After personally inspecting nearly 40,000 children, she pressed the board for day special schools and became a driving force in the establishment of the residential Sandlebridge Schools for the Permanent Care of the Feeble-minded. Opened in 1902 under the aegis of the Lancashire and Cheshire Society for the Permanent Care of the Feeble-minded [LCSPCFM] (Cruikshank, 1976; Jackson, 1996, 1997, 2000), Sandlebridge was the first institution of importance to be certified under the Elementary Education (Defective and Epileptic Children) Act, 1899 (Board of Education, 1910).[2]

Mary Dendy travelled widely both in Britain and abroad to propagate her views on the necessity for the permanent care of the feeble-minded. She became part of the growing international network of eugenicists,[3] speaking at international congresses, writing about the feeble-minded and visiting institutions for their care in England and abroad. She was a key witness to the 1908 Royal Commission on the Care and Control of the Feeble-minded [RCCCFM] and was present in the gallery of the House of Commons to hear her views discussed during debate on the 1913 Mental Deficiency Act (McLachlan, 1935). In its wake, she became the first paid commissioner under the Board of Control, the administrative body set up to regulate the 1913 Act. In this chapter, I locate Mary Dendy's ideas on the feeble-minded and their care within intellectual and social networks that were familial, local, national and international. I examine her views on feeble-mindedness and their relationship to citizenship as well as to casework practice. I look at how these underpinned the 'progressive' pedagogy, that she advocated at Sandlebridge.

Much of this story can be pieced together from Mary's published writings, particularly her evidence to the RCCCFM and from her papers at conferences and to learned societies, as well as from the printed accounts of Sandlebridge. Through these sources, Mary the woman reformer can be glimpsed. Mary left a diary that was available to Herbert McLachlan, who quoted directly from it in his biographical chapters on the Dendy/Beard family in 1935. Here, we see the public face of Mary's work and glean impressions of the private Mary on her foreign travels. Sadly, all efforts to locate this diary proved fruitless.[4] The expert Mary can be glimpsed as she performs in the institutionalized context of the RCCCFM. Here, we see evidence of her ability to represent herself as 'expert' in a public forum. The printed reports of Sandlebridge provide further evidence of Mary, the inveterate teller of a well-rehearsed tale geared to raising funds for Sandlebridge and the permanent care of the feebleminded. Here, she uses auto/biographical practices to interweave the establishment of Sandlebridge with her story of her public self. She presents a Whiggish trajectory of progress in the face of others' views of her expected failure and their initial unwillingness to assist. McLachlan notes that Mary was prone to melancholy. In the reports of Sandlebridge, she represents herself as prolific worker, engaged in heroic struggle with herself and with a public that required persuasion to support the work she held dear:

> All doing similar work must constantly find that they are up against a solid mass of incapacity, degradation and misery that it is very difficult indeed to better…. It was a very sad pilgrimage …The report I made [to the Manchester School Board] was discussed and we visited some Special Schools … but, we got no further … I saw nearly 50,000 children … It was a tiresome piece of work to write the report – I do so hate writing. I took that report to the Board, and they said … that as I was not a doctor, I could not know anything about the matter … Dr Ashby was interested … He said: 'Well, Miss Dendy, … if I begin on Monday, will you begin again… I made up my mind that we must have a permanent Home for defective children.… And I also made up my mind that we must have legislation … It was difficult. I had no money … It was a great struggle to get people to take my point of

view...One very kind-hearted man in Manchester, who could have given me substantial help, said, with tears in his eyes, 'Miss Dendy, you'll break your heart, and do nothing.' Well, I have not broken my heart: and I have done something...Of all those called together there was only one man in the meeting who would support me. They would not hear of permanent care...London would have none of us. They would not hear of it (LCSPCFM, *Annual Report* 1925, pp. 11–12).

In his scholarly study of the Sandlebridge Schools, Mark Jackson (2000) points to the importance for Mary's work of her location within a late Victorian and Edwardian nonconformist 'intellectual aristocracy': 'where family connections reveal some caucus of power or influence...which moulds the country's culture' (p. 39). McLachlan's (1935) biographical chapters on the Dendy/Beard family point to the contribution of her extended family to developments in education, social service and liberal religion. Mary's father, John Dendy, was both businessman and Presbyterian minister. Other family members were prominent Unitarians with an interest in education. Mary's uncle, Charles Beard (1827–88), minister of the Unitarian Chapel, Renshaw Street Liverpool, was a foremost proponent of higher education and heavily involved in the foundation of Liverpool University (Harrop, 1997). Mary's maternal grandfather John Relly Beard (1800–76), taught at Manchester's Owen's College, published widely on education and was a key figure in the Unitarian Home Missionary Board (Jackson, 2000). Her youngest brother, Arthur (1865–1925), was a zoologist, who held posts at London University and at Universities in Australia, New Zealand and South Africa (McLachlan, 1935). Her younger sister, Sarah Louisa (1856–1931), was assistant mistress at Manchester Girls' High School. Her youngest sister, Helen (1860–1925), who married Bernard Bosanquet, was a member of the Royal Commission on the Poor Laws from 1905–09 and became editor of the *Charity Organisation Review* (Lewis, 1991).

Mary was educated at home by her mother, Sarah (nee Beard, 1831–1922), and a German governess. Sarah had been well prepared for the educative role she undertook in the family. Her father, John Relly Beard, had 'modern notions about female education' (McLachlan, 1935, p. 111). Sarah went to Miss John's school, where she learnt Latin declensions from Valpy's Grammar, and when Miss John's school closed, spent a period at somewhat inferior girls' school before her father put her into classes in his school at Stony Knolls, where she did the same lessons as her elder brother (including mathematics and foreign languages) until the latter went to College. Sarah then spent a period as pupil at the school of the Misses Field at Leam House, between Warwick and Leamington. Prior to her marriage, she gained nearly two years' teaching experience back in her father's school, an education, she considered, made her a better mother for her children than any other training could have done. Prepared by her mother and her German governess, Mary attended Bedford College from 1874–75, where she studied mathematics, natural philosophy, French, Latin, English, literature and music and was the oldest boarder in residence.

After Bedford College, Mary returned to the family home at Monton, near Manchester. Here, she taught in the Sunday School, was a key worker in the Temperance Society and spent many hours writing and publishing verse, fiction and Sunday School lessons. When her father's business failed, Mary left Manchester for Braintree, Essex, in 1882, to become lady's companion to Sarah Ann Cawston, the adopted daughter of Samuel Courtauld. Here, too, Mary taught in the Sunday School and organized the school plays, one of which she wrote; conducted a sewing class for girls; established a club for elder scholars and teachers; checked the accounts of the Coffee House, day school and Sarah Cawston's farm; and managed Sarah Cawston's domestic staff. During this period, she published a short novel in the 1885 edition of *All the Year Round* (founded by Charles Dickens) and continued to write and publish Sunday School articles and stories.

On her death in 1889, Sarah Cawston bequeathed Mary an income that gave her financial independence. After Miss Cawston's death, Mary visited Australia to see her brother Arthur, who had married Ada Courtauld, Sarah Cawston's niece. On her return to Manchester, she worked with her sister Helen, as a founder member of the clubs for working girls and boys begun in 1885 at the Collyhurst Recreation Rooms. For a short period, like her sister Sarah Louisa, Mary lived with Elizabeth Day, headmistress of Manchester High School. Sarah Louisa was honorary secretary of the Manchester Girls' Club Workers Union (Goodman, 1997) and was deeply interested in social welfare, living for a time in the model dwellings at Ancoats (McLachlan, 1935). Mary became involved in the Manchester Society for Women's Suffrage and was secretary of the South Manchester Women's Liberal Association from 1892. She also acted as secretary to the Society for Women Guardians and made numerous visits to workhouses, cottage homes, model dwellings and industrial schools in various towns, as well as speaking on women's suffrage and education. She was co-opted to the Manchester School Board in 1896 in place of Rachel Scott. She was elected in her own right as member in 1900 (Goodman, 2000a). This combination of educational, political, religious and charitable work provided the background against which she developed her work for the feeble-minded (Jackson, 2000).

Mary Dendy and Eugenics

In his study of the fabrication of the feeble-mind in late Victorian and Edwardian England, Mark Jackson demonstrates how boundaries between the 'normal' and the 'pathological' were constructed in a social and political context in which difference became re-conceptualized as inferiority. Jackson traces how feeble-mindedness came to designate a borderland between 'normal' intellect and 'idiocy' and the categorization 'feeble-minded' was thought to connect disparate social pathologies, including criminality, poverty and promiscuity. This borderland 'functioned ... as a flexible and forceful metaphor for a wide range of social problem groups and as a powerful tool for the elaboration of class boundaries' (Jackson, 2000, p. 12). Those categorized as 'feeble-minded' were thought not capable of complete independence but able to manage themselves under supervision (Zedner, 1991). The Royal College of Physician's noted the feeble-minded were:

> Persons who may be capable of earning a living under favourable circumstances, but are incapable from mental defect, existing from birth or from an early age: (1) of competing on equal terms with their normal fellows, or (2) of managing themselves and their affairs with ordinary prudence (Bartley, 2000, p. 121).

Feeble-mindedness was formalized as a legal category in 1913 and 1914 (Jackson, 2000).

Mary Dendy shared the view of Charles Lapage, physician to the Children's Hospital at Pendelbury and a frequent visitor to Sandlebridge, that a backward child could be distinguished from a feeble-minded child because the *'power to develop'* was present in children who were backward but not in the feeble-minded (Lapage, 1920). Mary's writings demonstrate strongly held hereditarian views of feeble-mindedness, in which sexually active and prolific women constituted a danger to society (Dendy, 1908). Roy Lowe has illustrated how eugenic concern with national deterioration combined both hereditarian and strong environmentalist elements (Lowe, 1998). While stressing that feeble-mindedness was 'a question of inheritance, not surroundings', Mary argued that surroundings nonetheless 'played a very important part in bringing the feeble-minded to destruction'. In her view, what was needed for the feeble-minded was a totally different environment and form of care (Dendy, 1911). Mary told the RCCCFM that her ideal scheme was a combination of day and boarding special schools, with a labour colony[5] attached to provide an institutional structure in which feeble-minded children would remain for life (RCCCFM, 1908, i, Q.818, p. 41). She was adamant that education in a day special school with a view to returning feeble-minded children to ordinary schools, or to prepare the feeble-minded for work, was a greater danger to society than if the feeble-minded child had received no education. 'Many … who are really defective, are, at a very great expense of time and trouble, taught a certain amount of parrot-learning, and are made to appear for a time, very much like a low grade of mentally abnormal children.' In Mary's eyes, this made them a greater danger to society than they would have been without it; for their training made them look 'in outward appearance more like normal persons' (Dendy, 1908, p. 139). She thought this made it easier for them to have families than the 'idiot' who was easily recognizable and urged triennial certification for feeble-minded children. Sandlebridge was envisaged as a community separated from the outside world, in which children would remain for life and the sexes would be separated. This rendered marriage impracticable and provided the alternative environment Dendy thought necessary for the feeble-minded (RCCCFM, 1908, i, Q.980, Q.995, Q.1051; Dendy, 1908, 1920; Lapage, 1920).

Although Mary was involved with several Unitarian ventures, her hereditarian views present a disjuncture with earlier Unitarian views, which largely rejected notions of innate causes and drew on associationist theory and views of perfectability developed by David Hartley and Joseph Priestley. These built on John Locke's notion of the tabula rasa on which Experience must write (Watts, 1998a). Priestley argued that moral, religious and intellectual development could be realized through reflection, experience and intellectual education but not through innate cause (Watts, 1998a). In this view, human nature was malleable, the person educable and the development of virtue possible. Central to much associationist theory was the education of the will in the making of the virtuous citizen. Mary's views of the nature and educability of 'will' in her constructions of feeble-mindedness was in tension with this Unitarian stance. Mary consistently reiterated the view that an over-riding characteristic of the feeble-minded was their lack of will power:

> The main characteristic that is common to all feeble-minded people is a great weakness of will power. ... You can predict pretty certainly of normal children that under certain circumstances they will do a certain thing ... The only characteristics which feeble-minded children have in common is this great weakness of will-power. ... they will do anything that they are told (RCCCFM, 1908, i, Q.854).

This lack of will power was thought to result in the feeble-minded being easily led astray. It translated for feeble-minded women into the view that they were easily seduced (Lapage, 1920). This, in turn, fed eugenic concern, that feeble-minded women led to race deterioration by producing feeble-minded children at an unacceptable rate. In Mary's eyes, lack of will power meant that the feeble-minded were not able to control their 'animal' passions (Dendy, 1908). This underpinned her view that to be unmarried, pregnant and on poor relief constituted feeble-mindedness and denoted the need for institutional care.

With the loss of Mary's diaries, it is difficult to be ascertain how she came to this hereditarian and eugenic stance. How far she developed her ideas in relation to those of her brother Arthur, an evolutionary biologist, and how far Arthur's later ideas were influenced by Mary's work, remains open to conjecture. Arthur studied zoology at Owen's College under Milnes Marshall. Marshall had been a student of Herbert Spencer and Charles Darwin and was 'a fiery apostle with the new faith of biology' (Mulvaney and Calaby, 1985). After working on the editorial staff of the Challenger Expedition and in the Zoological Department of the British Museum, Arthur moved to Melbourne at a point when Australians were playing a role in constructing the background against which Darwinian theory was being developed (Butcher, 1992). Arthur was appointed demonstrator to the new professor of biology at Melbourne University, Baldwin Spencer. Spencer had an interest in Darwinian evolution and, like Arthur, had studied under Milnes Marshall at Owen's. With Baldwin Spencer's encouragement (Blainey, 1957), Arthur became a productive researcher and fellow of Queen's (Melbourne), undertaking research on sponges that resulted in major scientific papers, and making significant contributions to the knowledge of Australian fauna (Smith, 1981). As successive editions of the *Melbourne University Review*, the *Melbourne University Calendar* and the University student paper the *Undergrad* illustrate, Arthur was actively involved in discussions on mechanisms of evolution both within the University and the wider scientific community in Australia. He proposed a theory of heredity and evolution in which aspects of Darwinism, embryology and Mendelism were subsumed under a broader explanatory umbrella that was fundamentally Lamarckian (Butcher, 1992).[6]

Mary visited Arthur in Melbourne from January to August 1891 and again from November 1893 to July 1894 when he moved to his new post at Christchurch University, New Zealand (although she turned down his suggestion that she should move to New Zealand with his family). Arthur introduced Mary to marine biology during the excursions she made with him in 1891 along the shore in Australia, where they collected specimens together for dissection by his students. She became familiar with his research, copying his writings and acting as his amenuensis (McLachlan, 1935). Both Arthur and Mary spoke at the 1911 meeting of the British Association in Portsmouth, where Arthur commented on Mary's paper on the feeble-minded. Arthur's Presidential Address to the zoology section at the meeting of the British Association for the Advancement of Science held in Australia in 1914 was entitled: 'Progressive Evolution and the Origin of Species' (Dendy, 1915). In the 1920s, Arthur was concerned with the relation of biology and social questions, contributing 'Evolution and the future of the human race' to the *Eugenics Review* (1922–23). By 1924, he was publishing and lecturing at Kings College London (having been appointed Professor of Zoology in 1904) on 'the contribution of a biologist towards the discussion of those social and political problems which confront us today' (McLachlan, 1935, p. 220). While the hereditarian and eugenic views of both Mary and Arthur would not have accorded with those of Unitarian relatives such as Charles Beard, nonetheless, Arthur's practice of evolutionary biology and Mary's approach to her work reflected an earlier Unitarian concern to develop a rational scientific understanding of the world.

Auto/biographical Practices and Family Histories

From the earliest reports of her investigation of children in Manchester schools, Mary's 'scientific' approach to her task was reflected in the case-book type records she accumulated. At Sandlebridge, Mary compiled careful records of the first 284 children as they arrived between 1902 and 1911 (Sandlebridge, Album 1902–11). On separate pages, she entered the name and date of birth of each child and the source of maintenance fees (parents, education authority, guardians etc.). Apart from the few years when she was commissioner at the Board of Control, she added short comments on the child's physical appearance, behaviour and educational ability, their progress and, where applicable, a note on their discharge or death. Mary attended the examinations of 'defective children' conducted by Dr Henry Ashby, physician to the Manchester Children's Hospital (RCCCFM, 1908, v.1, Q.815) and assiduously collected family histories of children deemed to be feeble-minded, which she subsequently used to illustrate her addresses and articles.

Collecting family histories was a form of auto-biographical practice rooted in both the narrative practices of the administrative state and medical narrative practice. As Carolyn Steedman (2000) argues, the accounts told by the poor to the administrative state had well-established tropes: stories of seduction and betrayal; bastardy examinations conducted before justices of the peace; stories told to philanthropic societies in exchange for dole. Such narratives were produced by questioning but transcribed with the omission of the interlocutor:

> By these means, multitudes of labouring men and women surveyed a life from a fixed standpoint, told it in chronological sequence, gave an account of what it was that brought them to this place, this circumstance now (Steedman, 2000, pp. 29–30).

In the wake of the 1913 Mental Deficiency Act, the family history for those thought potentially feeble-minded formed a component of the larger case record and one element in the process through which certifying doctors 'stitched together' patients' complaints into a series of logical diagnostic clues that framed a recognizable clinical picture (Epstein, 1992, p. 32). This attested to the 'rightness' of certification as feeble-minded. Eliciting life histories was also used as tactic when individuals would not co-operate with the certifying practitioner. Inducing individuals to recount their life stories was thought one way to win confidence and had the benefit of revealing social and moral 'incompetence', as well as inaccuracies and inconsistencies to the trained eye (Squires, 1990). The life history also enabled the certifying doctor to trace an individual's school records and so to meet the statutory requirement to demonstrate the existence of a mental defect from birth or early age (Thomson, 1998).

In this context, the family history was a narrative, inter-subjective event, framed within unequal relations of institutional power (Stanley, 2000). For the certifying doctors, the family history operated in terms of scientific case reporting. Those providing the details of the family history – in the case of children, or those thought to be mentally defective, often a parent or carer – drew on narratives of sickness existing outside of, and generally formed prior to, the consulting room (Hogarth and Marks, 1998). They employed popular representations of personal meanings created from experiences of illness and health, in which pain, suffering and disability were placed within the context of wider lives, family stories and working conditions and access to the necessities of life. The story told and heard was transformed in the process of narration as the person collecting the family history interpreted the story according to strict rules of causality and signification not shared by the person telling the story. Events and descriptions in the family history told a story different from the one those representing the life-history believed themselves to be telling (Poirier *et al.*, 1992, p. 14). The 'scientifically' produced (medicalized) family history, in which the questions of the interlocutor were represented in the text by scientific headings, was meant for the professional reader only and was passed between administrative agencies.

Feeble-mindedness was deemed to be primary (from birth) or secondary (caused by illness of accident) (Thomson, 1998, p. 246). Sandlebridge case papers demonstrate that many parents of Sandlebridge children created their own personal meanings of mental deficiency, which equated to secondary feeble-mindedness. They variously attributed their child's condition to whooping cough, measles, father's heart disease or death, a fall on the head at birth or when very young; a fall downstairs, brain trouble in babyhood, shock at being scalded, or a fall or a fright received by the mother when pregnant (LCSPCFM, Case book 1914–30, 1920–35, 1931–36). Since these were all possible causes of secondary feeble-mindedness, such stories resisted the hereditary taint. Charles Lapage, physician to the Manchester Children's Hospital at Pendelbury and a frequent visitor to Sandlebridge noted that not too much importance was to be attached to these factors for parents were prone to exaggerate (Lapage, 1920, p. 219).

In her publications, Mary used the family histories she collected and recorded at Sandlebridge to demonstrate the primary, 'incurable' and hereditarian nature of feeble-mindedness and to argue that the 'defective' should not be left in society free to reproduce offspring:

> a great number of them live to have families, and their offspring are generally more feeble in every way than themselves. This would point to the conclusion that they would die out in the course of time, but unfortunately, they are not left to themselves, the strong and the bad mix with the weak and mad, and so the horrible story goes on (Dendy, 1899, p. 26).

In contexts where she was asking for money, or moving amongst 'experts' and 'professionals', Mary used her collected family histories to provide a pseudo-scientific legitimacy for her claim that the feeble-minded needed permanent care. She told the RCCCFM:

> Take the next case: the mother denied any history; she is the wife of a builder; they are very well off. She said there was nothing at all on her side of the family, but one of her husband's sisters had been queer for a bit. He referred me to the family doctor and he gave us the history: that the mother herself had been in an asylum; her mother was then in an asylum; her sister was in an asylum, and the father's sister was in an asylum. That kind of thing we find over and over again … If you look at Case 204, at Sandlebridge, we have there, a defective girl. Her father died in an asylum, her father's father died in an asylum, her father's sister died in an asylum, and her father's wife died in an asylum and her grandmother was paralysed (RCCCFM, 1908, Q.836).

She asked the 1911 Manchester conference on the care of the feeble-minded to examine the diagram of Ethel (case 204 presented to the RCCCFM) commenting:

> The most important results of permanent treatment cannot even be estimated in our life-time … You will see what would have been the chief practical result if the first-known degenerate of this family had been detained in a Colony for life. Instead of taking care of the grandfather, it was left to us to try to take care of the only two of the grandchildren we could reach. It has been found impossible to detain even these two. They are high-grade defectives of a very dangerous type (Dendy, 1911, pp. 45–6).

Mary also provided family histories for Karl Pearson and Ethel Elderton for a study investigating a possible link between parental alcoholism and mental deficiency or degeneration (Jackson, 2000).

In compiling her Album as a case-book, Dendy illustrated aspects of work practice that she held in common with her sister, Helen, and brother-in-law, Bernard Bosanquet, about the 'scientific' nature of case-work procedures. The Bosanquets were key advocates of case-work. They believed that 'thorough charity' required scientific investigation of circumstances and character and argued that case-work provided the means of discerning causes of distress and a methodology for 'scientific charity' (Lewis, 1991). As Jane Lewis notes, Bernard Bosanquet argued that Idealism combined faith in the world of facts with passion and wisdom 'because it had an idea, a principle, order and organisation'. In his view, 'social work needed to combine careful investigation with love', towards which the social worker would strive through the 'completeness of casework' (p. 161). Lewis argues that in popularizing such views, Helen Bosanquet wove her case-work data into a fabric of explanation dictated by Idealist philosophy. In Helen's view, the task of the social worker was one of changing the habits of the poor, strengthening their characters and enabling them to become independent and self-maintaining; for Idealism attributed to individual mind and will the key role in achieving social change (ibid.).

Mary's Album similarly adopted a 'scientific' stance to her task of investigating individual cases in order to provide permanent care for the feeble-minded. Mary wove her case-work data into a fabric of explanation dictated by hereditarian and eugenic views that posited a weakened and dysfunctional 'will'. Like Galton, who approved of her work, Mary was opposed to 'charitable mischief' (Dendy, 1908, p. 131). She viewed removal of the feeble-minded into 'permanent care' at Sandlebridge as a form of 'scientific morality' which would benefit both society and the individual by decreasing the suffering to the children themselves; bringing economic gain to the nation; and preventing the future deterioration of the race (RCCCFM, 1908, i, Q.858). As the first woman to address the Manchester Statistical Society in 1908, she told the society that the welfare of the nation depended upon taking 'rational action … in accordance with the laws of science', a duty owed to posterity, 'for we have interfered with the laws of natural selection in this matter and are responsible' (Dendy, 1908, p. 136). She advocated compulsory action on the part of the state, arguing that the hereditary and incurable nature of feeble-mindedness justified over-riding the responsibility of a parent for their child (ibid., p. 124). Indeed, compulsion was a 'kindness' to a mother, faced with the difficult decision of whether to send away her child. 'If the State made the decision for the mother the trouble would be done away with in a great measure' (Dendy, 1911, p. 26).

Mary's sister, Helen, who placed the family at the heart of her analysis and prioritized the fostering of active citizenship rather than material relief, was opposed to state intervention because she believed it threatened to undermine personal responsibility and character (Lewis, 1991). For those in the Charity Organisation Society, whose *Review* Helen edited, the state was to bolster schemes like Sandlebridge, rather than to replace them. Yet, when it came to the feeble-minded, a group thought not to be held responsible for their circumstances and lacking in the capacities of mind and will to engage in active citizenship and achieve change, Helen argued: 'We cannot hope to make them good citizens, to make them clever men and women, but we aim at keeping them innocent' (Thomson, 1998, p. 152). As Thomson argues, the use of the term 'innocent' here is significant. Rather than the feeble-minded being viewed as citizens, or even 'potential citizens in need of reform', care was to be provided 'as a paternal act and because of moral and eugenic concern to maintain the "innocence" of the feeble-minded' (ibid.). For Mary, 'true' liberty for the feeble-minded was the 'freedom' of the feeble-minded not to be taken advantage of. 'Liberty' therefore required the feeble-minded to be taken care of for their own sake as well as that of society. This reworked liberal notions of citizenship, in which bars to the exercise of individual liberty were to be removed.

Paula Bartley demonstrates how, for women like Mary Dendy, this 'preventative' stance towards the exploitation of female sexuality was compatible with support for women's suffrage (Bartley, 1998).

Community and Pedagogy at Sandlebridge

Sandlebridge was to provide an alternative community for individuals removed from society on the grounds of their seeming incapacity to play their part as the 'trained and self-disciplined citizen of modernity' (Peim, 2001). It was to be a self-supporting, self-contained colony, a 'little kingdom', in which each child was become a 'willing and happy subject' (Dendy, 1920, p. 207). For Mary, this was both an humanitarian aim and a necessity in the light of her views of the sexual nature of feeble-mindedness. Prior to the 1913 Mental Deficiency Act and the 1914 Education Act, education authorities had the power to make provision for, and to control, the education of feeble-minded children up to the age of sixteen. They could enforce attendance at a day special school. But if there were residential institutions they could only with the parents' consent send feeble-minded children to them up to the age of sixteen but were unable to legally enforce detention at any age. After the age of sixteen all legal control ceased (Lapage, 1920). The result, as Mary explained, was that parents wanting special education moved into districts where schools were provided; but more frequently, parents desiring to avoid special education evaded the law by moving just outside the boundaries.

Mary attempted to work the law in her favour. The fact that a boy over the age of fourteen and a girl over the age of sixteen had the power to choose their own place of residence, meant that they could not be removed against their will from an institution where they wished to stay (Dendy, 1908). Acting on the principle that 'there are no ideas in the heads of the weak-minded excepting those that are put there' (Dendy, 1908), she wished to instil in the children that they would remain for life. She noted: 'the principle upon which we have gone is to hold it out to them as a reward that they may stay there if they are good, and if they are naughty the chances are that they may get sent away' (RCCCFM, 1908, i, Q.822). She wished to gear institutional life to the happiness of the resident (Dendy, 1908, 1911). The children were to be given treats; the girls dressed in individual clothing; and all those that came into contact with the children were to make their world so interesting that they would not wish to leave (Dendy, 1920). Mary also saw constant supervision as vital for the control of their 'animal passions' (RCCCFM, 1908, i, Q.852, Q.857). The dual principles of 'kindly encouragement and strict supervision', surveillance and the creation of desire within the child to remain in the institution, constituted the key notes of the education and training (Dendy, 1920). Mary aimed to render the feeble-minded at Sandlebridge both happy and harmless (Dendy, 1908). Jackson's analysis of the retention patterns at Sandlebridge demonstrates that this was no easy task (Jackson, 1996). As the case books at Sandlebridge illustrate, rhetoric and reality were frequently at variance.

Mary's notion of the 'happy citizen' in their 'little community' resonated with Froebelian views of the kindergarten as 'a miniature state for children', propagated by Baroness Berthe von Marenholtz-Bulow (Allen, 1982). Marenholtz-Bulow conceptualized the kindergarten as 'a place of education ... which represents a miniature state for children, in which the young citizen can learn to move freely, but with concern for his fellows' (Allen, 1986). It resonated, too, with the sentiments of the Froebelian Middendorff, that the kindergarten produced self-motivated responsibility inspired by a sense of community: 'Every child follows joyfully ... the power of community leads even the inexperienced child back into the right path' (Allen, 1982). Mary moved within the circles of Manchester Froebelians. Her mother's closest friend, Sarah Howorth married the Reverend Samuel Alfred Steinthal, a foremost proponent of Froebelian education in Manchester. Caroline Herford, who lectured at the Manchester Kindergarten Training College and was headmistress of the Froebelian Ladybarn House, which she had co-founded with her father, William Herford, English translator of Froebel's *The Student's Froebel* (Brehony, 2000; Lawrence, 1952) had been a co-worker with Mary and Helen at the Collyhurst Recreation Rooms (Goodman, 1997). Mary's relative, Mary Shipman Beard, took over from Caroline Herford as headmistress of Ladybarn House, before moving to work with Michael Sadler at the Board of Education in the Department of Special Inquiries (McLachlan, 1935; Watts, 1998a). In 1911 and 1912, Caroline Herford brought parties of students from Manchester University to the Sandlebridge schools (Mary Dendy Hospital, Warford Hall Visitors Book 5 July 1910; 25 June 1912) and in 1922 Grace Owen, a foremost Froebelian (Brehony, 2000), then principal of the City of Manchester and Mather Training Colleges, also visited (ibid., 25 May 1922).

In Mary's 'little kingdom', children were to learn to respect each others' property and to share all gifts brought in for them by relatives and friends (Dendy, 1920). The 'unsocial disposition' was to be discouraged as children learned to take their share 'of rough and smooth in the little community of which they form a part'. Mary wrote that the aim of the education at Sandlebridge was to prepare each resident to become 'a more useful member of society; that is, of the little society in which he will have to live' (Dendy, 1911, p. 48). Whatever the ability of the child, it was to be 'communised' for the good of the whole. In this light, Mary saw great advantages in having boys and girls and men and women in the same colony; for the feeding of the girls provided a market for the produce of the boys' labour; while the making and mending and washing of the boys clothes provided work for the girls (ibid.). This, in turn, increased the potential for the colony's economic self-support and so the colony's separation from the world outside its borders. Care and control of the sexuality of the feeble-minded and the ambiguities of feminism and eugenics could both be accommodated in this alternative 'little kingdom'.

Successive annual reports of the Sandlebridge Schools demonstrate that while reading and writing was taught to those thought able to avail themselves of it, manual training was consistently stressed as the most suitable branch of education for the children. In Mary's view, training in hand and eye became increasingly important as feeble-minded children grew older (RCCCFM, 1908, i, Q.823, Q.979). In 1910, the Annual Report noted a scheme for training the senses. Mary spoke of her familiarity with Seguin's techniques in her evidence to the RCCCFM in 1904 (RCCCFM, 1908, i, Q.875). Seguin's manipulative material and games, which complemented his gymnastic exercises, included the peg board, buttoning and unbuttoning, and lacing and unlacing and threading of beads, feeling surfaces, smelling, tasting and eating, listening to music and voices and watching lights in dark rooms (Talbot, 1964). In 1848, Seguin emigrated to the United States, and assisted in developing the residential training school model that was adopted in Massachusetts (Winzer, 1993). The promotion of sense-training at Sandlebridge followed Mary's month-long visit in 1908 to the Massachusetts' Waverley school and colony for the feeble-minded. At Waverley, Mary particularly admired the organization of sense training – sight, smell, hearing, taste and touch, in which children fitted shapes into the hole in the piece of wood from which they were cut, smelled and tasted substances, listened to sounds and felt objects in bags (Dendy, 1920).

Materials made at Sandlebridge for use in the schools, similar to those in the sight cupboard at Waverley, were illustrated in the Sandlebridge Annual Report for 1910 (LCSPCFM, *Annual Report*, 1910). The 150 models made by the manual training teacher and his brother – and used particularly in the lessons on sight and touch – bear a great resemblance to the materials patented by Maria Montessori, based on her development of the work of Seguin. Montessori worked on her method for the education of the feeble-minded in parallel to Mary's investigation of the condition of feeble-minded children in Manchester board schools and her involvement in the establishment of the Manchester day special schools and the Sandlebridge Schools. Mary may have been present when Montessori addressed the English National Association for Promoting the Welfare of the Feeble-minded in 1899 (Kramer, 1976), but Montessori maintains that in 1899, when she visited London, Seguin's work was not understood in England (Montessori, 1920). It is more likely that the adoption of methods similar to those of Seguin at Sandlebridge were the result of Mary's transatlantic networks and visits.

As Mabel Talbot (1964) outlines, for Seguin the muscles and sensory organs were the means of offering material for reflection – as such they formed a conduit to the mind – and sense-training constituted an early stage of the harmonious development of physical, intellectual and moral capacities.[7] Seguin's view of education was influenced by Rousseau's *Émile* and by Saint Simon's *Nouveau Christianisme*, which posited education as physical, intellectual and moral development. Working with pupils unaware of responsibilities and duties, Seguin wanted to elicit willed responses from the child. The docile child, obedient to circumstances as well as to personal authority was not the end of the training. (Indeed, for the seduced feeble-minded girl, this was posited to be her condition.) Following Rollin, Seguin aimed to place volition and discipline within the child. Improvement depended on the development of willed action. His training in volition began with the first movements willed and exacted by the teacher and ended with the pupil's assumption of responsibility. Seguin termed the development of spontaneity or willed action, 'moral treatment'. For Seguin, 'moral treatment' drew on a Rousseauian view of morality as social responsibility, in which the individual exercised social duties as well as social rights. Moral training, therefore, was implicit in the physical and intellectual training.

For Seguin, attention to the development of the individual child, which accompanied his case study method, was vital; but the group situation was also a necessary part of moral education as the children worked together and helped each other. By 1846, Seguin included vocational tasks as part of the sense training that dealt with the child as a whole (ibid.). Seguin's view of 'morality' and Mary's view of 'work' in the Sandlebridge community resonated. For Mary, regular employment had a 'healing influence' (Dendy, 1899). For Mary, like Seguin, work continued the children's sensory learning. From their earliest days at Sandlebridge, little children polished floors, taps and tiles, laid tables and carried food as part of their role in the community. Work tasks were apportioned in relation to the assessment of individual character and 'needs' (RCCCFM, 1908, i, Q.823; Dendy, 1920). Older girls spent time in the laundry, boys on the farm. Work sent residents to bed 'healthily tired', but had to be carefully matched to the abilities of the children if health was to be built up. Despite providing crucial economic support to the institution, work was presented as a favour to the children (Dendy, 1920), part of the process by which they were 'produced' as 'happy citizens' of the 'little community'. In a process aimed to place volition and willed action in the child, the staff at Sandlebridge presented the possibility of a particular type of work to a child, but then witheld it to inculcate the desire in the child to take it on.

In line with the role of nurturant mother, the unmarried Mary portrayed the community of Sandlebridge as a family, in which both staff and pupils had to be willing to live together (RCCCFM, 1908, i, Q.859), and herself as surrogate, spiritual mother (Yeo, 1992, 1995). Each house was to have its own kitchen, which was both economical and convenient, and more home-like, with some food served in the kitchen and some at the table like a family (Dendy, 1920). Mary noted: 'I have my meals with the children when I go down to stay the night and they behave at table quite like little gentlemen or ladies' (RCCCFM, 1908, i, Q.822). The day room was to have a good solid table, chairs, a cupboard for toys, a piano, a couch for an ailing child to lie down on, pictures on the wall, a rocking-horse and a few of the best toys on the mantelpiece. Where the children were tiny, the large table was to be dispensed with to enable the children to play on the floor and very small tables and little bent-wood armchairs were to be available to be drawn close to the fire for invalid or delicate children. Toys, broken very frequently by feeble-minded children, were not to be put out of their way; for it was better in Mary's view for them to break them than for them not to play. While children were to learn to put away their toys, care was to be taken that too much was not sacrificed to tidiness. 'It is not possible that a large room, in which a number of children have for some time been play-ing happily, should look tidy' (Dendy, 1920). On 3 June 1902 she wrote in her diary, 'helped to bathe my boys and put them to bed. Stayed all night. Thank God for a beginning' (McLachlan, 1935, p. 174).

Pedagogy at Sandlebridge illustrates some ways in which within progressive pedagogies relations of power and desire interpenetrate in the production of subject positions (Walkerdine, 1990). It illus-trates, too, the tensions between care and control examined by Annemieke van Drenth and Francesca de Haan in *The Rise of Caring Power* (1999). Van Drenth and de Haan provide a gendered rework-ing of Foucault's notion of pastoral power. They argue that the gen-dered and pedagogical relations of care formed a new disciplinary force in the nineteenth century, characterizing evangelical philan-thropic work in general and the work of women in particular. In relations of care, aspects of power, identity, surveillance, subjection and subjectivity were interrelated in a process in which personal contact between carer and cared for and notions of morality played key roles. Van Drenth (forthcoming) has recently applied this frame-work to argue that in the domain of special education, medics and teachers, as agents of caring power, worked through persuasion and seduction based on their (expert) knowledge of the 'true' state of … individual's minds and bodies. In this process, medics and teachers evoked the development of a self in the physically disabled and mentally disturbed individuals who were their clients.[8] 'Scientific' casework played an important role in identifying the supposed curability of the few, which, in turn, confirmed the demoralized remainder and acted as a form of normalization.

The Home Office and the Education Department battled over the right to define special residential education (Thomson, 1998; Sutherland, 1984):[9] one aspect of the way the 'special' school can be seen – to rephrase Ian Hunter and Nick Peim – as the synthesis of an assemblage of ad hoc techniques (genealogy) arising in different 'departments of existence' which becomes integrated into the special 'purpose-built formative milieu' and 'the instrument and the effect of a bureaucratically organised pastoral governance of the popula-tion' (Peim, 2001, p. 185; Hunter, 1994). Caring power's Foucauldian framework provides one way of thinking about issues of subjects, self-regulation and citizenship for individuals placed in the 'alternative' community epitomized by Sandlebridge, with its ostensibly humanitarian objectives rather than the ostensibly punitive objectives of the reformatory. It points to the tensions in the special school as the outward regime of care which is also the regime of control and surveillance (Peim, 2001).

By 1910, when Manchester University conferred on Mary the degree of MA, she had examined 70,000 children scattered in elementary schools around the country. She showed many visitors round Sandlebridge and spent many days in the colony with the children and staff. After her period as commissioner at the Board of Control she returned to Sandlebridge and in 1921 took up residence at Greencote, a house she built on the estate and bequeathed to the colony, where she lived for the remainder of her days. By the end of her life, she had travelled far and wide and become a respected authority on the feeble-minded and had seen her views taken seriously by a Royal Commission. Her stance today on issues of sexuality appears harsh, particularly in respect of the women who came to be incarcerated under the 1913 Mental Deficiency Act in view of behaviour categorized as promiscuous. Yet, she had played a key role in putting the care of the less able children, foundering in the education system, or neglected by it, on the national agenda. Although the records of Sandlebridge attest to the difficulty of the undertaking, she worked hard to provide an education for them that she thought had their best interests at heart. Her work highlights the ambiguity of the institution's Janus-faced siting concerned with both care and with control, the public and the private.

Post-script

The stories of the Sandlebridge schools and colony intersect with the stories Mary told of herself and of the lives of the residents and their families that she had collected as family histories. Mary's auto/biographical practices – her variety of articulations at different levels in the social structure (Stanley, 2000) – were related to the social context in which such speech was possible. Hers were stories of her time, as she engaged with an evolutionary 'science' of hereditary that itself was evolving. The extent to which her self-representations and stories supported Sandlebridge as institution, and the extent to which they were stories that were 'tellable' in a particular time and context, are illustrated by the institution's subsequent fortunes after her death. When she died on 19 May 1933, aged 78, Mary had raised £35,000 from voluntary sources. Reports of the commissioners and inspectors from the Board of Control, over-ridingly positive about Sandlebridge during Mary's lifetime, show signs of criticism, beginning within months of her death. Although commissioners' reports remained largely positive about the happiness of the residents, the Sandlebridge managers were soon required to meet with the Board's commissioners to discuss how they would redress aspects of the institution that commissioners felt to be dated. Throughout the 1930s, commissioners voiced a litany of complaints, along with the suggestion that a few of the residents should be given a trial in the 'outside world' on license or guardianship – both contemporary methods of care in the community available during Mary's lifetime. Commissioners also pointed to the lack of opportunity for older residents to meet with the opposite sex, except at Sunday Service, and suggested that more opportunities for them to meet at social events should be considered. Both developments would have been an anathema to Mary and at variance with her stories of hereditary taint.

Having lost their most successful fund-raiser, from 1937 onwards the requirements of the commissioners and inspectors necessitated more funds than the committee could raise by voluntary subscriptions and donations. In 1939, negotiations were entered into with Cheshire County Council, who took over the institution in April 1941. In 1948, the Mary Dendy Homes came under the aegis of the National Health Service, were renamed the Mary Dendy Hospital and located within the Cranage Hall Hospital Group. An annex was opened in May 1955 but with the increasing shift to care in the community, the Mary Dendy Hospital ceased to exist shortly after.

6

Shena Simon (1883–1972) and the 'Religion of Humanity'

Shena Simon made a considerable contribution to educational thought and practice in twentieth-century Britain. The significance of her work was acknowledged when the Honorary Freedom of the City of Manchester was conferred upon her in 1964 – 40 years after she entered the City Council as a Liberal member of the Chorlton ward. In thinking about her life, this chapter attempts to explore certain central themes that informed her political practice (aims, visions and actions), moving on to assess her effectiveness and influence in achieving her goals. The opening largely concentrates on the thought and sensibility that contributed to her personal development and on the choices she was able to make as a result of her privileged education and assured social position. Notably, she was freed by affluence from having to support herself economically but so were other leisured individuals for whom activism was not a social practice. In her case, the injunction to promote the common good was not just an intellectual matter, but also a moral priority. Inspiration came from a concern with the social responsibilities of privilege; and by the 1920s, Simon publicly acknowledged the impulse to what she called the 'religion of humanity' (J. Simon, 1986, II, p. 36).

She was not a lone voice. In his analysis of the moral sensibility of the period, Stefan Collini (1993) argues that ideas of 'social duty' were particularly influential among Radical English intellectuals formed by the 'culture of altruism' that flourished between 1850 and 1880. This lay at the basis of much middle-class social involvement that relied upon an internalized ethic of service: the assumption that altruistic aims are sufficient to motivate to action. Its influence was apparent in the place held by the 'Religion of Humanity' devised by

Auguste Comte and espoused by the English positivists (attracted by the possibility of an ethical substitute for traditional Christianity). Its appeal meshed and intermeshed with the optimistic presumptions about the interplay of enlarged altruism, ethical imperatives and active citizen-participation that found expression in popular as well as academic studies. As Beatrice Webb so appositely remarked, 'it was during the middle decades of the nineteenth century that, in England, the impulse of self-subordinating service was transferred, consciously and overtly, from God to man' (1938, p. 123). Shena Simon was influenced by this point of view. She found her vocation in the membership of philanthropic and civic-reform associations and deplored those who did not share her behavioural norms and social-scientific idealism. The educated woman has no excuse for 'not taking her part' she wrote; to fight social injustice as a 'member of the city or town council' is 'better than playing golf or going to theatre matinees' (*Daily Dispatch*, 30 July 1922, cited in J. Simon, 1986, II, p. 37). But it was a long while before she would profess a surrogate 'secular religion'. Not for two decades would she spell out her convictions in these terms (affected by the ideology of Edwardian progressivism as well as the public-spirited enthusiasm of her spouse). In choosing the work of public service in education, she drew inspiration from the belief that schools could be used as agencies of social change to reduce social inequalities. Here, it will be argued that her three main contributions lie in the following areas: the fight against the application of a 'marriage bar' to prohibit married women from working as teachers, the fight on the Spens Committee for a single Code of Regulations for elementary and secondary education and the fight for comprehensive schools. A member of Manchester Education Committee from 1924–33 and 1936–70, her early advocacy of the comprehensive ideal is traced through two of her writings *Four Freedoms in Secondary Education* (1944) and *Three Schools or One?* (1947).

London Youth: in Public and in Private

Shena Simon was born Dorothy Shena Potter, daughter of Janet Boyd Thompson and John Wilson Potter, shipowner,[1] the second of nine children. At first sight, her parents seem to have shared the powerful orthodoxy that the education of 'ladies' was best conducted in a domestic setting. As a girl growing up in London in the

1890s, she lived inside dominant and class-based discourses – whereas the early education of the five Potter sisters took place at home, their brothers were sent away to school. This conventional pattern was broken when Shena was encouraged to attend Newnham College, Cambridge, to study economics. From here she went on to postgraduate studies at the London School of Economics in 1907.[2] In her study of British universities before 1939, Carol Dyhouse (1995) suggests the London institution offered a research environment that was relatively friendly to women. By contrast to Cambridge academic life, there was no informal social apartheid between the sexes and Shena had the distinction of registering for a higher degree under the supervision of Leonard Hobhouse, the first Professor of Sociology in Britain, and the Fabian Graham Wallas. However, she never completed her doctorate on Labour Party philosophy. Instead, she had training in social surveying with the National Anti-sweating League, a pressure group formed in 1906 which campaigned for the establishment of trade boards to protect unorganized low-paid workers and obtain for them minimum rates of pay. Shena worked with its secretary, Jimmy Mallon, studying wages and arbitration boards in Australia and New Zealand. She also joined the National Union of Women Workers, which worked to implement wide-ranging reforms with its support for women's rights and social welfare provision. Its annual conferences were well attended and attracted educated, activist women from across the political spectrum. Shena found a role model in Margaret MacDonald, wife of the Labour party leader, Ramsay MacDonald, who was extremely active, widely travelled and worked long hours despite being married with young children.

MacDonald came from a family keenly interested in community affairs. She was greatly influenced by her father, the nonconformist scientist Dr John Hall Gladstone, who served alongside Jane Chessar on the London School Board. Like her elder sister, Florence, she was encouraged to become a school manager giving her the opportunity to influence the daily experience of working-class children in school. By the age of 23, Margaret was taking classes for servant girls, co-operating in parish work and acting as a lady visitor for the Charity Organisation Society. She moved nearer to political activity, however, through direct contract with poorer women and girls in the course of voluntary work. In April 1896, she joined the newly formed Independent Labour Party, determined to diminish the deprivation of working women and bring her own direct experience to bear on policy making. Joan Simon (1986) comments that Margaret and Shena shared a special interest in child welfare, education, the problems women faced as employees, unemployment among women and the suffrage. Joining forces on the Legislation Committee of the National Union of Women Workers, they belonged to a movement of women that included Shena's friend from Newnham, Eva Spielman, now poor law guardian for Paddington (Harrison, 1987, p. 276).

In 1911, Eva married Bill Hubback, shortly to be appointed lecturer in classics at Manchester university (J. Simon, 1986, II, p. 2). Her new social contacts included Edith Eckhardt, another ex-Newnham student and cousin of the wealthy Liberal industrialist, Ernest Simon. Mary Stocks', Ernest's friend and biographer, observes that Ernest was a 'devoted adherent' of the ideas and practices of Beatrice and Sidney Webb of the Fabian Society, whose social reform programme based on voluminous researches 'precisely fitted his cast of mind' (Stocks, 1963, p. 23). But the admiration went beyond a shared interest in social questions. It offered a number of scripts for his personal life and direction. Writing to his mother in 1910, Ernest acknowledged his need for marriage and the kind of wife he wanted. She replied:

> Whenever you do marry it must be a woman who will help you and encourage you in all you care for. I am sure it is true, as you say of the Webbs, that the two together can do far more than twice as much as one – and there is absolutely nothing that so paralyses all one's best efforts as an unsympathetic (that is too strong a word) partner for life. Of course there cannot be the entire love and understanding unless you do care for and believe in the same things (quoted in Stocks, 1963, p. 25).

His ideal is very noticeable in his mother's assessment and it would seem that he wanted a close companionate relationship based on shared interests and values. Unaware of this correspondence but confident the 28-year-old Shena was the perfect wife for Ernest, Eva invited her to spend a weekend in Manchester. 'They had only to meet, she thought, and the thing would happen. It did' (quoted in Stocks, 1963, p. 33).

Surviving correspondence and Ernest's private diaries supply a vivid record of their courtship, which, while they may not be wholly representative, provide ample evidence of their goals for future life

together. Revealingly, the topics covered include collective ownership, democracy, Fabianism, the international labour question, the
institution of marriage, social reform and the women's suffrage
movement; as well as personal relations and friendship. For instance,
it will be recalled that Shena's idol was Margaret MacDonald. Shena
asked if Ernest had known Margaret and whether he would like to
see MacDonald's memoir of his late wife (quoted in J. Simon, 1986, I,
p. 31). Ernest was greatly influenced by Beatrice Webb, but Shena
thought Emmeline Pankhurst the 'greater person' (quoted in J. Simon,
1986, I, p. 34). Time and again they broached the question of the
women's suffrage movements (militant and non-militant) often to
Ernest's discomfort. Shena supported the suffragettes but had not
done anything militant:

> Mainly because my family objects so strongly and so long as I am
> economically dependent upon them I cannot do what they dislike.
> Some years ago, they objected to my speaking for the suffragettes,
> and then I made a bargain with them that if they allowed me
> to speak and walk in procession etc I would promise not to do
> anything actively militant (quoted in J. Simon, 1986, I, p. 30).

This was a young woman who, as her letters point out so clearly,
had a strong streak of rebellion and a concern for social justice.
Ernest proved especially hostile to militancy and felt a greater personal affinity with constitutional agitation so, they accommodate
viewpoints after a probing of each others position (Stocks, 1963,
p. 35; Tylecote, 1974, p. 2). The search for purpose is a prominent feature of their letter-writing and there is a strong sense of a marriage
of equals. As Ernest declared in his diary: 'I hope and believe that on
fundamentals we shall have an absolutely common creed – that we
shall really live a common life in perfect sympathy and with one
aim' (J. Simon, 1986, II, p. 5.) That one aim was based on a moral
sensibility whose guiding principle was 'the cause of humanity'
measured by 'the standard of the community' (Shena Potter to
Ernest Simon, 26 September 1912, quoted in J. Simon, 1986, II, p. 17).
Shena married Ernest on 22 November 1912 and for much of the
48 years of their life together continued to play a major role in
feminist and educational causes. In 1959 the Simons' were described
'as the Webbs' best pupils' (J. Simon, 1986, II, p. 3); but theirs was no
carbon copy of the Webb matrimonial pattern. First, it was not a
childless marriage and it may be that the tragedy of losing her only

daughter to cancer in 1929 led Shena to expand her activism to the work of national bodies. Second, Ernest and Shena were active on different issues: most particularly housing and education (Stocks, 1963, p. 39). Finally, place was important – Ernest was a Mancunian and Shena became one.

Manchester Politician: in Public and in Private

The Simon family had strong roots in the social, industrial and cultural life of Manchester dating back to 1860, when Henry Simon, educated as an engineer, settled there from Zurich (B. Simon, 1997). Born in Silesia, he became a highly respected Manchester citizen, who established two family firms and figured prominently in civic affairs, a generous and active benefactor of cultural life and educational facilities (especially the city's musical heritage and Owens College – now Manchester University). Ernest grew up in Didsbury, then a village some five miles south of Manchester city centre. Shena began married life in the home of her mother-in-law, but moved within a few months to Moorlands, Fog Lane, Manchester. Three years later the young family moved into Broom Croft:

> It was a very pleasant house – with outbuildings and a gardener's cottage at its drive gate, sufficient room indoors for entertaining after an extra wing had been added to it, and sufficient acreage out of doors for tennis, archery, and the cultivation of flowers and vegetables (Stocks, 1963, p. 79).

There was also a London flat; for a little over a decade a farm; and later, Hellsgarth, in the English lake district. The constant presence of domestic help gave Shena the freedom to pursue her political work but while they undoubtedly enjoyed a comfortable lifestyle the Simons' eschewed self-indulgence. Able to justify two cars and expensive holidays on the grounds of energy expended in public service, Ernest could not bring himself to apply the same principle to his premarital expenditure of £500 a year on polo (especially difficult when reminded by Shena that her personal allowance was £110 a year) (J. Simon, 1986, II, p. 7). Collini (1993, p. 83) has depicted 'the somewhat aggressive personal austerity' that often accompanied a 'concentration upon the duties of altruism to those below one in the social scale' and this fits in with what we know of the Simon household. Reading materials were one of the few unquestioned luxuries they allowed themselves, although security of wealth certainly reduced the constraints of domestic married motherhood. Mabel Tylecote commented in a memorial lecture: 'She had freedom to read and to write and she had secretarial help. Books could be bought that scholars must read in a library and a stream of blue books was delivered to order' (1974, p. 14).

The Simons enjoyed a singular position within Manchester politics and culture. Their roots in the city's German community brought many social contacts, plus a web of connections to the business world, politics and the press (B. Simon, 1997). Within easy reach were the staff of an expanding university and the personnel of the *Manchester Guardian*, who feature in the customary account of the Simons of Manchester:

> Here at Broom Croft with its wide grounds and its views over the River Mersey, gathered the Scotts, the Behrenses, the Godlees, and others of that powerful and influential 'Didsbury Set'. Here, and in their London flat, they would match their guests in brilliant discussion and argument, drawn together by common interests in liberal principles and by desire to find the best methods of promulgating them (Memorial Notice, *Newnham College Roll Letter*, 1973, p. 55).

This sketch of a social-cum-intellectual circle has all the appearances of the kind of permeation tactics so favoured by the Webbs. Of course, it may be a misjudgement. Shena herself said 'there was no Didsbury group' and Joan Simon considers the term a 'misnomer for the circle concerned which, however influential severally and together, was no tightly knit pressure group' (J. Simon, 1986, II, p. 43). Irrespective of how best to characterize this use of domestic space, however, Ernest had two close male friends who exercised a profound personal influence on Shena. The first was John Scott, in the same school house at Rugby, son of the newspaper's editor. The second was another Rugby contemporary, Richard Henry (Harry) Tawney, who went down from Balliol College, Oxford, to the East End's famous university settlement, Toynbee Hall. Like Margaret MacDonald, he served an apprenticeship with the Charity Organisation Society and, like her, made a dramatic break with their philosophy by joining the Labour Party. Tawney's friendship was particularly important for Shena due to his stance on educational reform and membership of key committees. Related to this was the influence of idealism, rooted in the social philosophy of Plato. Jose Harris has noted four aspects of Plato's thought that were especially attractive to idealists: first, the 'emphasis on society as an organic spiritual community'; second, his 'vision of the ethical nature of citizenship'; third, the 'focus on justice rather than force as the basis of the state'; and finally, 'his mysticism and anti-materialism' (1992, p. 128). According to Harris, citation of other Hellenic writers recurred in many social scientific and philosophical journals of the period who held out the figure of Pericles as a role model for 'modern youth' (op. cit., p. 130). Symbolically, the Christmas cards sent out to schools during the Simon's mayoral year carried a quotation from Pericles' Funeral Oration; and without wishing to overstate the case, it seems reasonable to add that a framed copy of the words hung in the children's bedroom (J. Simon, 1986, II, p. 36).

Ernest moved into Manchester politics with his unopposed election to the city council as Liberal member for Didsbury in 1911. He served without interruption until 1925, holding office as chairman of the housing committee 1919–23 and the youngest Lord Mayor the city had ever elected in 1921. In five years, between 1913 and 1917, Shena gave birth to three children. Her eldest, Roger, was born in 1913, Brian was born in 1915 and Antonia in 1917 (B. Simon, 1997, p. 6). She also pioneered the Manchester and Salford Women's Citizen Association, launched through the Manchester branch of the National Union of Women Workers. The aim was to help women use their growing civil rights to 'realise the power they possess as voters to press for the better consideration of all municipal affairs, and especially those which attract women and children' (Tylecote, 1974, p. 2). Poor health forced Shena to restrict her efforts some time later but as Lady Mayoress she again positioned herself as a change agent, using her public platform to challenge the 'natural order of things'. First, she refused to distribute Christmas presents at St Mary's Hospital for Women 'on the ground that there were no women either on its Board or its medical staff' (Stocks, 1963, p. 66). The attendant publicity meant two women were appointed to the governing body. Second, at the opening of a toy shop in December 1921, she advised that dolls be given to boys to encourage paternal instincts. Saying 'we do not want any sex monopoly in any of the occupations of life, and above all in the most important occupation of being good parents' (J. Simon, 1986, II, p. 38). Finally, at a prize giving ceremony in a girls' school she anticipated that by 2022 'half the House of Commons should be women and there should certainly have been "at least one woman Prime Minister" ' (J. Simon, 1986, II, p. 37). The basis of her familiarity with Manchester's educational system was recalled in an interview for the *Times Educational Supplement*:

> When you are the Lady Mayoress you can ask to see anything you want. I wanted to see schools, so they lent me an inspector and I spent a whole year going round looking and asking questions ('An 87-year old radical', *Times Educational Supplement*, 10 July 1970).

In November 1924, Shena fought the Council elections as a Liberal candidate for the Chorlton ward of Manchester. Her victory was a remarkable achievement in that Patricia Hollis (1987, p. 398) has suggested it was much harder for women 'to win seats on the great city councils. In Manchester, Birmingham, and Liverpool only women with an outstanding reputation were successful'. But what was the specific organizational setting to which she gained access?

Feminist critics of contemporary British politics argue that the distribution of political power reflects a certain bias in the way society is organized that makes it easier for some individuals and groups to see their objectives come to fruition (Lovenduski and Norris, 1996). Certainly, there was male bias in terms of the numbers of men and women on Manchester City Council at this time and men played the majority role in the policy-making process. Not until the 1930s were women promoted to full committee chairmanships: Mary Kingsmill Jones (Health, 1931) and Shena Simon (Education, 1932), areas that reflect traditional notions of the sexual division of labour. At first sight, this appears to prove that the female contribution tended to be concentrated in welfare but it is important not to exaggerate the male influence here. Simon *wanted* to speak on education, which she regarded as a specialty of hers, and was ready to champion the interests of women. In promoting 'social' and 'welfare' issues, she was playing a role she herself had chosen and capitalized on the opportunity to challenge the political agenda as defined by men. Proceedings on the Sanitary Committee reveal the culture of male fraternity:

> The aldermen loved their familiar and well-bred mares, and each committee began with a long report on 'the health of the horses.'

She used, unsuccessfully, to move its replacement by a report on 'the health of the men.' Regularly, too, little plates of oats were set before the committee members to 'inspect the feed.' 'Mr Chairman,' she said formally, 'I am afraid I don't see the value of this.' The chairman, a silver-haired alderman, sympathetically left his chair and standing behind her said: 'I understand my dear. No doubt you've not had much to do with horses. A lady too. Allow me to show you how to test the oats with your finger and thumb – thus. Now, I'm sure you see, don't you?' (Brian Jackson, 'retirement', July 1970).

Conscientiously Shena went so far as to judge the oats but decided against sticking her nose in chunks of hay when Alderman Swales emerged 'with a large scratch' (J. Simon, 1986, III, I, p. 3). On another occasion, the chairman arrived with a mare's kidney stone (wrapped in newspaper) to show why the animal had to be destroyed before the committee could vote on the recommendation. Not surprisingly, her advocacy of electric traction for the water and dust carts found little support until the death of the chairman and the resignation of the superintendent of the cleansing department (ibid.).

A very articulate, witty speaker, she found it less difficult to make her presence felt on the Education Committee. During the long period of high unemployment between the wars there were huge cuts in public expenditure, including education. Local authorities were under considerable pressure to produce savings and in 1925 this climate of economy threatened to halt a Manchester education programme covering ten years' development. The Finance Committee rejected the provisional education estimates and it was the newly elected Shena Simon, not the leading Liberal, who put the Education Committee's case to the full Council. More self-assured than the average woman, she had the advantage of a degree in economics and refused to concede finance as traditional male territory. She sought out the Scott's to get support in the *Manchester Guardian* but defeat did not dissuade her from standing up for her convictions when she saw fit. In 1970, when asked what she considered to have been her greatest contribution to education Simon remembered 'the success we had in 1928 when it became possible for married women teachers to stay in the profession after they were married' (Medlicott, 10 July 1970). It is to this that we now turn.

In 1910, Margaret Ashton, the only female member, unsuccessfully attempted to prevent the introduction of a ban on appointing married women (other than widows); although she did win a concession where a husband was 'incapacitated from work' (Bedford, 1998, p. 12). The authority encouraged women to return to teaching during the First World War but when hostilities ended they were only retained if their husbands were unable to maintain them, or on the grounds of 'good teaching ability' (Simon, 1938, p. 261). In Manchester, the question of the marriage bar was raised three times during the economic recessions of the 1920s and 1930s. In 1922 (the year most local authorities sacked married women teachers), Annie Lee (Labour) successfully opposed the Education Committee's recommendations regarding the reintroduction of the pre-war regulation; six years later Shena Simon took a lead in attacking attempts to clamp down on the employment of married women teachers. It was proposed that maternity leave last a compulsory 17 months (of which only three or four would be paid) and this put women's posts and pensions in danger. Simon failed to convince a majority on the Education Committee and subsequently challenged the ruling on the Council. Joan Simon sets the scene. On the one hand, Lee and Simon united across party political lines to protect women's employment. On the other, the newly elected Mary Kingsmill Jones (Conservative) supported the marriage bar. According to the Conservative chairman of the Education Committee, Alderman Woollam:

> the principle operated generally for the good reason that divided attention operated against efficiency and there were naturally difficulties when women had babies; a woman who married ought to look forward to being a mother and the council should not be prepared to encourage people who were determined not to have children (J. Simon, 1986, III, p. 11a).

At this point Shena Simon rose to her feet. She demolished the charge of absenteeism, the prescription of women's role as mothers and another customary rationale put by Kingsmill Jones that the marriage bar would protect single 'unsupported' women from competition for scarce jobs. Afterward, a majority of eight voted in favour of referring back the ruling and Manchester City Council adopted the regulations applied by Lancashire County Council: that is, two months leave of absence before a confinement and three months afterwards. When the opponents again raised the question in 1934, they had little success either in Committee or in the Council.

Nearly 40 years later, Simon recalled an argument put by an old
adversary on the education committee, Alderman Woollam
(Conservative), that escaped contemporary reporters:

'how dreadful it would be for the children, if, just when the
"scholarship" examination was being held, all the women teachers in junior schools were away having babies.' 'I was sorely
tempted to get up and say that I was sure they would arrange
things differently, but was only restrained by the fear that the
council would be shocked by any reference to birth control'
(J. Simon, 1986, III: 11–11a).

Shena Simon lost her seat in 1933. A year later she unsuccessfully
fought the Wythenshawe ward as an independent and in 1936 failed
to capture the Moston ward as a Labour candidate (Tylecote, 1974,
p. 3). She did not regain her elected status but served as a co-opted
member of Manchester Education Committee (nominated by the
Labour group) from 1936 to 1970. As a result, she could neither steer
proposals through the full Council, nor serve on the national committees of local government organizations.

Statutory Woman: in Public and in Private

One thus has something of a paradox, in that at national level she
found herself in a position of extraordinary influence on the
Consultative Committee of the Board of Education. Set up as part of
the Board of Education Act of 1899, by the late 1920s the
Consultative Committee had come to occupy a prominent place in
policy-making although strictly as an advisory body. The official
position, as articulated by R.H. Tawney, was that:

The Consultative Committee is neither the Treasury nor the
Cabinet. They will both have their say later. Its job is to see that a
policy is laid down in accordance with *the educational merits of the
case*. It is for the politicians to say later whether they will act on it.
Unless the Committee sticks firmly to that line, it can never consider subjects on their educational merits *at all* (R.H. Tawney to
S.S., 26 February 1936).

At the beginning of its life the traditional interests of the Church,
public school and ancient universities dominated but the Board was

soon ready to incorporate new interest groups like elementary school teachers, organized labour and women. Kevin Brehony (1994) has argued that the rules governing its composition corresponded to political necessities tied to two objectives: 'First of all the need to utilize greater inputs of knowledge and experience in the policy-making process and second, the need to permit a certain degree of representation to social groups, with an interest in education' (Brehony, 1994, p. 171). According to Brehony, 'the fact that members were selected, not elected, meant that power lay principally with the Board of Education rather than with those represented' (1994, p. 192). It follows that the Board's permanent officials were particularly receptive to appointments that were unlikely to give them problems. In 1914, for instance, the choice of Helen Smith, Lady Superintendent of the Borough Polytechnic, was disapproved by administrative civil servants when inquiries revealed that she had recently appeared in public in 'some feminist connection' (op. cit., p. 191). Robert Morant, as Permanent Secretary of the Board of Education from 1903, took full advantage of these possibilities. He personally selected his friend and acolyte Albert Mansbridge, founder of the Workers' Educational Association (WEA), to represent the views of the working classes (Mansbridge, 1940, pp. 161–2). In recruitment by patronage the key question is whether the person is 'one of us'. Mansbridge did not articulate a specifically socialist working-class politics and his was a voice they did not mind hearing. His successor, R.H. Tawney, was very obviously akin to senior officers of the Board in terms of familial background and education at elite institutions. When Tawney retired in 1931, he proposed that Shena Simon succeed him as a representative of what was now referred to as 'workers education'. Admittedly, her position as 'Tawney's disciple' (Simon, 1974a, p. 188) may have had some bearing on this but she was an experienced administrator whose opinion was listened to and noted. All this gave her political clout even if her feminism was regarded with suspicion.

It must be appreciated that the admission of women to the Consultative Committee can only be understood in the context of the fight for women's political enfranchisement and lobbying on the part of professional organizations like the Association of Head Mistresses. Suffrage arguments made great play of the distinctive character of the female contribution which was contingent upon a gendered and classed construction of 'special needs'. Girls were regarded as having different requirements to boys (either physical, emotional or intellectual) and women educationists found the conscious emphasis on women's contribution and skills useful. In trying to understand their appointment, it is important not to lose sight of two things: first, the dependence on male sponsors; and second, altered expectations contingent on 'expert' knowledge. Up to 1916, the selection criteria for the representation of women were 'connection to a particular sector of the education system' and lack of 'ties to women's organizations' (Brehony, 1994, p. 171). Fifteen years later, the re-constituted Spens Committee had four women members out of a total of nineteen. Only one, Shena Simon, was selected as an expert in administration rather than teaching. The others represented different sectors of education. They were Dorothy Brock leading member of the Association of Head Mistresses (secondary schooling), the Newnham-educated econo-mist Lynda Grier (university education) and Essie Conway anti-suf-fragist (elementary schooling). Conway died in office in 1934 and was replaced by Ada Phillips. In *Troubling Women* (1999, p. 3) Jill Blackmore argues that women who get into educational leadership occupy an ambivalent position 'as both insiders (as "managers") and outsiders (as women) in male dominated cultures'. The avail-ability of surviving correspondence of Shena Simon has thrown up issues pertinent to current debates about women in educational leadership and facilitated new interpretations of the relationship of women to power in the state apparatuses and bureaucracies. In a privileged position, with all the expectations that go with being one of a few, statutory women played a special role in educational deci-sion-making. They were not specifically responsible for questions relating to girls' schooling but as Brehony (1994, p. 191) points out, 'one member could represent more than one constituency'.

By 1934, the Committee had a new remit and a new chairman, Will Spens, Master of Corpus Christi College, Cambridge, as well as many new appointments since the publication of the Hadow Report on the education of the adolescent in 1926.[3] The extension of years spent in school heightened debate over the relation of the elemen-tary and secondary sectors, particularly the question of whether it was really possible to achieve parity of esteem between the alterna-tive forms of post-primary education. In this situation the Spens terms of reference were:

to consider and report upon the organization and inter-relation of schools other than those administered under the Elementary Code which provide education for pupils beyond the age of 11+; regard being had in particular to the framework and content of the education of pupils who do not remain at school beyond the age of about 16 (Maclure, 1965, p. 193).

Brian Simon has argued that it is possible to discern a 'doctrine' at the Board of Education, even though it was not supposed to have a 'policy of its own'. According to Simon (1974a, p. 257) this is evident in the fact that neither the Hadow nor the Spens committees were permitted to consider an integrated system of post-primary education. Essentially, the Board's line of policy was to sustain and protect the elite secondary sector, and the public school system, at the expense of the mass elementary sector. At the same time, the machinery of selection enabled a select few to sidestep into secondary school if they gained a free or 'special' place. Within the Consultative Committee there was a tension between two opposing views – those who wanted to change the status of technical schools and those who wanted to raise all post-primary schools to secondary schools. Her strong commitment to the policy proposals set out by Tawney in 1922, and published by the Labour Party under the title *Secondary Education for All*, placed Shena Simon in the latter camp. As is normal in politics, she sought to ally herself with other forces, particularly those representing local authority interests. Notable among these were William Brockington (Director of Education for Leicestershire 1903–47), Sir Percy Jackson (chairman of West Riding Education Committee 1917–37) and Ernest Rowlinson (Labour leader of Sheffield city council and chairman of the education committee). Rowlinson was invited to serve in 1936 but Brockington and Jackson had both produced reports under Hadow's chairmanship. The other experienced members were Dr H.W. Cousins (headmaster of a grammar school at Ulverston, Cumbria, to represent rural schools), Lynda Grier, Albert Mansbridge, H.J.R. Murray (former divisional inspector, a representative of the Board) and J.A. White (headmaster of a London central school). To achieve any sense of whose voices were heard most authoritatively we need to understand how the decisions were arrived at. In the surviving correspondence there are glimpses of the particular kind of skill in the management of committees at the heart of the business.

Here, the influence and policy priorities of Shena Simon will be considered in relation to two key points: the fight for a single Code of Regulations for elementary and secondary education and the abolition of secondary school fees. It is interesting that Shena feared the appointment of Spens as chairman. Her reservations were expressed in a letter to William Brockington:

> When the present chairman was appointed I heard from many people who had served under him that he was an excellent chairman, but that he was not always over scrupulous in the methods by which he gained his ends. When that is combined with a lack of knowledge of education – apart from Public Schools and Oxford and Cambridge – and with strong and well known conservative leaning in politics, I cannot help wondering whether his appointment was not meant to curb the progressive spirit, which has been the mark of the Consultative Committee's Reports up to the present. I may be quite wrong, but I am not alone in my suspicions (S.S. to W. Brockington, 19 November 1934).

Thus briefed, Brockington took pains to mollify her apprehension by confiding in his reply that Spens was 'not the first choice' (W. Brockington to S.S., 26 November 1934). Nonetheless, the implications of her doubts and uncertainties are consistent with the conclusion that the Board was inclined to give credence to particular outside voices (Hunt, 1991; Simon, 1974a). Shortly afterwards, a caucus of Brockington, Spens and the secretary to the Committee, R.F. Young (a Board official), met to establish due process and enable the chair to control deliberations more tightly. This triumvirate prepared a draft report which they then read to Shena in a private meeting. That Simon was accorded this privilege is a further indication of her ability to make her presence felt in political decision-making. In the face of this regard, how did she respond? It seems that she was alarmed by the presumption that minds were made up and this decision to re-visit the principal recommendations of the Hadow Report: notably the raising of the minimum leaving age to fifteen and the institution of secondary education for all children at the age of 11-plus. Afterwards, she confessed to Tawney that she 'was rather rude' because she 'felt the whole procedure was wrong' but wise enough to want to conciliate Brockington who thought her 'very intransigent'.

Sometime earlier, she showed herself ready to challenge institutional procedures in defence of a principle she believed in – the proposal that all post-primary schools should be equal in amenities.

It was she who intervened to challenge the chairman's agenda which gave priority to the question of the multilateral school. Her move succeeded. Sir Percy Jackson, Ernest Rowlinson and J.A. White all supported her and after a morning's discussion the chairman endorsed her proposal to set up a Code Sub-Committee composed of himself, Brockington, Jackson, Simon and White. Undoubtedly pleased with the outcome, Shena reported to Tawney that Brockington's attitude was the 'only disappointment' but she was hopeful: 'Sir Percy and I between us will be able to strengthen him' (S.S. to R.H. Tawney, 22 February 1936). The Tawney/Simon correspondence shows the part he played in helping Shena to wield political power in an area where her expertise was acknowledged and her influence already in evidence: 'The right line, I think, is to insist on deciding *first* what is desirable on grounds of educational policy' (emphasis in original, R.H. Tawney to S.S., 26 February 1936). To press the demand for equality between the different post-primary schools she should 'make Young' collate the weight of supporting evidence (he thinks 'he did something of the kind for us before') and focus attention on the 'educational merits of the case' (R.H. Tawney to S.S., 26 February 1936). Above all, she should distance the argument from party politics.

With Tawney's backing, Shena played a leading role in the deliberations of the Code Sub-Committee. Members decided (20 March 1936) to take the question of the multilateral school first, despite protests from Jackson and Simon that this was a special case (in line with Tawney's advice to move from the general to the particular). Internal relations were expressed in terms of differing stances on educational reform between two adversarial pairs: Brockington and Spens versus Jackson and Simon. An early example was class size. Spens argued for the continuation of larger classes for the non-academic pupil, whereas Jackson and Simon successfully opposed this view. Much of the debate focussed on secondary school fees – Brockington and Spens argued that grammar school fees were justified, since that type of education cost more, but this was anathema to their opponents. Jackson adopted an interesting psychological technique. To Spens' discomfort, he prefaced every remark with a statement like 'As we are going to recommend that all post primary education shall be secondary' (S.S. to R.H. Tawney, 25 July 1936), when the Committee was actually undecided. Nonetheless, while it seemed that at first there would be no clear statement on the abolition of fees in all state-aided secondary schools; by August 1937 the tables were turning. Spens asked Brockington and Simon to prepare memoranda on the opposing points of view. Typically, she wrote:

> Personally, I believe that in time, other forms of post-primary education, raised to the level of Grammar Schools, including the Technical High Schools, will make good, and parents, rich and poor alike, will come to select the school that best fits their child. Until then, let us have as many Grammar School places as there are children ready and qualified to fill. This will not mean a wasteful provision, because we are recommending that all post-primary schools should be equal in amenities i.e. size of classrooms, number in class, salaries of teachers, provision of playing-fields, gymnasia, dining halls, libraries etc., etc. (Memorandum in favour of 100 per cent Special Places in all Maintained and Grant-aided Grammar Schools, pp. 5–6).

This judgement of equivalence between different types of post-primary education makes clear that she thought it possible to foster parity of esteem between alternative forms of secondary school. It was an assumption she came to regret. When the Report was at its final stage she expressed her disappointment to Tawney:

> I wish I had fought 'parity' earlier. I am afraid that I let it go, and now it is so deeply embedded in the Report that it would be impossible to get it changed. I think the chairman and Brockington feel that 'equality' smacks too much of Bolshevism! (S.S. to R.H. Tawney, 17 October 1938).

Moving towards membership of the Labour Party (she joined in 1935), on a spectrum of opinion from broadly socialist to conservative, she stood at opposite ends to some of her colleagues. She fought crucial contests during the years of deliberation and won some important victories: notably the introduction of a common code and the recommendation (strongly opposed by Brock and Grier) that *all* secondary school places be 100 per cent 'special places' awarded on merit. At times she stood alone and Ernest Rowlinson acknowledged her contribution:

> I am grateful to know that you championed the 100% position, and I am amazed beyond measure that certain people are willing

and desirous of insisting that, all other things being equal, the scholar with known assessment of ability to take advantage of higher education, shall deliberately be caused to make way for the 'inferior brain', because some unknown trait in his character, may bring 'tone' to the school (Alderman Rowlinson to S.S., 4 May 1937).

In a similar fashion, Tawney congratulated her after the Report was published: 'I know how wearing and disillusioning a single-handed struggle on a committee is', he told her, 'and I felt for you in the battle. You can, at any rate, feel that it has had valuable results' (R.H. Tawney to S.S., 3 January 1939).

Most importantly, proposals on how best to secure parity of status between the different types of school were set out in an administrative chapter, that dealt, at some length, with the need for a common code, recommended the abolition of secondary school fees and the raising of the leaving age to sixteen. The placing is significant, for it may have eased the completion of a united report. At one stage, it had seemed inevitable they would 'divide' on the issue of fees but how much significance should be attached to the chairmanship of Spens? Joan Simon (1977a,b) has carefully analysed the shaping of the Spens Report. She has found that he 'canalized discussion in a way that avoided confrontation and adhered to a mode of approach bringing recommendation within the reference to neutralize official objections' (1977b, p. 180). Whether the unanimity came about because he manipulated the committee remains open but Shena conceded the achievement, given the basic disagreement: 'many members don't really believe in the administrative proposals and I want to keep all types in the same school' (S.S. to R.H. Tawney, 11 January 1939). This was a stance she retained to the end of her life. Like her political mentor, Tawney, she strongly criticized the endurance of social distinctions in the field of education.

The Comprehensive Ideal

We can trace the development of her views about secondary education as they were represented in *The Four Freedoms in Secondary Education*, published in March 1944, and the short book *Three Schools or One?* published in 1947. *Four Freedoms* belongs to the period of educational inquiry leading up to the 1944 Education Act. In it, she sets out the view that the issue of control needs connecting to the issue of representation. One consequence of the abolition of fees was to focus attention on the future status of the 232 direct grant schools. Many had their origins in old-established endowed schools and they were all free from external control. The 1944 Bill proposed the abolition of fees in all state-aided secondary schools but at the time of writing, the question of fees in direct grant schools was unresolved. So, too, was the contentious issue of their independent status. In the minds of opponents the two were intimately connected and Simon examines the implications of local authority control for institutional autonomy. It was hoped and expected that this might defuse opposition to the abolition of fees in direct grant schools. The independent sector resented this kind of 'political interference' and fiercely contested any loss of autonomy that might interfere with the freedom the schools had hitherto enjoyed. Protagonists argued this freedom was made up of three parts: the freedom of the governing body (power of appointment, control over admissions policies and finances), the freedom of the headmaster (power to appoint and dismiss staff) and the freedom of the parents (to express a preference of school). In her opinion, it was a charade to use a vocabulary of rights to defend such privilege and she has no truck with this elitist wing of educational thinking. She writes about the influence of the 'old school tie' in private school appointments as well as the freedom of the assistant staff, rarely mentioned, against arbitrary action by the head. The implications of parental choice are noted, as she went on to ask how can it be 'choice' when the freedom to exercise these rights is dependent on the ability to pay? In her view, the changing relations of power and control may remove an obstacle to active citizen-participation:

It is as true of local, as of central government, that the nation (or local community) gets the government it deserves. Many of those who are loudest in attacks on local education committees could not name the chairman of their local committee, and few of them take an active part as citizens in the selection of candidates for their local council, or in their election and subsequent support. Such people have surely forfeited any right to attack LEAs and perhaps one of the advantages that will result from the abolition of fees, will be that leading citizens, whether governors, teachers or parents will realise in future that the personnel of an education committee is not a matter for abuse, witticisms or indifference, but

one of vital importance to them as individuals, if not as citizens
(Simon, 1944, p. 32).

Three Schools Or One? sets out alternate conceptions of the future
structure of the secondary school system. Initiatives are considered
in terms of their historical lineage and there is a comparative analysis based on visits to American city high schools in 1942, and
Scottish schools in June 1947. Reviewing the data on participation in
education, Simon points out that American high school fees were
abolished about 1870, the minimum leaving age was 16 in 39 of the
48 States, and between 70 and 75 per cent of the age range 14 to 17
were attending high school in 1942 (in England the figure was 10 per
cent in 1938). In a further comment on educational provision and
social opportunity, she uses statistical evidence to contrast patterns
of admission to higher education. In this respect, England and
Scotland lagged far behind their American counterparts, of whom
eight per 1,000 of the population managed to get to university, as
opposed to one per 1,000 and two per 1,000 respectively (pp. 20, 26).
Unusually for the time, Simon did not ignore the weaknesses and
shortcomings of the 1944 Education Act with regard to its ambiguity in certain key areas of provision: notably, the exact structure of
the secondary school system for *all* children over the age of eleven.
For instance, in a shrewd critique of a recent Ministry pamphlet, *The
New Secondary Education* (1947), she questions the idea of three types
of mind and the validity of intelligence testing. She objected strenu-
ously to the proposal that selection for the grammar school be based
on the 11-plus process supported by a parental promise that the
child will stay on until they are eighteen. Does the Ministry mean
working-class children should go to the modern school she asks – if
so, the 'grammar schools will once again become class schools'
(Simon, 1947, p. 54). Less than ten years after the publication of
the Spens Report she identifies the contradictions at the centre of
tripartitism:

> But will not a school which alone leads eventually – if only for the
> few – to the highest educational institution in the land, and for the
> many, to secure white-collar occupations, not carry a prestige
> higher than the school which leads to manual work, although
> skilled, and one which leads to nowhere in particular but will
> obviously include all the children who are going into unskilled
> and perhaps blind-alley occupations? (Simon, 1947, p. 43).

Simon strongly opposed the dominance of the classical tradition and was not at all convinced of the virtues of the British grammar school. In her opinion, the grammar school curriculum was too much dominated by the university requirements that bedevilled the English qualifications system and helped preserve the elite hallmarks of a highly stratified system of schooling.

By the end of the 1940s, Simon's vision of public education as central to democracy was well developed. She wrote that separation (whether along lines of attainment, social class, gender, culture or wealth) is undemocratic and suspected the confusion of intellectual ability and social class retained by those who took an elitist position. Her goals were very different to those who favoured the traditional emphasis on character formation and social leadership for the academic elite. As we have seen, she was committed to a belief in the educability of *all* children and the principle of everyone of secondary school age going to schools designed for all abilities. She was optimistic that the common school could create social cohesion and provide the arena in which a really democratic community could be attained. It was the responsibility of the school to meet the needs of all children and she looked forward to 'the time when we can build new secondary schools, to a new standard which will express a new set of educational and social values' (p. 95). She lived long enough to see the movement to establish comprehensive schools win official recognition in 1965, as well as the transition to comprehensive education in Manchester two years later (Kerckhoff *et al.*, 1996).

An analysis of Shena Simon's life and work reveals something of her idealism. It shows, also, her extraordinary spirit of optimism and hope. She was among the young women who first attended universities and her philosophy of life owed not a little to the historical moment in which she lived. The 'religion of humanity' provided an intellectual schema for her social activism and it seems entirely plausible to argue for a link between Simon and the idealist ways of thinking that fired Tawney while an undergraduate at Balliol College, Oxford. The influence of Thomas Hill Green, Fellow of Balliol, until his death in 1882, is of particular interest given his focus on the importance of *patriots*, whose lives promote the well-being of the state, both by social service and participation in democratic government at different levels (op. cit., p. 45). In many ways, Shena Simon exemplified Green's ideal, with her involvement in the local community on the one hand, and political activity on a national scale on the other. But what did she get in return? Green's strategy appealed to the intellect and to the emotions: the socially privileged 'would gain that release from bad conscience' and 'that moral development which comes from living in a moral society where all men are treated as agents, each of whom is an end equally to himself and to others' (Richter, 1964, p. 135). But did she embrace this rationale? Could she be assured of its meaning and efficacy?

In a lifetime of activism she consistently endorsed a more equal and socially inclusive education system to accommodate change. On the one hand, she became a committed socialist with a class perspective on education reform. On the other, she was overtly feminist. Unlike her great mentor, Tawney, her egalitarianism did extend into a championing of gender issues. She fought against contemporary attitudes between the wars, especially in promoting opportunities for women and opposing public spending cuts. Unusually for the time, she also appreciated how the underlying theme of differentiation was going to be hard to shift. Indeed, she began arguing for common secondary schooling in the 1930s and thereafter tried to promote the abolition of selection as a co-opted member of Manchester Education Committee. Spurley Hey, the Director of Education with whom she first served, wrote in 1928 to her:

> I like to think of those who have been kind to me personally, interested in my work, and enthusiastic on behalf of the great cause of education. On these grounds I think first and longest of you, and I want you to know how greatly I appreciate your kindness to me personally, and still more gladly I pay tribute to the work you have accomplished on behalf of education. I have never known a better member of an Education Committee … you will be the first woman chairman of the Manchester Education Committee and the first woman President of the Association of Education Committees. You may not count these as great honours but I do, and I hope to see them realized, in my own day, if possible (quoted in Tylecote, 1974, pp. 6–7).

Hey did not live long enough to see her win the first of these honours in 1932. The second was denied her after the electoral defeats. Simon made her political career by building up a reputation for her ability to use committee machinery and to lobby and pressurize, to change the order of things. Her success was a sign of her tenacity, her grasp of detail and her personal circumstances that made her a far more independent person than the career politician.

7

Margaret Cole (1893–1980): Following the Road of Educational and Social Progress

Soon after the Second World War, Margaret Cole, historian of the Labour movement, journalist and author, wrote a single volume of autobiography entitled *Growing Up Into Revolution*. In the preface, the reader is invited to accept that in writing it her 'intention is not merely to recount the events of one not particularly important life, but to present a picture, as seen through the lens of one mind and one set of experiences, of the revolution of our times' (1949, p. v). The life is described in some detail but it is interwoven with reflection on major shifts in early twentieth-century Britain. Margaret Cole's writing suggests she was influenced by Beatrice Webb's autobiography, *My Apprenticeship*, published in 1938. In her biography of the Fabian sociologist who became her close friend and research mentor, Cole makes a case for *My Apprenticeship* as 'an autobiography of a remarkable kind'. First and foremost it shows no personal malice, has a historian's eye for narrative and a sociologist's experience of presenting the individual as a social being. For these reasons, it 'is far from being a book of simple reminiscence' (Cole, 1945, p. 153). Emulation of this exemplar aside, it follows that Margaret Cole's generic labelling of her own 1949 autobiography as 'reminiscence' is significant. This chapter argues that her life-writings provide a particularly clear case of the interstices of biography and autobiography, history and subjectivity, theory and experience. How to interpret the autobiographical is the chapter's theme.

Autobiography belongs to a narrative tradition that we can use in the spirit of C. Wright Mills' (1959) vision of the 'sociological

141

imagination': to draw the connection between 'personal troubles' and 'public issues'. For years this meant looking at the productions of men; for the woman's writing voice was written out of what Jane Miller (1986) has called that 'learned androgyny'. But things have moved on and feminist criticism has exposed how autobiography as a distinct literary genre privileged the masculine subject. Attention has been drawn to the 'absence of women writers from the autobiographical canon, or of gender from critical accounts of autobiography' (Anderson, 1997, p. 2). Bjorklund (1998, pp. 31–2) wrote that 'the problem of being interesting' related to what counts as an eventful life. These critics also put into question the construction of women as autobiographical subjects. The challenge for women as writers and readers of autobiography is that men have been linked with the capacity to advance our understanding of how people give meaning to the world and male authors are generally regarded as the writers of representative autobiography. Marcus notes the extent to which the genre of autobiography 'and theories of autobiography in general, derived almost entirely from texts by male authors, and a very selective group of male authors at that, acquired an intrinsic andocentric bias' (1994, p. 230). Discussing a group of modern critics writing in the 1960s and 1970s, she points out the politics of genre at work. Citing Pascal on the concept of 'intention', the following quotation is taken as emblematic. 'The first condition is the seriousness of the author, the seriousness of *his* personality and of *his* intention in writing' (Pascal, 1960, p. 60, my emphases). In the light of all this, it becomes apparent that writing autobiography is a social, ideological activity. A certain conception of authorship delegitimizes the writing of women and the development of a narrative for the self has to be understood as both cultural product and social act.

This takes us to questions of interpretation: the genre of autobiography has been seen as providing a reasonable index to cultural values and assumptions. As Stanley remarks: 'Women who might be famous if they were men remain *women* and therefore by definition secondary to the great and famous of their day' (1988, p. 68). Hence the historical tradition of autobiography came to be equated with the lives of 'great men' who were, I may add, mostly Western and middle class. The centrality of sexual difference means control of the more powerful discourse lies with men. 'Serious' autobiographies become cultural artefacts contributing to the valorization and dominance of certain experiences. For Miller (1986) this is to be expected so long as the dominant modes of ordering and categorizing experiences exclude women from being representatively human. This raises questions about the relation between subjectivity, representation and narrative. We all build narrative accounts of our lives in which we portray ourselves for different purposes and with different audiences in mind. We select what is important and what is to be left out. Margaret Cole did not lead an uneventful life and unlike most of her female contemporaries there is a sense in which she lived and worked as an honorary male. Choices about how to write the preface to *Growing Up* indicate decisions made about how to take up a position in her culture as a woman. They may, perhaps, suggest she felt the need to place a disclaimer to assure her readers of her womanliness and disarm critics who would otherwise charge that she was egotistical. Using this kind of approach the information presented may signify the dilemma of how to locate herself as an autobiographical subject. The notion of a witness to change seems to offer her a way out – a means of personal justification – an authorial space in which the subject could create herself in the masculine field of autobiography.

Similar tensions are revealed in the public autobiographical writing of Beatrice Webb, who excelled in the private writing of diaries (which were never published in her lifetime). Taken together, these total works establish that she certainly regarded her own life worthy of recall and daily documentation; but she still gestures towards defence or apology at the start of *My Apprenticeship*:

> I have neither the desire nor the intention of writing autobiography. Yet the very subject matter of my science is society; its main instrument is social intercourse: thus I can hardly leave out of the picture the experience I had gathered (1938, p. 17).

The irony is that Cole and Webb had each established a reputation as a writer. By placing a disclaimer in their autobiographies, they construct a portrait of self that masquerades as personal expression and may be read as essentially performative. This implies that they had some difficulty in making claims about their own importance. It implies, too, that they want to persuade readers that they were not, in some crucial way, flouting contemporary conventions and stereotypes about femininity and the appropriate behaviour of women. This is a strategic presentation of self that relates to the effects of prevailing assumptions about their social and cultural positioning. They were well aware of the crucial influence of society and the importance of impression management. As women, the available vocabularies of self were constrained by an entire system of conventions that drew woman as the necessary counterpart to man. On the one hand, the feminine subject radiated selflessness, modesty, and passivity. On the other, the masculine subject exuded acts of self-promotion, interest, egotism and aggression. From a historical perspective it follows that self-assertive women autobiographers were more likely to be viewed pejoratively by readers and critics alike. So, the choice of vocabulary may give clues that suggest a desire to find a language, or form of expression that protected them from charges of abnormality and allowed them to colonize alien spaces: both discursive and political. Besides vulnerability to the charge of autobiographical vanity around their right to assert the importance of their particular experiences, it is inconceivable that these left-wing intellectuals were ignorant of the cultural devaluation of women's lives and actions. That they should have felt the need to justify their action in writing their life stories is a measure of the extent to which gender-power dynamics affect self-narrative. The combination of theory and experience become very important in thinking about these women writers, especially when speculating about definitions of self and questions of gender. Margaret Cole was a feminist in the sense that she believed women were equal, and given the opportunity could do as well as their male counterparts. Yet, I suspect, this politically deft woman tones down the claim of achievement because of conventional value-systems. Self-justification aside, this eminent campaigner and public figure did much to advance women's interests, and made a considerable impact on the development of socialism, London education and the scholarship of labour historiography.

The chapter is organized in three main sections. In the first section I set out the analytic framework with reference to metaphors of space, voice and social career. In the second part I explore the presentation of self in Margaret Cole's biographical and autobiographical writings. A variety of images or autobiographical memories are used to review 'ways of seeing' this woman's life (Grosvenor and Lawn, 2001). To try to do justice to her many-faceted activism, section three examines her contribution to campaigns in favour of equal pay and London's response to the 1944 Education Act. I argue that she wanted to improve the conditions of women's varied existence but had clear views about the ways in which feminists organize, or think they ought to. Thus, those dilemmas over women's politics in the postwar world raised issues of contradiction that still leave the contemporary women's movement uncertain and confused.

Writing Women's Lives: Subjectivity, Representation, Narrative

The connection between autobiography and biography have been described by Liz Stanley (1990) using the term auto/biography. This connection is implicit and often explicit in the historical writing of Margaret Cole. So, too, is the relation between the authorial voice and empowerment. To varying degrees Margaret Cole subverted the more powerful discourses in writing the life of others. This elision of forms helped her create spaces within spaces to colonize. I use the metaphor of 'auto/biographical spaces' to deconstruct the conditions and limits of this conceptual divide. A possible framework for exploring the meanings of self displayed in Margaret Cole's writing voice that examine this narrative conjuncture is suggested by Carolyn Steedman's *Landscape for a Good Woman: A Study of Two Lives* (1986). Steedman writes at the interstices of autobiography and biography, case history and social history. As Steedman suggests in her biography of Margaret McMillan:

> The shade of an autobiography – a story of the self presented as a biography of another – has moved through the preceding pages; and that shade has been a major source for the writing of this book. In her *Life of Rachel McMillan* (1927) McMillan purported to write the biography of her sister, and in fact wrote her own (Steedman, 1990, p. 243).

There is a sense in which a similar kind of 'shade' moves through the succeeding pages. Margaret Cole wrote a biography of her husband, Douglas, which looked at the man as well as the socialist intellectual but within the social history of the period. When he died in 1959 they had become one of the most famous radical partnerships of the twentieth century. So it is perhaps inevitable that her *Life of G.D.H. Cole*, published in 1971, blurred the distinction between autobiography and biography. We have seen that the practice of writing about oneself both reflected and defined questions about women's place in cultural production and literary traditions and the ways in which masculinity and femininity was represented culturally. Speculation about 'the problem of being interesting' can be weighted with an extract from the preface to *Life*. Here she notes: '*As a person*, he had said time and again, he was of no interest whatsoever ... I did not myself share this Judgement – nor, I may say, did anyone who had known him personally' (1971, p. 9). Contrast this with the somewhat defensive explanations in her own 1949 autobiography, where she stressed connectedness to her times. To this extent she might appear at times to be complicit in, and colluding, with dominant male auto/biographical spaces, while accommodating and challenging the doubts and negative voices from both within and without.

The accompanying emphasis on 'voice' is taken from Stefan Collini's (1993) dissection of educated political debate in the decades before the First World War. It includes a number of elements: the identity that the subject chose to present, besides a fabric of assumptions, values, ideas and associations. Collini uses the metaphor of 'voice' to convey something of 'the implied presence of an audience, whether addressed in a conversational or didactic or hortatory or other mode' (1993, p. 3). Tellingly, the declaimer to *Growing Up* suggests tensions, as Margaret Cole struggled to contend with her own objections as well as with readers in her autobiographical practices. This consideration of a general audience is similarly evident in a 'snapshot' recollection she presents there of the Labour MP, Susan Lawrence, who said:

> There are three stages in the life of any woman with a public life. In the first, she is 'that charming and intelligent girl'; in the second, she becomes 'that rather frightful woman'; and in the third she is 'that very interesting old lady.' *I* am in the third stage now; *you* – with a hoarse happy chuckle – 'are just in the second' (Cole, 1949, p. 207).

Margaret was probably in her forties when this exchange took place but with this choice of epigram she was alert to the extent that women's entry into public space was viewed with condescension, redolent with prevalent stereotypes of femininity. Expressed in terms of her relation to men, the developmental narrative places the woman with a public life in a particular frame of time–space that registers representations of aging and gender. The rhetorical form of linearity are followed through in Vernon's 1986 biography of Cole, written in the conventional 'record of achievement' type pattern (Evans, 1993). Time passes as the reader trundles through the childhood and youth of Miss Margaret Postgate, moves into

Mrs G.D.H. Cole, Mrs Margaret Cole, Dame Margaret Cole and inevitable assessment. This characterization is too simple, of course, but the social organization of sexual difference is glimpsed in the titles above, since men and women have rather different relationships to the 'proper name'. Part of my argument will be that the social construction of Margaret Cole can tell us something about the social situational constraints of impression management related to the contradictions and inconsistencies in representations of gender. In exploring the movement from high school teacher to educator activist I use the notion of 'social career' to open spaces, to eschew linearity and attempt to inscribe flux and process as I raise questions about subjectivity, representation and narrative. Here, I first look briefly at Cole's life and work. Then, informed by Steedman's (1990, p. 11) writing on biographical questions and history writing, a selection of Cole's texts will be read 'as historical entities in their own right, rather than as the transparent illuminator of anterior historical reality'.

Introducing Margaret Cole: Biographical Notes

Margaret Cole was born in Cambridge in 1893. Her mother, Edith Allen, attended one of the new high schools associated with the nineteenth-century women's movement, the North London Collegiate School for Girls, and was Girton-trained. Her father, John Postgate, was classics lecturer at Trinity College, Cambridge, and subsequently Professor of Greek at Liverpool University. At the age of ten, Margaret won a scholarship to Roedean School, from where she won another scholarship to read Classics at Girton. There she joined the Girton dramatic society, the debating society and in 1914 was placed in the First Class of the Classical Tripos. Although she had taken the degree examination in exactly the same way as her male counterparts, she was not awarded a degree, or even a degree title. Her father suggested that she obtain her degree with extra study at Liverpool but she refused. Having taken advantage of higher education for women, Cole availed herself of new opportunities for physical and social mobility and secured an appointment as classics mistress at St Paul's high school for girls in London.

When Margaret Postgate moved to London in 1914 it was the undisputed capital market of the world, the centre of the British state and high politics, the legal system and the learned professions.

All of this meant that it enjoyed greater wealth, prestige, fashion and social status in comparison with that of other regions of the country. The strength of the pull fluctuated over time but José Harris argues 'London in the 1890s and 1900s was a much stronger magnet for the educated and ambitious middle classes than it had been a generation before' (1993, p. 22). London's geography precipitated new expectations and new possibilities for Margaret's preoccupations and purposes. She shared a flat with St Paul's gym mistress, the daughter of a Russian revolutionary; joined the National Union of Teachers; and saw the metropolis as a place of opportunity – a site for self-development. Work colleagues included the Fabian freethinker Edith Moor, who invited her to her Oxfordshire cottage. There, from Edith and a friend, she first heard of Douglas Cole (Cole, 1949, p. 57). The experience of war confirmed her in her chosen political convictions. In the spring of 1916, her younger brother Raymond, then a first year student at St John's College, Oxford, was called up for military service. Despite familial disapproval and the unpopularity of the anti-war stand in the wider community she travelled to Oxford to offer moral support. His prison sentence was the catalyst that led her directly into socialist politics:

> I did not realise, until I had heard the old man with the long beard hanging over the edge of the Bench pronounce sentence, and seen Ray disappear through a kind of pantomime trap-door in the floor, what a large slice of England there was that was either actively opposed to the war or very doubtful about its conduct; but it is almost literally true that when I walked away from the Oxford court-room … I walked into a new world, a world of doubters and protesters, and into a new war – this time against the ruling classes and the government which represented them, and *with* the working classes, the Trade Unionists, the Irish rebels of Easter Week, and all those who resisted their governments or other governments which held them down (Cole, 1949, p. 59).

Immediately she started out as a voluntary worker in the Fabian Research Department, then dominated by guild socialists committed to political action by the industrial wing within the labour movement. Their goals were transferring the ownership and control of industry to the workers organized in their trade unions. Afterwards the workers would form producers' guilds in their respective industries, whose job it would be to organize and manage production.

Apart from Ray's Oxford friend, Alan Kaye, the Department's key officers were Robin Page Arnot, an expert on the mining industry; Douglas Cole; and William Mellor, later editor of the *Daily Herald* and afterwards of the *Tribune* weekly (Cole, 1961, p. 151). Margaret found this a welcoming and congenial political space and at the age of twenty-three resigned her teaching post to join the paid staff at a salary of £104 per annum. Involvement in mixed-sex politics furnished a formal introduction to her future husband, then honorary secretary of the Department and research officer to the Amalgamated Society of Engineers, whom she married on 14 August 1918. They had three children – two daughters and one son – all born in the 1920s.

After her marriage Margaret continued as secretary for the Fabian Research Department, editing their *Monthly Bulletin* and tutoring for the WEA. Her husband was director of tutorial classes in London University for three years before he returned to permanent teaching in Oxford, first as Reader in Economics in 1925 and from 1944 as Professor of Social and Political Theory. In the 1920s and 1930s the Coles collaborated on one detective novel a year but after several years in Oxford the young family returned to London. Initially to a big house in Hampstead and then, in 1935, they moved to Freeland, in Hendon, which became the family home for over twenty years. Their circle of friendship now encompassed Naomi and Dick Mitchison, Daisy and Raymond Postgate, *New Statesmen* writers, Oxford literati like Gilbert Murray and his wife, Mary, fellow Fabians Beatrice and Sidney Webb, as well as WEA students and tutors. The Coles gave parties and shared holidays with the Mitchisons, as Margaret and Naomi juggled the demands of marriage, motherhood, politics, private friendships, public service and writing. Both make it pretty clear neither would have been satisfied with a purely domestic existence for themselves. Like Margaret, Naomi started life in a privileged position. She was born into the Haldane dynasty and family ties were very significant in the move into public life. Her father was the Edinburgh physiologist and philosopher John Scott Haldane; an uncle was Lord Chancellor in the first Labour government. In a lifetime of activism, Mitchison helped run a pioneer birth control clinic; became an energetic farmer; stood unsuccessfully for parliament; served on Argyll County Council and the Highlands and Islands Development Council; managed to write prolifically; and brought up five children (Jeger, 1999). In a posthumous tribute, Naomi recalled Margaret's 'incisive eloquence' at an election rally for Dick that 'shook' her into joining the Labour Party in 1931 (Mitchison, 1982, p. 18).

The 1930s were years of intense political and intellectual activity pressing the twin causes of workers' education and workers' control. In this decade, also, Margaret embarked on some of the literary activities that would make her famous in her own right. On top of three large-scale collaborative history books written with Douglas, there were two edited collections resulting from Fabian activities, besides *Women of Today*. This consisted of ten biographical vignettes of suitable role models, including three socialist women: Annie Besant, Mary Macarthur and Beatrice Webb. It is notable that Margaret shared her ideas about appropriate gender roles and behaviour in the first full-length book that she wrote without Douglas, *Marriage*, published in 1938. Among other things she particularly focused on the issue of dependency within marriage, the sources and implications of women's economic independence, women's 'dual role', childcare policy, the socialization of housework, female sexuality, birth control and divorce reform. In sum, Cole offers a unique examination of ideas of motherhood, employment and domesticity but she does so with circumspection. Having set out what the book is about she writes:

> I do not claim, therefore to be impartial, but only to have tried to see what there is to be said from more than one angle. If I seem to have given much space to changes in the position and capabilities of women at the present time, it is because I do not think that they have received enough attention, not because I think that the results will necessarily be what the Utopian pioneer hopes, or because the results, whatever they are, are yet patent in the thought or behaviour of women; for those who are chiefly affected are not forming theories just yet and not at all certain what they want (Cole, 1938, p. 9).

This claim could be read in various, not necessarily mutually exclusive, ways. A strength, implicit here, is the recognition of the very different experiences, situations, and needs of different groups of women, albeit with a particular concern with class. There is then the hint at British feminists' engagement with socialism. At the same time, there is the vexed question of compromise and the radical potential of feminist activism to effect change.

Introducing this woman's life through metaphors of space promotes the discussion of continuities and discontinuities through putting her into motion rather than taking up a settled position. To follow the train of thought, for Margaret Cole, finding a voice in discursive space was accompanied by the taking of physical space in organizational structures in order to challenge institutionalized power. She was the catalyst behind the weekend political schools held at Easton Lodge, the country house belonging to an aristocratic devotee of socialism, Lady Warwick (Cole, 1961, p. 222). Disillusioned with the performance of the second Labour minority government elected in 1929, Fabian and non-Fabian intellectuals went there for lectures and discussions. They built up a reputation as the 'Loyal Grousers' and the key circle comprised the Coles, Lance Beales of the WEA, Mostyn Lloyd of the *New Statesmen*, and Dick Mitchison whose socialism was attributed mostly to Margaret (Vernon, 1986). As a group, they initiated two main forums for debate and drafting of policy outside the Labour Party. The first was the Society for Socialist Enquiry and Propaganda, founded in June 1931 to revive the Party's 'faith and drive' and lasting little more than a year. The second was the New Fabian Research Bureau that eventually amalgamated with the revived Fabian Society in 1939. Margaret was the moving spirit of the Bureau, working alongside R.H. Tawney and Barbara Drake, the favourite niece of Beatrice Webb. Afterwards, Margaret consolidated her position when honorary secretary of the amalgamated Society from 1939 to 1953.

In the 1940s she extended her sphere of influence to educational policy-making and administration. In 1941 she was co-opted by the majority Labour group to serve on the London County Council (LCC) education committee and served without interruption until 1967, when she retired. In office, Margaret joined Labour friends like Helen Bentwich, Helen's brother Hugh Franklin, Molly Bolton long personal secretary to the Webbs, Barbara Drake, Lady Eleanor Nathan and R.H. Tawney. Membership of the Fabian Women's Group also connected Bolton, Cole and Drake with another female colleague Leah L'Estrange Malone. By 1951 Cole was chair of the further education subcommittee, a position she held until 1965 with one year's break when Douglas died. She was elected an alderman in 1950 and when the Council was abolished in 1965, under the London Government Act of 1963, she was on the new education authority for London as vice chair of further and higher education. At one time she chaired the governing body of the Holloway School and two teacher training colleges. She also served on the governing body of the Regent Street Polytechnic. At a national level, she became an exponent of the British comprehensive reform. At a local level, she was a keen supporter of adult education. Towards the end of her life, she saw her career and achievements widely honoured and recognized by the governing and cultural elites of the period. She amassed an OBE, a DBE, was elected a Fellow of the Royal Historical Society and made an honorary Fellow of the London School of Economics. Still mentally alert, Margaret Cole died at a nursing home at Goring on Thames on 7 May 1980, the day after her eighty-seventh birthday. She spent this attended by her only son, Humphrey, and her best friend, Naomi Mitchison (Vernon, 1986).

Ways of Seeing I: Auto/biographical Spaces

These are the broad outlines of Margaret Cole's social career. Next I use a variety of narratives of selfhood to focus on the question of identity formation (the workings of language) and its relationship to the category 'woman' and the construction of gendered subjectivities. Movement as Cole passes into, between and across auto/biographical and political spaces is implicated in the specificities of 'place and politics' (Steedman, 1986, p. 6); reflections on the various representations of self address a rethinking of the questions of autobiographical subject, of authorial 'voice' and of material location. So the analysis of Cole's political journey moves among three questions she put to other people and their life writing. 'First, who and of what kind were his family? ... Secondly, what was his social class ... thirdly, what was his physical home, if he had the same home for long enough for it to leave an impression on him?' (Cole, 1949, p. 1).

The male cast of Annan's (2000) famous article on the English intellectual aristocracy includes no Postgates but deals with the ramifications of the Haldane–Burdon–Sanderson marriage following 'the gradual removal of the regulations requiring celibacy of Oxbridge and Cambridge dons' (Dyhouse, 1995, p. 56). The Allen–Postgate marriage took place shortly after and the couple belonged to a circle of families intimate with the new status group sketched by Annan. Margaret was the eldest of six children embracing four brothers and one sister. She grew up in a solid middle-class world, materially secure, never rich but, equally, never having to worry. The Postgates were affluent although not ostentatiously wealthy:

> We belonged to a special group, that of the professional academic, and we lived in a university town. The importance of this is that

we were brought up in an atmosphere of comparative equality. The range of university salaries is not – or was not – enormous; and few of the parents with whose children we went to school and parties had noticeable private means. There was some difference of course ... But the difference lay in the frills, not in the essentials; we all had nurses and servants and seaside holidays, and all went to upper-class schools and had dancing and drawing classes (Cole, 1949, p. 9).

In telling her story, Margaret reveals self-consciousness and a need to sift through her girlhood to show how this homogeneity made her a natural egalitarian. It follows that she felt little sympathy for Roedean, the prestigious independent school she was sent to in September 1907 as the winner of the single annual scholarship. Unpopular and unhappy, she reacted against the tradition of a school, where the development of middle-class femininity seemed more important than the aim of academic excellence. The obsession with hockey seemed especially banal:

It was all like the Boys' School Story raised to the *nth*. I have no personal objection to games as such ... But I do feel that the games-worship at Roedean gives some support to the complaints of anti-feminists that women ought not to be allowed to do the things that men do, because they have no sense of proportion and drive everything to death (Cole, 1949, p. 30).

In looking back, the autobiographical intention is powered by the struggle to understand this exercise of parental choice. It is difficult to speculate to what extent her parents valued the ideal of ladylike behaviour but she claims never to have 'felt any acute sex disability other than the youthful and inescapable one of being a girl in petticoats' (Cole, 1949, p. 43). Even so, her father had some strange inconsistencies. First, John Postgate was an anti-suffragist, who opposed the admission of women to degrees at Cambridge, and yet paid for his daughter's higher education. Second, he was an atheist who 'thought religion good for women' but took exception to Margaret's childish fancy to be a 'Golden Sunbeam':

child subscribers to a cheap periodical who enrolled themselves as willing to bring the word of God to a child in another district – the East End of London, probably – I was very firmly discouraged; and when, having read an appallingly sentimental book entitled

Bruey: a Little Worker for Christ (she died, of course, at an early age), I tried to follow her example, I found that Little Workers for Christ were definitely at a discount in the home circle (Cole, 1949, p. 22).

Finally, her father was a classicist who promoted the conversational method to teach boys Latin and seemingly did not entertain the idea of pedagogy for girls in his educational thought and practice. At home, Margaret wrote of how the little Postgates, the 'Other' who ate in the upstairs nursery, were allowed down on Sundays. Unimpressed, she resented the requirement to speak Latin to avoid going hungry. 'I still remember the awful occasion on which, at the age of six or thereabouts, I asked for "the beef" instead of "some of the beef," and my father pushed the huge sirloin on its dish in my direction' (Cole, 1949, p. 5). In sum, there were equivocal, contradictory and rather inconsistent aspects to her father's position.

Until she reached Girton, Margaret was largely ignorant of public affairs. Suffragettes figured in jokes between childhood girlfriends, Roedean did not have a debating society and the only whisper of politics was a display of anti-Disraeli feeling from a young history teacher. In contrast, her first impressions of college were of freedom from the constraints of school (despite careful supervision and chaperonage) and of many, many more friends. She enjoyed the company and life of a Cambridge she later described as 'next door to Utopia' and fell 'passionately and fruitlessly in love' with a 'very personable Jewish girl, who wore picturesque flowing frocks and a necklace of great fire-opals' (Cole, 1949, p. 38). Unusually among intellectuals in Victorian and early twentieth-century Britain, she did not struggle with an antidote to doubt. Consider, for example, the terms in which she reflected, in 1949, when she was in her fifties, on her loss of religious faith. 'I did not ever like the hero of Mrs Humphrey Ward's best selling novel *Robert Elsmere* and other earnest works, suffer from "religious doubts"; as soon as religious doubts appeared upon the horizon I gladly yielded to them' (Cole, 1949, p. 41). Similarly, in explaining why she chose socialism, she looked back nostalgically to reading H.G. Wells, which made her a socialist and a feminist overnight. Careful to distance herself from his portrayal of the 'new woman', she does not attack conventional marriage; and the boundary between the middle-class worlds evoked by Cambridge is implicit in her construction of wartime London social life.

An old school friend and drama student, Phyllis Reid, shared a studio with Stella Bowen a South Australian student at the Westminster School of Art and 'broke every convention in the book as they mingled with London's avant-garde' (Mckinnon, 1997, p. 205). As part of their artistic and literary circle Margaret went to dinners, poetry readings and parties with T.S. Eliot, Wyndham Lewis, Ezra Pound and W.B. Yeats. Let us compare the narrative images of Phyllis and Stella constructed in Margaret's autobiographical narrative. Metaphorically, they offer points of entry into the connection between ideas, comradeship and personal freedom. Phyllis, 'who possessed in abundance what we had not yet learned to call either S.A., or It, or Oomph' is presented as being particularly adventurous: 'ready to take on anything in trousers'. In contrast, the text contains a number of 'silences' notably about Stella's preparedness to transgress social mores which led eventually to a sexual relationship outside marriage with writer Ford Madox Ford. 'Living together' was morally unacceptable and perhaps it is agreement with the need for an equal moral standard that underscores Margaret's representation of Ford as a selfish individual more concerned about his stomach than Stella's welfare. A house guest of the Coles during the difficult (and presumably dangerous) birth of their daughter, Ford took to bed (in sympathy?) demanding devilled sirloin when meat was rationed (1920) and oyster soup (Cole, 1949, pp. 82–3).

Despite this friendship network, the move to London disorientated Margaret. She found the world of boarding houses 'dreary after dark' and felt uneasy negotiating the wartime metropolis at night. Possibly she was not prepared for the sense of loss as she learned to understand a new spatial location. The wide open spaces of East Anglia were a haven and a stepping-off point. She remained thoroughly rooted there:

As soon as I get on the raised highway, with the white posts marking its corners, that runs through Hereward's country, and from six miles away, through a gap in the hedge, catch sight of the Octagon of Ely, fullest of light of all English cathedrals; or stand on Fleam Dyke, the low earth rampart that runs for miles beyond Fulbourn and still grows wild flowers which you can pick nowhere else in the county; or see the huge expanses of sky... something moves in me that is as old as my birth, and my senses recognise that I have come home (Cole, 1949, p. 3).

Accepting this statement about the geographical spaces of her child-hood, what about her political journey? How did she put her new politics into practice?

Margaret Cole's rendering of her life and actions suggest histori-cally specific gendered aspects of the process of politicization. She took a tremendous risk in choosing socialism, for she gave up the economic security she enjoyed as a schoolteacher and alienated her father. Looking ahead and related to this, the young Postgates were expected to share their parents' Tory values and marry according to their father's lights. As a consequence, when Margaret challenged his authority he disinherited her and refused to allow her mother to stay at her house (he died in 1926). What were the consolations? Above all, there was the comradeship offered in the pioneering days of 'the Movement':

> Though we would not have called ourselves a 'thin red line of heroes,' being very suspicious of emotional appeals, we did really believe that it mattered enormously for the future of mankind that we should stick up the last press-cutting and check the last signif-icant fact; we were ready to spend ourselves up to the limit in the service we had voluntarily entered – and who is prepared to say that we were wrong? Being so dedicated, we were extraordinarily happy, so happy that we never realised it fully, but worked our-selves into states of tremendous agitation over minute differences in the philosophy of Guild Socialism and its application to imme-diate problems of the day (Cole, 1949, p. 73).

There can be no denying shared optimism as central to her experi-ence. In the words of Naomi Mitchison: 'we felt we had a cause worth living for, even worth dying for' (1979, p. 205). Theirs was a visionary socialism and they were confident of achieving the co-operative commonwealth. Margaret enjoyed the comradeship of shared activities; of dining 'in groups or en masse in Soho' the choice of restaurant dictated by degrees of economic hardship and relative poverty (Cole, 1949, p. 71). However, she does not display the qual-ity of self-importance. Writing how 'we small fry' tried to pursue research and propaganda there is a tendency to diminish the self in her account of 'the Movement'.

Fortunately Rowland Kenney, a comrade in the pioneering days of guild socialism recaptured the girl-self in his autobiography published in 1939. Kenney writes:

> She was wearing a rough felt hat, from under which fell black locks, surrounding a vital, vivid face, out of which stabbed a pair of blazing dark eyes. Everything about her was intensely, exceedingly alive, ready for anything, particularly – or so it seemed to me – for a fight to the finish on any point about which her opinion differed from that of anyone else in the room. You felt that she had no use for the velvet glove. And she looked, if I may assume such a creature, like a provocative elfin-tigress. And there seemed nothing incongruous in the fact that she was smoking a big cigar; it helped to complete the picture Margaret made (1939, pp. 204–5).

This rich textual image offers a sense of desirable womanhood that links this desire with images of power and sexuality associated with nature, which in themselves reflect the values of the masculine and the feminine. Cole's biography of her husband has a chapter entitled 'Through the eyes of others' where one finds a similar presentation of the girl-self to that found in Beatrice Webb's diary which Margaret edited in the 1950s but previously unavailable. In this elision of forms, written at the interstices of autobiography and biography, the process of becoming Margaret Cole is defined through the eyes of Webb. Apparently she 'recognized the young woman as possessed of some personality' and warned Douglas to look out for 'possible sexual entanglements' (Cole, 1971, p. 89).

As a journey the movement from professional to political space suggests rather special claims for herself – claims that involved dedication and hard work. In her *Life of G.D.H. Cole*, however, Margaret gives the impression that she became interested in the labour movement because of her spouse. 'It's a Man', her father declared when she gave up teaching (Cole, 1971, p. 90). Here Margaret's political journey is a narration embedded within Douglas' story. It is, of course, also a love story written in a way that uses humour as an ironic counterpoint to intimacy. So, what intrudes in another auto/biographical space, *Growing Up Into Revolution* is the 'normal' prospects of marriage to a man:

> I very clearly recollect writing the words 'Mrs G.D.H. Cole' on a piece of paper in the St Paul's staff-room and hastily crumpling it up; and when I first set eyes on him – in the room of a friend of Ray's in St John's, the winter before Ray was called up – I thought

that his face and appearance were exactly what I should most like to look at for the rest of my days. I set eyes on him then, but I did not actually 'meet' him; it was afterwards reported to me that, on being asked, 'Would you like to be introduced to Postgate's sister?' he replied emphatically, 'No, I should *not*' (Cole, 1949, p. 75).

Might this passage suggest emotion was the motivation of her life whereas the lived experience was actually a good deal more complex? What interpretation might Douglas' response be given?

Readers of *Life* are told that he identified two kinds of women. They all wanted 'to distract man from his proper work, either directly, or (if "good" women) by giving a man "a stake in the country" which turned him into a "stick-in-the-mud"' (Cole, 1971, p. 92). Perhaps this was what he feared of 'Postgate's sister'. At any rate, he would not readily compromise. His words suggest he feared the possibility that a conventional marriage started with a man's concessions. Apparently he never seemed to have any interest in embarking on sexual relationships with any woman besides his wife and generally to 'regard them as rather a low type of being' (Cole, 1971, p. 92). Jane Austen aside, he did not think highly of women writers, thought most women unintelligent and reactionary, but wanted them to become voters as a matter of socialist principle. In saying this, he understood that Margaret would have a public life and the way in which he approached questions of the sexual division of labour was consistent with the notion of companionate marriage popularized in the 1940s. Furthermore, his income meant they could benefit from the long period of high unemployment between the wars and the flight of political refugees from Nazi Germany as a source of cheap labour (Cole, 1971). Initially, it was the services of a working-class woman as cook-housekeeper; later there was a nurse for the children and an unemployed miner and his wife who ran the house. This freed Margaret, to some extent, from domestic responsibilities, providing the opportunity to pursue a political career, though care of Douglas (particularly after his diabetes was diagnosed in 1931), is represented as creative activity in her 1971 biography. Certainly, that support task must have absorbed large parts of Margaret's creative energies. We can identify in her telling of his story the discourse of the feminine caring person, whereas his failure to recognize it opens up the question of his own needs and masculine viewpoint.

In contrast, Margaret positively rejected the domestic home-based roles of women in her 1949 autobiography. She did not give up politics while her children were young and indicated that 'the Movement' initially meant more to her *'conscious* self' than her daughters (Cole, 1949, p. 103). Not surprisingly, she struggled to resolve the tensions between the achievement of personal autonomy and the patriarchal traditions of a university community such as Oxford (see Dyhouse, 1995). She was in a particularly difficult position as a don's wife:

> In London, I had had a job as well as a family, and a place in the front row of whatever was going on; if there was an interesting discussion I was in the middle of it. But in Oxford, it seemed to me, all the really interesting discussions, the occasions when something important was done, took place in colleges where women could not enter; even if you entertained a distinguished visitor, say R.H. Tawney, in your own home, you were only expected to feed him; after dinner, if not before, he went off and talked in a male common-room. I did not find the routine occupations of female Oxford – taking lessons in Spanish, for example, going to listen to Magdalen Christmas carols in a high cold loft reserved for Ladies, having children to tea-parties, and escorting one's own to Greek Dancing lessons, dressed in tomato-coloured silk frocks – at all satisfying (Cole, 1949, p. 110).

Nonetheless, it was an extension of her political hostess role that enabled her to pass as an honorary male. Shifting from anger to accommodation she successfully created a discursive space in the salon around Douglas that met on Monday evenings at their home and developed into the 'Cole Group'. Former members praised her skill as a hostess, enjoying the atmosphere and centre for informal socialist discussion (Vernon, 1986, p. 56). Tutoring for the WEA provided another space within which to develop an independent, professional identity. Yet in telling her story she fails to emphasize her own importance. In 1949 she wrote 'I have contributed less than many of my colleagues and I claim no particular credit for my educational services' (p. 215). In *Servant of the County* (1956) she found indirect means of describing the dialectic between the two roles she played out in her life, one as wife-carer-mother, and the other as public-political-subject. Here she uses words of self-deprecation to tell us public service was skewed towards the leisured with private incomes, including the category of women members 'married to men who can afford to keep them and to pay for domestic assistance' (p. 182).

Ways of Seeing II: Political Spaces

Margaret Cole had extensive feminist connections. She numbered the feminists Stella Bowen and Naomi Mitchison amongst her close friends and her sister-in-law Daisy (her father, George Lansbury, led the Labour Party in the early 1930s) was a militant suffragette. Daisy, Margaret and Naomi all combined their role as a wife and mother with some political work on behalf of the Labour Party, although it should be stressed that for Margaret, loyalty to the Labour movement largely precluded any challenge to the *status quo*. She regarded herself as an emancipated woman, yet avoided the techniques and methods of some political women's practice. So, while sympathetic towards women's claims, she disapproved of the noisily assertive attitudes of certain colleagues on the LCC, which caused the Education Committee to be dubbed 'the Shrieking Sisterhood' (Vernon, 1986, p. 76). At the same time, she recognized that women have found it difficult to convert theoretical equality into real power (which she thought important for democracy) and implied some possible explanations. For instance, she took a negative view of 'the lack of interest shown by the Webbs in young women in comparison with young men' (1949, p. 159) and wrote to her brother Richmond in 1945:

> The pre-1914 suffragettes did have a hell of a time, though you don't have to take Vera Brittain *au pied de lettre*, because she's an emotional ass ... but the whole revolt of women is historically and sociologically very interesting, for they were being double-crossed by a Parliament of males ... but we haven't solved the problem ... Now we have got to try again to make the forms fit the values (cited in Vernon, 1986, p. 76).

In the statements above, the implicit questions concern the male political establishment in Britain and the response to feminism. They imply that men are the 'gatekeepers' and this is why it is difficult for feminism to enter the parliamentary arena. However, it is worth briefly exploring why Vera Brittain (another child of the

1890s) is singled out for criticism here. Taken together, their lives illustrate the dilemmas in combining marriage and children with public participation. As individuals, they were very different personalities. This translated into both auto/biographical and political spaces.

In the 1930s, Brittain wrote what Virginia Woolf described as an 'anguished' autobiography *Testament of Youth*, where the story of her wartime experience is told in detail and without reserve (Anderson, 1997, p. 77). By this time, Brittain had drifted away from the separate women's organizations and her record of Labour Party membership was inconsistent (Pugh, 1992, pp. 262–3). In contrast, Cole's writing was never 'anguished'. She maintained a lifelong involvement with the more party political Fabian Women's Group and never broke faith with the Labour movement. At the end of her autobiography she emitted the heartfelt plea:

> I still hope that, before I die, I may see this revolution working itself to rest, and the cause which I have believed in all my life triumphing over the difficulties and disasters which so few of its ardent protomartyrs foresaw (Cole, 1949, p. 219).

Nonetheless, like Brittain, there were women-centred issues, such as married women's right to work and equal pay, which Cole pursued before and after the Second World War. Accepting that most women would follow a primarily domestic role while children are young, she wanted women to have the right to compete on equal terms with men in the paid workforce. In *Marriage* she condemned the practice of firing married women when the economy slumped and unemployment rose. Far from seeking an alternative to labour market participation, she wanted to find ways of making the married woman's role compatible with a successful career. This led her to reject advocacy of family allowances to raise the status and financial security of women's work as homemakers and mothers. Significantly, she wrote: 'As a Socialist, I think that people ought to earn their keep, and that the existence in society of a large number of parasites or semi-parasites is both offensive to the sight and a danger to the body politic' (Cole, 1938, p. 200).

During the Second World War the drive to recruit women into jobs usually performed by men gave a boost to the demand for equal pay but a lobbying campaign met with only limited success. When the Conservative Thelma Cazelet-Keir carried by one vote an amendment to the 1944 Education Bill that would have given equal pay for women teachers, the decision was reversed following a vote of confidence in the government. The uproar that followed was contained by means of appointing a Royal Commission; and the Fabian Women's Group was among a number of organizations to give evidence (Briar, 1997). Margaret Cole continued the propaganda in a pamphlet, *The Rate for the Job*, based on their research. She found the anti position weak on a number of points. For instance, there were those habits of prejudice and exclusion captured in the evidence of the National Association of Schoolmasters (NAS). 'Rarely has there been a more deplorable exploitation of a helpless section of the community for personal and sectional ends than is evidenced by this callous disregard of the needs and rights of thousands of boys in this country' (Cole, 1946, p. 16). The men's union reasoned men teachers needed more money to keep a family at home. This provided some leverage for Cole to expose the fallacy behind their objections. Using historical and comparative evidence, she argued that working women were proving themselves to be at least equal and often superior. She treats with derision the suggestion that women *need* less pay than men: 'one might as well suggest that all male workers weighing say less than nine stone and measuring less than 5 feet 4 inches should be paid some fraction of the standard rate' (op. cit., p. 18). Again, humour is her chosen weapon to counter claims that working women are unreliable: 'no one has proposed to remedy absenteeism in the coalfields by lowering miners' wages' (op. cit., p. 20). Her response to claims of female wastage is supremely understated: 'we must point out that it is a little unreasonable for the civil service to dismiss women who get married and then to complain that women leave their employment on marriage' (ibid.). Cole's solution was to advocate equal pay for the same work, free and open competition between and among the sexes for all jobs and proper social recognition of women's unpaid workload. Her approach is emblematic of how Fabians used socialist 'social science' to convert others to the conclusion they were reaching.

The post-Second World War years were characterized by the greater recruitment of married women into the paid labour force. In *Marriage* Cole put forward ideas for communally provided and state-funded childcare, laundries and restaurants but her agenda for a change in policy direction was not adopted. Though the principle of equal pay for women in public sector employment was included in the election manifestos of all the major parties in 1950, it was not until 1954 that the Conservative government approved the gradual introduction of equal pay in the civil service. Even then it only applied in grades where there was common recruitment of men and women (Briar, 1997). In 1962, when the *Political Quarterly* invited Cole to assess the long-term political impact of the woman's vote, she suggested the female franchise had brought only limited change in terms of the extent of progress women had made politically, economically, educationally or socially. Cole refrained from exploring the factors that helped, or hindered the achievement of full citizenship but pointed to the mistaken assumption, on the part of militants and non-militants alike, that the vote would dramatically improve their status as women and benefit humanity as a whole. What women voters *had* achieved, in her opinion (apart from the abolition of the penny charge which women had to pay at the turnstile entrance of most municipal women's toilets), was family allowances and equal pay in the public sector.

Cole tried to rethink and reformulate gender questions but the question of loyalties was troublesome. She, like her predecessors in June Hannam and Karen Hunt's study of socialist women in Britain, from the 1880s to the 1920s, 'still faced the question of how to make socialism sensitive to gender inequalities and how to ensure that women played a full role in political life' (Hannam and Hunt, 2002, p. 205). In some ways she emphasized the collective interests of women as a sex by rejecting her husband's generalization that the great majority were unintelligent and reactionary. In another way she could not forget:

> Conservative Party Conferences at which embattled Tory ladies screamed for immediate increase in floggings, birchings, and hangings, or other less-publicised occasions on which 'representative' (?) women did not show themselves, to put it mildly, strong champions of the right to life, liberty, and the pursuit of happiness (Cole, 1962, p. 82).

Judging from Cole's struggle to construct a coherent argument, we see here the possibilities but also the limitations of a strictly equal-rights approach. She fails to question directly the patriarchal culture and sometimes what she says is ambivalent and confusing. Tensions between the equal-but-different position also affected the way in which she approached questions of gender in education both in theory and practice.

As described earlier Margaret Cole recognized the implications of the notion of women's dual-roles (paid work and the family) that was popularized after 1945. She talked about the likelihood of greater participation by women in the workforce, made more possible by the improved educational opportunities offered to women (Deem, 1981). Anticipating that more girls would combine a career with motherhood and marriage she laid great emphasis on the need to challenge the targeting of housecraft and other domestic subjects at working-class girls and those deemed 'less academic'. At issue was the differential subject status between curriculum areas and she wanted to see 'modern housekeeping' become 'a subject of as much educational repute as, say, geometry' (1938, p. 269). Preparation for marriage and a family was part of the life-plan she offered and she did not share a view of domestic science as essentially incompatible with academic objectives. Commenting on the late Mary Macarthur, leader of the National Federation of Women Workers, whose home-running 'looms like a horror in the eyes of themselves and their friends' (ibid.), she emphasized the necessity for the next generation to receive an education that prepared them for this future dual-role. There is a sense here of the wide gulf in class and social background that differentiated Cole from working-class girls and women. She did not have to do her own housework and she does address the question of shared housework. So, what was she able to accomplish in local labour politics and municipal government? What role did she play in policy-making decisions relating to the educational opportunities of London women?

Following the passing of the Education Act (1944), which introduced compulsory free secondary schooling, a major priority was to produce local development plans suited to London's needs. Published in 1947, the London School Plan for developing secondary education proposed a shift in policy in favour of comprehensive schools intended to redress inequalities experienced by working-class children. It was to be an uphill struggle, hampered by the inevitable bomb damage. Besides the 174 all-age elementary schools waiting to be absorbed into the school reorganization, there was desperate need for a renovation and building programme. The agenda for change included the replacement of outdoor sanitation, the removal of the gallery (long fixed forms which rose in a tier) from 2,000 classrooms and the installation of electricity in 326 gas lit schools (Maclure, 1990, pp. 150, 170). By the time the first purpose-built comprehensive, Kidbrooke School, was ready to open there had been a change of government and a direct challenge from Florence Horsbrugh, the Conservative Minister of Education, who refused to allow the incorporation of a girls' grammar school in the new comprehensive. Margaret Cole, pressing for a common secondary school, became London's foremost publicist. She urged the inevitability of change, prompted by a belief that: 'This is the road of educational and social progress. Let us follow it to the end, confident, as Socialists, that we have an educational programme in this great capital county worthy of the Labour cause' (Cole, 1953, p. 16). In the 1960s, Cole defended Labour education policy in a *Plebs* pamphlet, 'Comprehensives in London', claiming it 'was not merely right in principle but is proving itself in practice' (1967, p. 20). Apparently, she was prepared to challenge state policy on secondary education in the 1950s, but what about developments in her particular realm of responsibility – the education of adults?

Then, as now, feminists grappled with arguments of equality versus difference in the political arena. We know Cole came to identify concerns about class inequality in education policy but seemingly her writing on women and education was couched in terms of prevailing ideologies about women's role in society. How did she translate the theory into practice as chair of the LCC further education subcommittee? Mary Hughes (1992) answers this in a most emphatic way. Looking at a policy decision taken in 1957, the closure or merger of London's Women's Institutes, set up to provide nonvocational, evening education for women and girls, she suggests women in local government 'appeared to uphold the dominant ideology, supporting educational policy which enhanced the domestic home-based roles of women' (1992, p. 54). Besides the loss of a female cultural space, Hughes argues women principals and adult educators also lost out in the reorganization which threatened promotion opportunities. Given Helen Bentwich and Margaret Cole then held office as leader of the LCC and further education committee respectively what does this say about what difference women in power make? When women aspirants largely depend upon men for promotion to influential positions, it underlines the fact that the successful ones were likely to be acceptable male surrogates making it no doubt inevitable that they should reflect the official policies and priorities closely. This is why, despite a high proportion of women councillors, Hughes concludes there were no overt moves to 'extend the educational boundaries of working-class women in London' (ibid.). In Cole's case, acceptance of co-education may have been grounded in actual experience of single-sex schooling as a child. At any rate, she did not show any recognition for gender inequalities in her writing on the origins and development of mass state schooling, which 'alone escaped this sex-differentiation' (Cole, 1938, p. 93). The class nexus she acknowledges; the gender dynamic she ignores. Yet, while the principle of compulsion underpinning the educational legislation of the 1870s made no distinction of sex, the outcome of state policies on education for girls and boys was not identical. In practice, a pattern was soon established that rendered the expansion of the girls' curriculum gender specific. But this is not an issue if one accepts notions of women's equality based on the equal but different approach.

Making Connections between Auto/biographical Spaces

There are several generalizations to be made from Margaret Cole's auto/biography. She was an educated, middle-class socialist who held prominent positions in labour politics and opposed sex-based protective legislation. Marriage to Douglas meant that she did not have to earn a living but no lessening of her ambition. For both of them, political work came first and this made their marriage a partnership of equals of an extraordinary kind, even though Margaret took on what was assumed to be the roles of the wife. She had a household to run and a family to look after. Later, she nursed Douglas tenderly and was good at coping with what his diabetes involved in the way of caring in a practical way. In retrospect, Naomi Mitchison wrote that her friend would have been a good principal of a women's college but for the problematic of combining the role 'with being an adequate wife, mother and political hostess' (1982, p. 19). There was also the injustice of being judged against the underlying premise that Douglas was superior to her. Perhaps Shena Simon had this in mind when she observed in a letter of condolence; 'we know how much of his work was shared by you, and that even those books which bore only his name were joint in the deepest sense' (Vernon, 1986, p. 165). In the end, her struggle to create an autonomous self is built into the very 'silences' in the histories of socialism. Ironically, this extends to the space accorded Douglas in the introduction to Vernon's biography of Margaret written by Michael Foot, then a backbench Labour MP (Vernon, 1986, pp. 1–3).

Talented and strong-minded, Margaret Cole was a major figure in the Labour movement for 50 years. Yet, she does not display any distinct sense of her individual destiny or self-importance in her auto/biographical writings. Instead, the reader is made aware of rhetoric of uncertainty about the self, the value of womanhood and the proper balance of private life and public spirit. We are aware of dialectic between the 'ordinary' woman merging her own memories with an extraordinary record of achievement as she passes into, between and across auto/biographical and political spaces. We are aware, too, of a paradox of power and marginality. Secure by virtue of her personal position, she owed her co-option on to the education committee to the patronage of Herbert Morrison, who won the LCC for Labour in 1934 (Vernon, 1986, p. 125). Morrison was unusual. The 'male as norm' political establishment in Britain is constructed to position all women as 'Other'. The women who inhabit it are relatively privileged but have to live with the dilemma that there are relative degrees of power available and this power is contingent. The Edwardian generation of activist women had come far in a short space of time but, as Smith noted of the Canadian situation in the 1970s, 'this participation was within marked boundaries. Among the most important of these boundaries, I would argue, is that which reserves to men control of the policy making and decision making apparatus in the educational system' (1978, p. 281). Within the LCC Margaret was part of the male structure, always in the minority on the committees except for a brief period in the 1950s when women achieved equal representation on the education committee and then lost ground again (Hughes, 1992). Her work and activism were remarkable, but today women are still under-represented at the top of political parties, national governments, regional governments and local governments.

For much of her active life, Margaret Cole combined the roles of the 'good' wife and mother with public work. Looking across the whole period, she denied there was a serious obstacle 'to a woman doing what she likes, provided she wants to do it, and can' (1962, p. 83). To this extent, her published views were consistent with most of the feminists of her generation, who defined the goal in terms of balance between men, marriage and family on one hand and career on the other. Interestingly, it was Douglas who dreaded the possibility of self-sacrifice and deferred needs in contemplating marriage but his concern was for potential husbands and fathers. Margaret fostered a modern ideal of womanhood which preserved the primacy of domesticity, but ultimately this was a heritage that rebounded, to cement rather than transcend the gender division of labour. On the arrival of children, an equal entitlement to the full range of career and family experience is not always realizable in practice. Fatherhood and motherhood continue to be seen as having different implications and British women still have less free time than men. The adoption of an equal rights approach was destined to produce few measurable results and the lives of many have remained unaffected by the women's movement.

8

Conclusion: Individual Lives and Educational Histories

We have been looking at auto/biographical practices in the research we have recounted thus far. So what of our own auto/biographical practices as authors who grew up in teaching families in post-war Britain? In Chapter 1, we discussed how the 'auto/biographical I' places the voice of the author at the centre of the knowledge production process and gives the reader access to the value commitments, stylistic and political preferences, which design and colour 'the findings', the outcomes. Our investigation of women who form the subjects of our research involved a rethinking and re-seeing of issues to do with gender and career, gender and life course and gender and self in the 'lives' we have portrayed. In this conclusion, we scrutinize the personal dimensions that have informed our collective biography. We draw upon our own auto/biographical practices to explicate what has so far been implicit. In the preceding chapters, we have looked at how female subjectivity is produced in, and for, particular historical moments. What does the positioning of the personal say for our individual and collaborative struggle to find a voice, our struggle for self-definition? Our own autobiographical starting points are written with the aim of articulating a 'self-consciousness about women's identity both as an inherited fact and as a process of historical construction' (Heilbrun, 1989, p. 18). This takes us back to the web of identity, back to the invisible bonds underpinning gender projects. In what follows, we relate some of the experiences that led us, individually, to the conversation and personal thrill of intellectual discovery of 'forgotten lives' we now share and which have framed discussion and analysis in the book.

Autobiographical Starting Points: Jane – Chemistry Lessons and Egalitarian Projects

Consider the following *post hoc* construction of the teenage Jane and her experience of mixed chemistry lessons in an English comprehensive school in the 1970s. She could accumulate neither knowledge nor understanding in science per se and was particularly dismal at chemistry. Lessons were anticipated with fear and loathing in equal measure. In time, another girl and Jane learned to accommodate the classes by booking violin lessons during the chemistry slot. Later in life, as an undergraduate, I worked out the failings were not mine alone. To locate the teenage Jane through a particular slice of linear time, refracted through a preoccupation with auto/biography as method, is one means of understanding something of the interplay between the present self and the self recalled.

Within the patterns of another time and place, my undergraduate reading drew me to the feminist critique of girls' curricula and education generally. Reading the literature I was particularly struck by accounts of the chilly classroom climate for girls. Like the teenage Jane, the girls in the studies had not come to the realization that in education gender makes a significant difference. As feminist historical researcher, however, I am most influenced by my mother's story. As a child, I learned of her family's experience of being denied a secondary education that fuelled her class and political consciousness. Growing up in a single parent household in the 1930s, she passed the scholarship examination making her eligible for secondary school. However, failure in the oral examination meant she did not qualify for financial assistance and family circumstances prevented her achieving this goal. Instead, she went to the local central school, offering advanced training to working-class children. The weaving of these educational histories is linked to the great betrayal of keen and interested students like my mother, who were taken out of school to begin wage-work at the age of fourteen. It is linked to her sense of loss and frustration at the sacrifice of education and recognition of the political and social role of education. Like Kate Rousmaniere (1999) and Kathleen Weiler (1999) the kind of history writing I want to develop is of radical women who see education as a way of changing the world.

Autobiographical Starting Points: Joyce – Illusions and Contradictions of Female Authority and Becoming a Professor

My brother and I went to the school where Dad was head and my mother the secretary. Children referred to Mum as the headmistress because of her relationship to Dad, an intermingling of private and public relations and illusion of female authority that masked the extra hours she worked to support Dad for no extra pay. My curiosity about women educators was sparked by what was probably an apocryphal story of two mops told to me by my Dad. These mops lived at either end of a school corridor in an infant school and in Dad's story the prime concern of the infant school headmistress who 'reigned' over this school was that the mops were correctly placed at their respective ends of the corridor after use. Dad used this story to support his view that women head teachers were more concerned with detail (and the domestic) than with the 'big educational picture'. Whether Dad's story was apocryphal or not, later in life as a teacher I worked for female heads who fitted Dad's pattern and ones who didn't: the head who insisted I scrubbed my classroom wall to remove spatters of my reception children's paint and who constantly inspected my classroom floor for specks of sand and drops of water (for everything had to be in its place); and her antithesis, the head who sat on the floor with the sixth form girls discussing philosophy. Dad was drawn to feminist theology, but whether he changed his views on women's tendencies to adopt particular styles of educational authority I know not. But his story of the two mops, the ambiguities of living as the child of the head and pupil in his school, and my own experience of education in a girls' grammar school and later as parent and teacher, left me with an abiding curiosity about educational authority, particularly its gendered manifestations.

I worked on the introduction to this book at the same time as preparing for my professorial interview – an elicited auto/biographical practice and practice of authority if ever there was one! It was not just the story of my research that I was to tell. The telling would also count. How was I going to present this particular version of my audit self? Which clothes? Which story? Which bits of my career? The frequent new starts as I followed my own interests and coped with life as full-time/part-time teacher, corporate wife, mother, single parent, mature student, researcher, lecturer? Practising my story with a mentor/friend, I repeated the tensions of Heilbrun's (1989) women, who found it difficult to admit into their autobiographical narratives the claim of achievement, the admission of ambition, and the recognition that accomplishment was neither luck, nor the result of the efforts, or generosity, of others (p. 24). I put my 'success' down to hard work and being in the right place at the right time. Inwardly acknowledging that this may not have been the case and outward display were two different things. (Significantly, I still find it difficult to write 'my' – my educational leadership, my accomplishments in this account.) Fragmented selves and 'female' career I recognize as strength and sources of stress – as well as the way that I have made choices that have been crucial to my life in circumstances not entirely of my own making. I see the ways these have affected who it is I have 'become'. In my research, I am interested in contradictions and tensions of female authority, as they play out in the lives and work of women who worked for educational change.

Our Autobiographical 'Turn'[1]

Our autobiographical turn at the start of this chapter is part of our engagement with the feminist critique of the neutrality and objectivity of researchers, and the understandings we have gained from engagement with feminist theory of the ways we are implicated in the subject of our research and writing. It forms part of our understanding that auto/biography as practice denotes the active, inquiring presence of researchers in constructing, rather than 'discovering' knowledge. The metaphor of 'turn' is illuminative, here. When used in woodworking, 'turning' is a wasting process, in which layers of wood are removed at different depths, revealing on the wood the profile on which the turner has worked to pick out a shape that serves his or her purpose. This purpose may be explicit, as when a turner follows a pre-planned design, or implicit as the turner works on something free-form until it is pleasing aesthetically. Like the turner of wood, we have brought both purpose and receptivity to the intellectual work of this book. We have turned the raw material (primary source/historiography/theory) in relation to our purpose, discarding the extraneous and picking out the shape to construct our narratives. The metaphor of 'turn' also relates to 'turn-taking', or ordering. That is, it is also about ourselves as writer-readers – for the process in which we bring experience to theory, historiography and primary sources also works reciprocally on our (researcher) 'selves'. The metaphor of 'turn' is also about you as reader-writer in the process of reciprocity that lies at the heart of auto/biography as method.

We have made the 'auto/biographical I' explicit in this final chapter to aid the process of reflection on the women's lives, our writing of them, and the conclusions that we draw. Stanley's (1991) injunction that researchers produce 'accountable' knowledge by making clear their own intellectual biography and researcher presence is not simply a matter of researcher 'confession'. Our 'auto/biographical turn', forms a part of the development of 'personal criticism' and 'critical auto/biography'. This development critiques as pseudo objectivity the 'theoretical evacuation of the social subjects producing theory' (Marcus, 1994, p. 283) that relegates aspects of the personal to the margins of texts (Anderson, 2001). In this, we draw on a long tradition of women illuminating their own relation to the creation of ideas. Take, for example, the autobiographical passages in Harriet Martineau's non-fictional *Household Education* (1848), which Charlotte Bronte recognized uncannily recounted her own childhood experiences (Peterson, 1999). So, our auto/biographical 'turn' also recognizes and re-valorizes the writing practices of women educationists whose theoretical texts have often included the practical and auto/biographical in a disruption of the theory/practice binary. In this, we have been influenced by Carolyn Steedman and Morwenna Griffiths who use individual experience and theory in a process of reflection and rethinking which includes attention to politically situated perspectives.

The 'Turn' of the Six Auto/biographical Women

The female educators we chose all shared a novel political and administrative experience and their autobiographies speak of the relationship between political thought and actions and wider social and cultural change. They operated in differing social, economic and politic contexts and assigned education a major role in challenging the status quo and building a new social order. Their educational philosophies and practices and the way they negotiated political contexts and educational authority to effect educational reform demonstrate commonalities as well as difference across a period of nearly two hundred years.

Material circumstances formed an important background against which they developed their work in and for education – both economic vulnerability and economic security. Elizabeth Hamilton, Jane Chessar and Mary Dendy were single and from middle-class backgrounds where the economic vulnerability of the single 'redundant' woman can be glimpsed. Hamilton lived with her aunt Marshall until the success of her first book and then the provision of a Civil List pension provided her with the funds to move into single lodgings. Economic vulnerability may well have led Jane Chessar to study at the Home and Colonial, since many daughters of impecunious professional men expected to teach if they did not marry (de Bellaigue, 2001).

Economic vulnerability dogged Sarah Austin throughout her married life but Mary Dendy illustrates the effects of both economic vulnerability and economic security. Dendy's small legacy from Sarah Ann Cawston enabled her to embark on the work for the feeble-minded for which she became well-known. Similarly, security of wealth meant that the married Shena Simon could devote herself to public work, aided by domestic help, secretarial assistance and blue books delivered to order. Margaret Cole's contribution to public service was also effected with the help of domestic servants. In this, both Simon and Cole illustrate how some women participated more as active citizens but something more than economic security motivated their life in public work. Dendy shared an ethic of service that Shena Simon would have recognized, inspired as she was by the 'religion of humanity'. Naomi Mitchinson described the visionary socialism of herself and Margaret Cole as 'a cause worth living for, even worth dying for' (1979, p. 205). Indeed, Cole's devotion to this cause meant that prior to marriage she gave up her economic security for the cause she held dear. Fervour of diverse kinds – whether the 'religion of humanity', 'socialism' or that inspired by more traditional Episcopalian views, were important motivating factors in these women's lives. Her religious beliefs drove Hamilton increasingly to the religious introspection that fed off and into her metaphysical study of the human mind. Some, like Cole, moved away from the religious beliefs of their families. But engagement with public work was deeply rooted in familial 'intellectual aristocracies': the Taylor–Martineau–Reeves network; the Dendy–Beard–Bosanquet coterie; the 'Didsbury Set'; and the intimacy of the Allen–Postgate circle with the Haldane–Burdon–Sanderson circle.

Public life was not only the preserve of the single. Austin, Simon and Cole were all well-educated, intelligent wives. Sarah Austin's courtship prepared the ground for the future partnership she and John envisaged, as Sarah sent John her thoughts on the texts they were both reading. Before marriage, Shena and Ernest Simon conversed on topics as diverse as collective ownership, democracy, Fabianism, the international labour question, the institution of marriage, social reform and women's suffrage. An intellectual partnership, however, could bring tensions, as Margaret Cole's autobiography shows, particularly when the wife wanted to rework the mothering-role and reorganize her family life to reject the domestic home-based role. It could also inform the reflection that prompted more public work. Cole's *Marriage*, published in 1938, focused on the issue of dependency within marriage, the sources and implications of women's economic independence, as well as issues of motherhood, employment and domesticity. But as the life of Sarah Austin in the mid-nineteenth century demonstrates, here is no comfortable trajectory of 'progress' and 'enlightenment' in women's juggling of family and public and professional responsibilities as they enter the public world. While Sarah gradually took over the breadwinning role, she juggled her roles as wife, mother, writer and occasional teacher and the young Lucie could be found besides her mother as she worked into the late hours on the translation of the latest book.

A solid education, broadened by future study can also be glimpsed. Sarah Austin, Mary Dendy and Shena Simon were all educated at home. Elizabeth Hamilton and Jane Chessar attended small private schools and Margaret Cole Roedean, the prestigious girls' boarding school, which she hated. None attended the new 'public' high schools for girls, though Margaret Cole's mother had been to the North London Collegiate. Like many women of her day, Hamilton furthered her own education by reading extensively and corresponding with intellectual men, who advised her on her reading and commented on her work. Sarah Austin's courtship reading extended the advanced education for an early nineteenth-century girl that she had received and the early form of further education for women she gained in the cultural and intellectual circles of Anna Barbauld. Chessar, Dendy, Simon and Cole all tapped into the more formal further and higher education opportunities for women as these developed: Chessar at the Home and Colonial; Dendy at Bedford College; Simon breaking the gendered pattern of education within her family to attend Newnham and then registering for a higher degree at the London School of Economics; and Cole at Girton.

A key argument of this book is that education played a central role in these women's social vision. A hundred years apart, Austin in the mid-nineteenth century and Simon in the mid-twentieth both publicly argued that education was one way of bringing about social cohesion. Austin thought universal primary education the only guarantee of social and stable government, Simon that secondary education for all was central to the democracy that would increase educational equality. Both believed in the educability of the working class. Significantly, however, class analysis inflected their argument in divergent ways. While Austin was committed to an education for the working classes based on the development of rationality and the intellect, she thought it misplaced to instil in the minds of working people that education was the way to advancement; that knowledge was power and that to better oneself one needed learning. Writing in the context of 1830s fears of working-class radicalism, she wanted a national system of popular education that would lead working people to recognize their 'best interests' and defer to an intellectual elite. Simon, in contrast, was opposed to the traditional emphasis in education on character formation and leadership for an academic elite. Writing in the aftermath of the Second World War and in a context keen to build a 'New Jerusalem', she believed that schools could be agencies of social change to reduce social inequalities. Her vehicle was the common school, which would provide the arena in which a really democratic community, and so social cohesion, could be attained. Like Simon, Cole, too, became an exponent of the British comprehensive reform and its foremost publicist in London.

Simon and Austin demonstrate how closely allied to aspects of citizenship and state formation some women's arguments for reform of education were. Ideals of citizenship, and views on education's relation to the state, also reflected the centrality of notions of gender to active citizenship. Elizabeth Hamilton wrote about aspects of national identities in a context in which fears for the nation in the face of the rumblings of the Napoleonic wars were acute. Like Pestalozzi, she portrayed the mother of the family as central to the constructions of national identity and stability. For Hamilton, the 'new woman', and ironically the woman 'metaphysician', was a danger to the nation. Her argument that domestic virtue constructed national identity and brought national prosperity or decline gave women a central role in nation-building, while her novel *Glenburnie* constructed a particular version of Anglo-British identity. Sarah Austin, too, portrayed 'new' women like her cousin Harriet Martineau bringing national discontent through the subversion of domestic ideals. A hundred years after Hamilton, Mary Dendy's eugenic analysis reflected the negative aspects of Hamilton's concerns with her argument that sexually active 'feckless' women undermined the national stock. Both Hamilton's and Dendy's act of publicly making such arguments exemplified the ambiguities of women, as active citizens, speaking publicly on a platform that strongly supported gender differentiation. Less controversially 'strange' to our eyes today, the 'religion of humanity' that inspired Shena Simon was explicitly geared to promote the collectivist state's well-being, while Margaret Cole's socialism was fired by the commitment of socialists to political action to bring change in the state.

The ways these women operated to bring about change demonstrates how the means and channels through which they expressed their ideas were embedded in social, cultural and political contexts in which their arguments were developed. Key here, was the incursion of the state into education and the development of an educational bureaucracy that progressively distanced women from the centre of decision-making and which they had to learn to negotiate. Writing prior to state involvement in education, Hamilton produced a cultural analysis against the background of the rumblings of the Napoleonic wars. Austin, an advocate of state involvement in education used extra-Parliamentary influence to bring about national reform of education. Similarly, Dendy was committed to state intervention. As an elected representative in the wake of the Municipal Franchise Act of 1869, Chessar was one of the early women to negotiate the local educational bureaucracy. Dendy, Cole and Simon followed this path: Dendy onto Manchester School Board and then like Simon onto Manchester Education Committee; Cole onto the Education Committee of the London County Council. Adept at working in male-dominated bureaucracies, Dendy and Simon, particularly, demonstrated an ability to use committee machinery and lobbying pressures to effect change at local and central government level. Dendy became an expert witness to a Royal Commission and then commissioner at the Board of Control; Simon, an influential figure in national policy-making through the Consultative Committee of the Board of Education, where she was selected on the basis of her expertise in educational administration.

Party politics played an important role in the abilities of women like Cole, Simon and Dendy to propagate their views. Dendy's affiliations were Liberal. Simon's initially Liberal, although from the 1930s she was a Labour nominee on Manchester Council. Cole's socialist politics led to both a paid political post and an introduction to her future husband. But the activities of Sarah Austin, with her correspondence networks, salons, travel and writing, demonstrate ways in which social politics gave women an entrée into the male political world prior to their incursion and acceptance in organized politics. Social politics contained a range of strategies, which women who gained access to the machinery of the educational bureaucracy and corridors of government power continued to employ.

Women like Jane Chessar exemplified the type of trained, professional, expert teacher for which Austin called. As Hamilton's exhortations to mothers about the early education of their children demonstrate, however, a desire to professionalize women's work with children was a strong theme prior to the development of later formal training for teachers. Reformers like Simon and Cole took up the cause of teachers as professionals and were trenchant in their critique of the unequal mechanisms of pay, appointment and advancement for women teachers that militated against the professional lives of women. Indeed, Shena Simon thought her greatest contribution to education was her success in 1928 in getting agreement for women to remain in the teaching profession after they had married, a victory gained in the face of opposition from fellow Manchester councillor, the Conservative Mary Kingsmill Jones. Margaret Cole used historical and comparative evidence in her pamphlet *The Rate for the Job* to expose the fallacy of the objections of the National Association of Schoolmasters to equal pay for women teachers. But Austin's role as incipient comparative educationist points to the difficulties that women experienced as 'officials of the state'. The educational inspectorate, which Austin advocated, proved one of the most intractable areas for women.

The centrality of child-centred methods to the professionalization of both motherhood and teaching is a key theme in the work of Hamilton, Austin, Chessar and Dendy, particularly the ideas of Pestalozzi and Froebel. The emphasis of women writers on the role of the 'mother made conscious' was far from a sentimentalized approach. Austin's insistence on the importance of Pestalozzi was accompanied with a conscious acknowledgement of the double-edged nature of Pietist methods for promoting both submission and autonomy. Indeed, this formed part of her view of the manner in which education could 'accommodate' the poor to the rule of their betters through the creation of 'intelligent' loyalty. Her Pestalozzian stance ran alongside the tenets of education as 'positive science' that underpinned her use of comparative education methodology. A similar combination of science and a Froebelian approach characterized Dendy's work, with its dual aim of making the feeble-minded happy and harmless. Although Dendy's analysis of the need for state intervention was in tension with aspects of Idealist belief, her casebook approach to the feeble-minded shared similarities with the Idealism that underpinned the social investigation of her sister, Helen Bosanquet. Idealism and social investigation figures, too, in the work of Simon, whose 'religion of humanity' was influenced by Comte, at whose feet Sarah Austin sat in Paris. Austin's metaphor of the social body reflected Comte's organic models. But at the start of the nineteenth century Hamilton, too, stressed science – the science of the mind – demonstrating the way in which the long-standing interest of women in child-centred pedagogical methods was based on close study and first-hand observation of how children learn.

For some of these women, the importance of travel for the acquisition of educational expertise is clear. Hamilton learned secondhand of Pestalozzi's method from Maria Edgeworth, who had met Pestalozzi in Paris while travelling with her father. Austin's extensive travels provided her with first-hand information, friendship and the correspondence networks that lay at the heart of her ability to propagate Continental views on education and earn her living as a translator. Always frail, it was while in Brussels at an educational congress that Chessar died. Dendy developed her Darwinistic ideas and gleaned important educational ideas on travels to Australia, New Zealand and America. More unusually, Simon combined firsthand knowledge of Soviet and American schools. The Simons visited the USSR in 1936 and in 1955 Shena was the only prominent educationist to accept an invitation from the Academy of Educational Sciences in Moscow to study the Soviet education system (J. Simon, 1986). It is easy to slide, here, into whiggish trajectories of women's freedom to move across geographical spaces: to take on a view of travel in terms of a trope of 'self-realization in the spaces of the Other'. This understanding of 'travel as freedom' is a particularly European understanding which Grewal (1996) argues 'became an ontological discourse ... by which knowledge of a Self, society and nation was, within European and North American culture ... understood and obtained' (p. 4). How significant is it that Austin was loathe to leave England but was forced abroad by financial need? That Dendy travelled to visit her brother in Australia at a crisis in her life on the death of Miss Cawston?

Particular geographical spaces fostered women's ability to effect educational reform. Scotland, home to key late eighteenth- and early nineteenth-century philosophers and of significant University reform, where dissenters went in numbers for University study, produced Hamilton, Chessar and her friend Mary Sim. Metropolitan London, centre of the British state, with its wealth, prestige, fashion and social status acted as a magnet for many women. The Austins' home in London's Queen's Square, where they were neighbours of Mill and Bentham, placed them at the centre of mid-nineteenth-century Utiliarian networks. Chessar was part of the London metropolitan women's movement that underpinned the work of women on the London School Board and much feminist activity. Until 1990, London was the largest local education authority in England and the Coles' home in Hammersmith placed them at the centre of national organizations. The Simons, too, had a London base. But the stories of Dendy and Simon also point to the importance of Manchester – another early home of the suffrage movement, where Emmeline Pankhurst sat on the Manchester School Board alongside Dendy. Symbol of a new industrial age, Manchester was a thriving cultural centre. Like London, it had a large émigré community where Froebelian educational ideas were espoused and into which the Simons had an entree as a result of Ernest Simon's roots in the city's German community.

Domestic space continued to be important as well. Hamilton's home became a respected space, where the Edinburgh intelligentsia met to exchange ideas. Austin's London and Paris homes were distinguished for their salon culture and intelligent conversation. In her early married life, Simon established her home as a focal point for a social-cum-intellectual circle embracing Manchester's German community, besides providing a web of connection to the worlds of business, education, politics and the press. Similarly, Cole mirrored this use of the home as intellectual space, with the Cole group that met around her husband on a Monday evening. This proved one means of counteracting her life as the wife of a don in Oxford, where the expected feminine role went against the grain.

Networking and institution-building were closely linked and demonstrate women's ability to effect their plans in the borderland between the voluntary and local government apparatus as it developed. Dendy's community of Sandlebridge grew from the Lancashire and Cheshire Society for the Permanent Care of the Feeble-minded. She was also a member of a range of organizations for the care of the feeble-minded, through which she pressed for parliamentary reform. Simon, too, was active in both philanthropic and civic reform associations. She worked through the National Anti-sweating League, the National Union of Women Workers and the metropolitan women's movement and then established the Manchester and Salford Women's Citizen Association. Cole was active in the weekend political schools, which led to the foundation of the Society for Socialist Enquiry and Propaganda as well as the New Fabian Research Bureau. Both provided fora for debate and drafting of policy outside the Labour Party.

Through this activity and through their achievements, indications can be glimpsed of tensions experienced by women working on what was often masculine terrain. Sarah Austin's worries on the reissue of *On National Education* under her name were clear. It was not just the issue of being gunned down for holding unpalatable views. It was the fact that, as a woman, she was daring to put herself in the firing line by publishing political polemic. Her fears speak of the ambiguities of women's relationship to the signature and the proper name, particularly in the early and mid-nineteenth century. This was despite the public recognition that Austin gained – as her obituary and Civil List pension demonstrate. Even in the middle of the twentieth century, Cole was ambivalent about her authorial voice on the grounds of vanity – and impression management was still problematic.

Such tensions illustrate how closely public work in and for education and the concept and category of 'woman' intertwine, both in respect of public and personal perceptions of women's roles and citizenship. The six women related to the concept of feminism and 'the woman question' in their own ways; and as noted earlier, their public personae and their views on women (their education and their lives) were at times at variance or downplayed. Some, like Hamilton and Austin, professed themselves opposed to the feminist movement but readings of their lives demonstrate how hard a line predicated on woman's 'difference' was to sustain. Hamilton focussed on a range of Enlightenment discourses but walked a tightrope as a woman metaphysician who critiqued women philosophers and feminists through the philosophical devises and genres she deplored. At the same time, her writings on 'domestic woman' were geared to raising the status of women. Particularly in later life, Austin, was scathing of women who adopted a feminist stance. Yet, she held to the importance of an intellectual education for women and her adoption of the public role of 'partner' to her husband, when he was commissioner to Malta, resulted in her lampooning by the Maltese press. Dendy was a member of the suffrage movement, yet has gone down in history as the architect of a policy of sexual control for women that incarcerated women in mental hospitals for being single, pregnant and on poor relief – a policy that continued to resound until widespread community care closed the larger mental hospitals.

Both Simon and Cole specifically addressed the status of women in their research. Drawn to suffrage militancy, the pact Simon made with her family, on whom she was economically dependent, meant that she did not join the militant campaign of the Edwardian era. Crucially, even though divisions over tactics were a source of disagreement with Ernest, Shena continued to play a major role in feminist causes throughout her married life. Margaret Cole, converted to socialism and feminism overnight on reading H.G. Wells, carefully distanced herself from Wells' portrayal of the new woman. A lifelong member of the Fabian Women's Group, she was sympathetic towards women's claims but disapproved of her more outspokenly feminist colleagues on the LCC Education Committee. Yet, she consistently pursued married women's right to work and equal pay and wanted to find ways of making married women's role compatible with a successful career, a stance that she portrayed as compatible with her socialist views.

From Hamilton, Austin and Chessar, to Dendy, Simon and Cole, the women we have discussed were active in bringing about educational reform, albeit in a range of ways, with different projects, differently defined, in different contexts and with different outcomes. Their political manoeuvring illustrates shifts and tensions within and between the equal-but-different position and the equal rights approach to women's place in reform of education and to reform of women's education. While ambiguous, some of their achievements have been remarkable – both for their time and for pointing up ways in which women have traversed the political and the boundaries of the public and the private. Here, Sarah Austin is instructive. Her civic disabilities notwithstanding, she used a range of social and cultural approaches to bring her views on the importance of continental approaches for education to audiences that eventually stretched from Britain to the United States and Canada, where her translation of Cousin's work influenced the course of educational legislation. To reconstruct her work in educational reform, however, it is necessary to find new ways of seeing. Given the state of political representation today, it is clear that women still have considerable distance to travel for their voices to be heard with equal weight with those of men when it comes to educational reform. Rather than producing a programme of prescription for this journey, we offer this auto/biographical study in the spirit of conversation. We hope that your engagement with the text as reader-writer – as it has been for us as writer-readers – will prove a step on the journey towards this end: an end that can and should expect to produce a range of views on education, and a range of strategies for effecting educational change, that place due weight on the social, cultural and political context, as well as the visionary.

Notes

2 Elizabeth Hamilton (1758–1816) and the 'Plan of Pestalozzi'

1. This and the next paragraph draw on Kelly (1993) and Benger (1818).
2. The account of Pestalozzi's work draws on Silber (1960).
3. Silber notes that 'Anschauung' has no real English translation. It encompassed a range of mental activity through which the transition was made from simple receptive and unconscious processes to full mental awareness and activity: sense-impressions, observation, contemplation, receptivity, perception, apperception, intuition, imagination (Silber, 1960, p. 138).
4. Associationist theory built on Locke's view of association. Associationism is 'psychological theory which postulates that all mental phenomena arise from the association of ideas. These ideas are originally formed from sensations caused by the impression of external objects on the senses'. (Watts, 1998, p. ix).
5. This account of common-sense philosophy draws on Brodie (1998) and Rendall (1978).
6. As Jane Rendall noted in discussion after her paper at the Institute of Historical Research (Rendall, 2002).
7. The analysis of Glenburnie here and in later paragraphs draws on Kelly's excellent analysis (Kelly, 1993).
8. This summary draws on Silber (1960).

3 Sarah Austin (1793–1867): 'Voices of Authority' and National Education

1. In recounting Sarah's background, I have drawn here and elsewhere on Hamburger and Hamburger (1985). This is particularly the case in my description of John Austin and his work.
2. Lucie became Lady Duff Gordon and died in Egypt. Like her mother, she worked as a translator and is best known for her *Letters from Egypt* which Sarah edited.

5 Mary Dendy (1855–1933) and Pedagogies of Care

1. This chapter draws on records of the Mary Dendy Hospital, Great Warford, Alderley Edge, Cheshire, 1902–86, NHM11/3837, Cheshire Record Office. I am grateful to the East Cheshire National Health Care Trust for granting me access to the closed records in this archive.
2. As Sandlebridge children grew older, additional houses were built to accommodate feeble-minded women and men apart from the children;

a separate school, a house for very young children, a laundry, work-shops, a farm, a hospital wing and recreation facilities were gradually added in the grounds. Numbers of children in residence rose to 204 by 1909, 283 in 1919 and by 1929 there were 362 residents (Jackson, 1997).

3. Galton coined the term eugenics to frame 'knowledge of and control over human procreation'. His guiding principle was that the only way to improve human life was to ensure that the 'fittest' members of the population reproduced more than the less fit. His successor, Karl Pearson' headed the Eugenics Laboratory at University College, London (Burdett, 1998a,b).

4. I would like to thank the members of the Dendy family who were most helpful in my fruitless quest to find the diary.

5. The colony, with villas' was one form of residential care. Care in the community was also widely practised, through supervision and guardianship.

6. Mendel proposed a model of heredity based on the assumption that inheritance is divided up into units (now called genes) each of which determined a particular character. Most organism had two copies (alleles) of each gene transmitted to offspring with equal frequency. He argued that combinations of alleles remained distinct. This was the opposite of Darwin's scheme of blending inheritance. It was also the opposite of the inheritance of acquired characters proposed by Lamarck. Lamarck posited an original creation of life but his mechanism of adaptive evolution based on the inheritance of acquired characteristics lacked any idea of selection. Some form of vital striving took the place of Darwin's natural selection (Rose, 1998, pp. 35–6, 39–40, 76–7).

7. The descriptions of Seguin's method draw on Talbot (1964).

8. I would like to thank Annemieke van Drenth for sharing with me an early draft of 'Sweet-tempered but persistent': gender and professionalism in nineteenth-century special education in the United States.

9. The Board of Education's largely environmentalist views of the causes of mental deficiency were at variance with the more hereditarian views of the Board of Control. As Gillian Sutherland and Matthew Thomson both demonstrate, this resulted in a struggle between the two Boards as to whose province it was to certify and provide for children. Thomson argues that a desire to protect its own administrative territory, and concern over the rights of defective children and their parents, meant that the Board of Education was often unwilling to pass on children to the mental deficiency authorities and that this seriously undermined the attempt to set up a comprehensive system of care (Thomson, 1998; Sutherland, 1984).

6   Shena Simon (1883–1972) and the 'Religion of Humanity'

1. In recounting Shena's background, education and private life I have drawn here and elsewhere on Joan Simon (1986) 'Shena Simon: feminist and educationist' (privately printed). The pagination relates to discrete

chapters. I would like to thank Shena's younger son, the late Professor Brian Simon, for his helpful and insightful comment, enthusiasm and encouragement of this work as it developed.

2. Beatrice and Sidney Webb founded the London School of Economics and Political Science in 1895. It grew very rapidly to be a centre of social science research and teaching that attracted students from all over the world.

3. The new appointments were: Dr Dorothy Brock; the Rev. Professor Joseph Jones (of the Free Church Federal Council, Breconshire education and the Association of Education Committees); Hugh Lyon (headmaster of Rugby); J. Paley Yorke (of the LCC School of Engineering in Poplar); Ada Phillips (vice-principal of Avery Hill Training College, executive of the National Union of Teachers); T.J. Rees (director of education for Swansea); R.L. Roberts; Alderman E.G. Rowlinson; Dr H. Schofield (of Loughborough College); Lady Simon; J.H. Simpson (principal of the College of St Mark and St John). This account of the composition of the Spens Committee draws on Simon (1977a).

Conclusion: Individual Lives and Educational Histories

1. We borrow this phrase from Cotterill and Letherby (1993). The metaphors of woodturning were the result of a conversation with Bndget Egan, which we acknowledge with thanks.

Bibliography

Manuscript Sources

Emily Davies papers, Girton College, Cambridge.

Girton College Register, Girton College, Cambridge.

Jane Chessar election manifesto, Emily Davies papers, ED/LSB 58, Girton College, Cambridge.

Lady Simon of Wythenshawe papers, M14/2/1/2 retirement, Manchester Central Library.

Helen Taylor papers, London School of Economics, London.

Lancashire and Cheshire Society for the Permanent Care of the Feeble-minded, Case book 1914–1930, NHM11/3837/56; Case Book 1920–1935; NHM 11/3837/57; Case Book 1931–36, NHM 11/3837/58.

Mary Dendy Hospital, Visitors Report Book, NHM 11/3837/20, Cheshire Record Office.

Mary Dendy Hospital, Warford Hall Visitors Book 1910–12, NHM 11/3837/19, Cheshire Record Office.

National Union of Women Workers papers, London School of Economics, London.

Newnham College Roll Letter, Newnham College, Cambridge.

Sandlebridge Schools, Album, 1902–11, NHM/11/3837/42, Cheshire Record Office.

Published Reports

Board of Education, *Annual Report for 1908 of the Chief Medical Officer of the Board of Education* (London: HMSO, 1910).

Consultative Committee, *Report on Secondary Education with Special Reference to Grammar Schools and Technical High Schools* (London: HMSO, 1938).

Dendy, A. 'Progressive Evolution and the Origin of Species. Presidential Address to Section D (Biology), *Report of the Eighty Fourth Meeting of the British Association for the Advancement of Science* (London: John Murray, 1915).

Dendy, M. 'Feeble-minded children', *Transactions of the Manchester Statistical Society* (1899) 21–40.

Dendy, M. 'The problem of the feeble-minded', *Transactions of the Manchester Statistical Society* (1908) 121–47.

Dendy, M. 'The care of the feeble-minded', *Manchester and Salford Sanitary Association, Proceedings of a Conference on the Care of the Feeble-minded held in Manchester, 4 May 1911* (Manchester: Sherratt and Hughes, 1911) 43–6.

Lancashire and Cheshire Society for the Permanent Care of the Feeble-minded, *Annual Reports*, 1910, 1925.

Royal Commission on the Care and Control of the Feebleminded, vol. 1, cd4215 (London: HMSO, 1908).

School Board for London, *Minutes*, 1870–80.

School Board for London, *First Report of the Scheme of Education Committee*, 1871.

Tredgold, A.F. 'The problem of the feeble-minded', *Manchester and Salford Sanitary Association. Proceedings of a Conference on the Care of the Feeble-minded held in Manchester, 4 May 1911* (Manchester: Sherratt and Hughes, 1911) 5–19.

Journals and Articles

Allen, A.T. 'Spiritual Motherhood: German Feminists and the Kindergarten Movement, 1848–1911', *History of Education Quarterly*, 22 (3) (1982) 319–39.

Allen, A.T. 'Gardens of Children, Gardens of God: Kindergartens and Day-care Centers in Nineteenth Century Germany', *Journal of Social History*, 19 (3) (1986) 433–50.

Austin, S. 'National System of Education in France', *Cochrane's Foreign Quarterly Review*, 11 (June) (1835) 260–301.

Barkin, K. 'Social Control and the Volksschule', *Central European History*, 16 (1) (1983) 31–52.

Bartley, P. 'Preventing Prostitution: the Ladies Associations for the Care and Protection of Young Girls in Birmingham, 1887–1914', *Women's History Review*, 7 (1) (1998) 37–60.

Bedford, J. 'Margaret Ashton: Manchester's "First Lady"', *Manchester Region History Review*, XII (1998) 3–17.

Brehony, K.J. 'The "School Masters' Parliament": the Origins and Formation of the Consultative Committee of the Board of Education 1868–1916', *History of Education*, 23 (2) (1994) 171–93.

Brine, J. 'Equal Opportunities and the European Social Fund: Discourse and Practice', *Gender and Education*, 7 (1) (1995) 9–22.

Brinkman, W. 'A Historical Introduction to Comparative Education', *Comparative Education Review*, 3 (3) (1960).

Caine, B. 'Love, Friendship and Feminism in Later 19th-Century England', *Women's Studies Int. Forum*, 13 (1–2) (1990) 63–78.

Clegg, S. 'The Feminist Challenge to Socialist History', *Women's History Review*, 6 (1997) 201–14.

Cole, M. 'What is a Comprehensive School?' (London: London Labour Party) (1953).

Cole, M. 'The Woman's Vote: What has it Achieved?', *Political Quarterly*, (33) (1962) 74–83.

Cole, M. 'Comprehensives in London', *Plebs*, (April) (1967) 13–20.

Cruikshank, M. 'Mary Dendy 1855–1923', *Journal of Educational Administration and History*, 8 (1) (1976) 26–9.

Cunningham, P. 'Innovators, Networks and Structures: Towards a Prosopography of Progressivism', *History of Education*, 30 (5) (2001) 433–52.

Curtis, B. 'Preconditions of the Canadian State', *Studies in Political Economy*, 10 (1983) 199–211.

de Bellaigue, C. 'The Development of Teaching as a Profession for Women Before 1870', *Historical Journal*, 44 (4) (2001) 963–88.

Deem, R. 'State Policy and Ideology in State Education of Women, 1944–1980', *British Journal of Sociology of Education*, 2 (2) (1981) 131–43.

Edgeworth, E.M. 'Memoir of Mrs Elizabeth Hamilton', *Monthly Magazine*, XLIII, Part 11, 1816.

Educational Paper of the Home and Colonial Society, 1860–80.

Educational Times, 1860–80.

Eisenmann, L. 'Creating a Framework for Interpreting US Women's Educational History: Lessons from Historical Lexicography', *History of Education*, 30 (5) (2001) 453–70.

Ellis, A.C.O. 'The Training and Supply of Teachers in the Victorian Period', *History of Education Society Bulletin*, 24 (1) (1979) 22–38.

Englishwoman's Review, 1860–80.

Epstein, J. 'Historiography, Diagnosis and Poetics', *Literature and Medicine*, 11 (1992) 23–44.

Eugenics Review, 1911–22.

Evans, M. 'Reading Lives: How the Personal Might Be Social', *Sociology*, 27 (1) (1993) 5–13.

F.H.E. 'Memorial Notice of Dorothy Shena Simon', *Newnham College Roll Letter*, (1973).

Goodman, J. 'Girls' Clubs in Late Victorian and Early Edwardian Manchester', *History of Education Society Bulletin*, 60 (1997) 4–13.

Goodman, J. 'Languages of Female Colonial Authority: the Educational Network of the Ladies Committee of the British and Foreign School Society, 1813–1837', *Compare*, 30 (1) (2000a) 7–19.

Goodman, J. and Martin, J. 'Breaking Boundaries: Gender, Politics and the Experience of Education', *History of Education*, 29 (5) (2000a) 383–88.

Gordon, L. 'Response to Scott', *Signs*, 15 (1990) 852.

Grosvenor, I. ' "There's No Place Like Home": Education and the Making of National Identity', *History of Education*, 28 (3) (1999) 235–51.

Grosvenor, I. and Lawn, M. 'Ways of Seeing in Education and Schooling: Emerging Historiographies', *History of Education*, 30 (2) (2001) 105–08.

Harris, J. 'Political Thought and the Welfare State 1870–1940: an Intellectual Framework for British Social Policy', *Past and Present*, 135 (1992) 116–41.

Haywood, C. and Mac an Ghaill, M. 'Materialism and Deconstructivism: Education and the Epistemology of Identity', *Cambridge Journal of Education*, 27 (2) (1997) 261–72.

Heward, C. 'Men and Women and the Rise of Professional Society: The Intriguing History of Teacher Educators', *History of Education*, 22 (1) (1993) 11–32.

Hilton, M. 'Revisioning Romanticism: Towards a Women's History of Progressive Thought 1780–1850', *History of Education*, 30 (5) (2001) 471–87.

Hughes, M. 'London Took the Lead: Institutes for Women', *Studies in the Education of Adults*, 24 (1) (1992) 41–55.

Jeger, L. 'Among Us, Taking a Century's Notes', *Guardian*, 13 January 1999.

Jones, J. and Williamson, J. 'The Birth of the Schoolroom', *Ideology and Consciousness*, 6 (1979) 59–110.

Lady Simon of Wythenshawe, *Three Schools or One?* (London: Frederick Muller, 1947).

Lowe, R. 'The Educational Impact of the Eugenics Movement', *International Journal of Educational Research*, 3 (2) (1998) 647–60.

Martin, J. 'Entering the Public Arena: the Female Members of the London School Board, 1870–1904', *History of Education*, 22 (3) (1993) 225–40.

Martin, J. 'To "Blaise the Trail for Women to Follow Along": Sex, Gender and the Politics of Education on the London School Board, 1870–1904', *Gender and Education*, 12 (7) (2000a) 165–181.

Martin, J. 'Reflections on Writing a Biographical Account of a Woman Educator Activist', *History of Education*, 30 (2) (2001) 163–76.

Melbourne University Calendar.

Melbourne University Review.

Mitchison, N. 'In retrospect' in Vernon, B. (eds) *Fabian Tract 482. Margaret Cole 1893–1980*. (London: Blackrose Press, 1982) 18–19.

Peim, N. 'The History of the Present: Towards a Contemporary Phenomenology of the School', *History of Education*, 10 (2) (2001) 177–90.

Poirier, S., Fosenblum, L., Ayers, L., Brauner, D.J., Sharf, B.F. and Stanford, A.F. 'Charting the Chart – an Exercise in Interpretation(s)', *Literature and Medicine*, 11 (1) (1992) 1–22.

Pope, R.D. and Verbeeke, M.G. 'Ladies Educational Organizations in England 1865–1988', *Paedagogica Historica*, 16 (1972) 336–61.

Queen, 1860–80.

Ribbens, J. 'Facts or Fictions? Aspects of the Use of Autobiographical Writing in Undergraduate Sociology', *Sociology*, 27 (1) (1993) 81–92.

Russell, R. 'Elizabeth Hamilton: Enlightenment Educator', *Scottish Educational Review*, 18 (1) (1986) 23–31.

School Board Chronicle, 1860–1880.

Scott, J. 'Social Network Analysis', *Sociology*, 22 (1) (1988) 109–27.

Simon, J. 'The Shaping of the Spens Report on Secondary Education 1933–38: an Inside View: Part 1', *British Journal of Educational Studies*, XXV (1) (1977a), 63–80.

Simon, J. 'The Shaping of the Spens Report on Secondary Education 1933–38: An Inside View: Part 2', *British Journal of Educational Studies*, XXV (2) (1977b), 170–85.

Simon, S.D. *The Four Freedoms in Secondary Education* (London: The University of London Press, 1944).

Simon, S.D. *Margaret Ashton and her Times* (Manchester: Manchester University Press, 1949).

Smith, D. 'A Peculiar Eclipsing: Women's Exclusion from Man's Culture', *Women's Studies International Quarterly*, 1 (4) (1978) 281–96.

Steedman, C. ' "The Mother Made Conscious": the Historical Development of a Primary School Pedagogy', *History Workshop Journal*, 20 (1985) 135–49.

Tylecote, M. *The Lady Simon of Wythenshawe Memorial Lectures. The Work of Lady Simon of Wythenshawe for Education in Manchester* (Manchester Education Committee: 1974).

Victoria Magazine, 1860–80.

Watts, R. 'Some Radical Educational Networks of the Late Eighteenth Century and Their Influence', *History of Education*, 17 (1) (1998a) 1–14.

Willis, R. 'Professional Roots: The Royal Incorporated College of Preceptors and Private Teachers from 1846–1850', *History of Education Society Bulletin*, 64 (1999) 91–101.

Willis, R. 'W.B.Hodgson and Educational Interest Groups in Victorian Britain', *History of Education Society Bulletin*, 67 (2001) 41–50.

Yeo, E.J. 'Social Motherhood and the Sexual Communion of Labour in British Social Science, 1850–1950', *Women's History Review*, 1 (1) (1992) 63–87.

Yeo, E.J. 'Gender and Class: Women's Languages of Power', *Labour History Review*, 60 (3) (1995) 15–22.

Chapters in Books

Aiken, L. 'Memoir of Miss Benger', Preface to Benger, E. *Memoirs of the Life of Anne Boleyn, Queen of Henry VIII* 3rd edition (London, Longman, Rees, Orme, Brown and Green, 1927).

Biklen, S.K. 'Feminism, Methodology and Point of View in the Study of Women Who Teach', in Yates, L. (eds) *Feminism and Education, Melbourne Studies in Education* (Bundoora: La Trobe University Press, 1993).

Bloomfield, A. ' "Mrs Roadknight Reports ... "': Jane Roadknight's Visionary Role in Transforming Elementary Education', in Hilton, M. and Hirsch, P. (eds) *Practical Visionaries: Women, Education and Social Progress 1790–1930* (London: Pearson, 2000).

Brehony, K. 'English Revisionist Froebelians and the Schooling of the Urban Poor', in Hilton, M. and Hirsch, P. (eds) *Practical Visionaries: Women, Education and Social Progress 1790–1930* (London: Longman, 2000).

Burdett, C. 'Eugenics. Introduction', in Bland, L. and Doan, L. (eds) *Uncensored. The Documents of Sexual Science* (London: Polity, 1998a).

Burdett, C. 'The Hidden Romance of Sexual Science: Eugenics, the Nation and the Making of Modern Feminism', in Bland, L. and Doan, L. (eds) *Sexology in Culture. Labeling Bodies and Desires* (London: Polity, 1998b).

Chalus, E. ' "That Epidemical Madness": Women and Electoral Politics in the Late Eighteenth Century', in Barker, H. and Chalus, E. (eds) *Gender in Eighteenth-Century England: Roles, Representations and Responsibilities* (London: Longman, 1997).

Chalus, E. ' "My Minerva at my Elbow": The Political Roles of Women in Eighteenth-Century England', in Taylor, S., Connors R. and Jones, C. (eds) *Hanoverian Britain and Empire: Essays in Memory of Philip Lawson* (Woodbridge: Boydell, 1998).

Clarke, K. 'Public and Private Education: Infant Education in the 1820s and 1930s', in Steedman, C., Urwin, C. and Walkerdine, V. (eds) *History Workshop Series. Language, Gender and Childhood* (London: Routledge and Kegan Paul, 1985).

Cooke, E. 'Introduction' to Pestalozzi, J.H. *How Gertrude Teaches her Children. An Attempt to help Mothers to Teach Their Own Children and an*

Account of the Method (London: Quantum House Reprints, 1966, trans. L.E. Holland and F.C. Turner, with introduction by Cooke, E. first published 1805).

Dendy, M. 'On the Training and Management of Feeble-Minded Children', Appendix to Lapage, C.P. *Feeble-mindedness in Children of School Age* (Manchester: Manchester University Press, 1911 (1920 edn)), appendix.

Dyhouse, C. 'Miss Buss and Miss Beale: Gender and Authority in the History of Education', in Hunt, F. (eds) *Lessons for Life: The Schooling of Girls and Women 1850–1950* (Oxford: Blackwell, 1987).

Eisenstein, H. 'Femocrats, Official Feminism and the Uses of Power', in Watson, S. (eds) *Playing the State* (London: Verso, 1990).

Gleadle, K. 'British Women and Radical Politics in the Late Nonconformist Enlightenment, c.1780–1830', in Vickery, A. (ed.) *Women, Privilege and Power. British Politics 1750 to the Present* (Stanford: Stanford University Press, 2001b).

Goodman, J. 'Women School Board Members and Women School Managers: the Structuring of Educational Authority in Manchester and Liverpool, 1870–1903', in Goodman, J. and Harrop, S. (eds) *Women, Educational Policy-Making and Administration in England: Authoritative Women since 1800* (London: Routledge, 2000b).

Goodman, J. ' "Their Market Value Must be Greater for the Experience They Have Gained": Secondary School Headmistresses and Empire 1897–1914', in Goodman, J. and Martin, J. (eds) *Gender, Colonialism and Education: The Politics of Experience* (London: Frank Cass, 2002).

Haggis, J. 'Good Wives and Mothers or Dedicated Workers: Contradictions of Domesticity in the Mission of Sisterhood, Travancore, South India', in Ram, K. and Jolly, M. (eds) *Maternities and Modernities: Colonial and Post-Colonial Experiences in Asia and the Pacific* (Cambridge: University Press, 1998).

Hilton, M. and Hirsch, P. (eds) 'Introduction', *Practical Visionaries: Women, Education and Social Progress 1790–1930* (London: Pearson, 2000).

Hogarth, S. and Marks, L. 'The Golden Narrative in British Medicine', in Greenhalgh T. and Hurwitz, B. (eds) *Narrative Based Medicine: Dialogue and Discourse in Clinical Practice* (London: BMJ Books, 1998).

Hunter, I. 'The Pastoral Bureaucracy: Towards a Less Principled Understanding of State Schooling', in Meredyth, D. and Tyler, D. (eds) *Child and Citizen: Genealogies of Schooling and Subjectivity* (Queensland: Griffith University, 1993).

Jackson, M. 'Institutional Provision for the Feeble-Minded in Edwardian England: Sandlebridge and the Scientific Morality of Permanent Care', in Wright, D. and Digby, A. (eds) *From Idiocy to Mental Deficiency: Historical Perspectives on People with Learning Disabilities* (London: Routledge, 1996).

Jackson, M. 'Images from the Past: Using Photographs', in Atkinson, D., Jackson, M. and Walmsley, J. (eds) *Forgotten Lives: Exploring the History of Learning Disability* (Kidderminster: Bild, 1997).

Johnson, R. 'Educating the Educators: "Experts" and the State 1833–9', in Donajgrodzki, A.P. (ed.) *Social Control in Nineteenth Century Britain* (London: Croom Helm, 1977).

Koven, S. 'Borderlands: Women, Voluntary Action and Child Welfare in Britain, 1840–1914', in Koven, S. and Michel, S. (eds) *Mothers of a New World: Maternalist Politics and the Origins of Welfare States* (London: Routledge, 1993a).

Koven, S. and Michel, S. 'Introduction: Mother Worlds', in Koven, S. and Michel, S. (eds) *Mothers of a New World: Maternalist Politics and the Origins of Welfare States* (London: Routledge, 1993b).

Marcus, J. 'Invincible Mediocrity: the Private Selves of Public Women', in Benstock, S. (ed.) *The Private Self: Theory and Practice of Women's Autobiographical Writings* (London: Routledge, 1988).

Marcus, L. *Auto/biographical Discourses* (Manchester: Manchester University Press, 1994).

Martin, J. ' "Women Not Wanted": the Fight to Secure Political Representation on Local Education Authorities', in Goodman, J. and Harrop, S. (eds) *Women, Educational Policy-Making and Administration in England: Authoritative Women since 1880* (London: Routledge, 2000b).

Mason, M.G. 'The Other Voice: Autobiographies of Women Writers', in Olney, J. (eds) *Autobiography: Essays Theoretical and Critical* (Princeton: Princeton University Press, 1980).

Passerini, L. 'Women's Personal Narratives: Myths, Experiences, and Emotions', in Personal Narratives Group (eds) *Interpreting Women's Lives: Feminist Theory and Personal Narratives* (Bloomington, IN: Indiana University Press, 1989).

Poovey, M. 'Figures of Arithmetic, Figures of Speech: the Discourse of Statistics', in Chandler, J., Davidson, A.I. and Harootunian, H. (eds) *Questions of Evidence: Proof, Practice, and Persuasion across the Disciplines* (Chicago and London: University of Chicago Press, 1994).

Prentice, A. 'Workers, Professionals, Pilgrims: Tracing Canadian Women Teachers' Histories', in Weiler, K. and Middleton, S. (eds) *Telling Women's Lives: Narrative Inquiries in the History of Women's Education* (Buckingham: Open University Press, 1999).

Rendall, J. 'Citizenship, Culture and Civilisation: the Languages of British Suffragists, 1866–74', in Daley, C. and Nolan, M. (eds) *Suffrage and Beyond: International Feminist Debates* (Auckland: Auckland University Press, 1994).

Rendall, J. 'Writing History for British Women: Elizabeth Hamilton and the *Memoirs of Agrippina*', in C. Campbell Orr (ed.) *Wollstonecraft's Daughters: Womanhood In England and France, 1780–1920* (Manchester: Manchester University Press, 1996), 79–93.

Richardson, S. ' "Well-Neighboured Houses": the Political Networks of Elite Women, 1780–1860', in Gleadle, K. and Richardson, S. (eds) *Women in British Politics, 1760–1860: The Power of the Petticoat* (London: Palgrave, 2000).

Roland Martin, J. 'Excluding Women from the Educational Realm', in Roland Martin, J. (ed.) *Changing the Educational Landscape: Philosophy, Women and the Curriculum* (New York: Routledge, 1994, first published, 1982).

Rousmaniere, K. 'Where Haley Stood: Margaret Haley, Teachers' Work and the Problem of Teacher Identity', in Weiler, K. and Middleton, S. (eds) *Telling Women's Lives: Narrative Inquiries in the History of Women's Education* (Buckingham: Open University Press, 1999).

Scott, J. 'Experience', in Butler, J. and Scott, J. (eds) *Feminists Theorize the Political* (London, Routledge, 1992).

Smith, B. 'J. Arthur Dendy', in *Australian Dictionary of Biography vol. 8* (Melbourne: Melbourne University Press, 1981) 279–80.

Spacks, P. 'Selves in Hiding', in Jelinek, E.C. (ed.) *Women's Autobiography* (Bloomington: Indiana University Press, 1980).

Stanley, L. 'Feminist Auto/biography and Feminist Epistemology', in Aaron, J. and Walby, S. (eds) *Out of the Margins. Women's Studies in the 90s* (Lewes: Falmer, 1988).

Stanley, L. 'From "Self-Made Women" to "Women's Made Selves"?', in Cosslett, T., Lury, C. and Summerfield, P. (eds) *Feminism and Autobiography: Text, Theories, Methods* (London: Routledge, 2000).

Steedman, C. 'Enforced Narratives: Stories of Another Self', in Cosslett, T., Lury, C. and Summerfield, P. (eds) *Feminism and Autobiography: Text, Theories, Methods* (London: Routledge, 2000).

Thane, P. 'Women in the British Labour Party and the Construction of State Welfare, 1906–1939', in Koven, S. and Michel, S. (eds) *Mothers of a New World: Maternalist Politics and the Origins of Welfare States* (London: Routledge, 1993).

Theobald, M. 'Teachers, Memory and Oral History', in Weiler, K. and Middleton, S. (eds) *Telling Women's Lives: Narrative Inquiries in the History of Women's Education* (Buckingham: Open University Press, 1999).

Turnbull, A. '"So Extremely Like Parliament": the Work of the Women Members of the London School Board, 1870–1904', in London Feminist History Group (eds) *The Sexual Dynamics of History. Men's Power, Women's Resistance* (London: Pluto, 1983).

Walkerdine, V. 'Femininity as Performance', in Stone, L. (eds) *The Education Feminism Reader* (New York: Routledge, 1994) 57–69.

Weiler, K. 'Reflections on Writing a History of Women Teachers', in Weiler, K. and Middleton, S. (eds) *Telling Women's Lives: Narrative Inquiries in the History of Women's Education* (Buckingham: Open University Press, 1999).

Wyse, T. 'On the Present State of Prussian Education', in *Central Society of Education, Third Publication, Papers* (Essex: Taylor and Walton, 1839, Woburn Reprint).

Books

Aldrich, R. and Gordon, P. *Dictionary of British Educationists* (London: Woburn Press, 1989).

Anderson, L. *Women and Autobiography in the Twentieth Century: Remembered Futures* (London: Prentice Hall, 1997).

Anderson, L. *Autobiography* (London: Routledge, 2001).

Annan, N. *The Dons* (London: Harper Collins, 2000).

Austin, S. *On National Education* (London: John Murray, 1839).

Austin, S. *Fragments from German Prose Writers* translated by Sarah Austin, illustrated with notes (London: John Murray, 1841).

Austin, S. *Germany, from 1760 to 1814; or Sketches of German Life, from the Decay of the Empire to the Expulsion of the French* (London: Longmans & Co., 1854).

Austin, S. *Two Letters on Girls Schools and on the Training of Working Women, with Additions* (London: Chapman Hall, 1857).

Autobiography of Mrs Fletcher with Letters and other Family Memorials, edited by the Survivor of her Family (Edinburgh: Edmonston and Douglas, 1876).

Bartley, P. *Prostitution: Prevention and Reform in England, 1860–1914* (London: Routledge, 2000).

Bateson, M. (eds) *Professional Women Upon their Professions* (London: Horace Cox, 1895).

Benger, E. *Memoirs of the Late Mrs Elizabeth Hamilton, with a Selection from her Correspondence and other Unpublished Writing* (London: Longman, Hurst, Rees, Orme and Brown, 1818).

Biklen, S.K. *School Work: Gender and the Cultural Construction of Teaching* (New York: Teachers College Press, 1985).

Bjorklund, D. *Interpreting the Self* (Chicago: Chicago University Press, 1998).

Blackmore, J. *Troubling Women, Feminism, Leadership and Educational Change* (Buckingham: Open University Press, 1999).

Blainey, C.A. *Centenary History of the University of Melbourne* (Melbourne: Melbourne University Press, 1957).

Brewer, W.V. *Victor Cousin as Comparative Educator* (New York: Teachers College Press, 1971).

Briar, C. *Working for Women? Gendered Work and Welfare Policies in Twentieth-Century Britain* (London: UCL Press, 1997).

Brodie, A. *The Scottish Enlightenment. An Anthology* (Edinburgh: Canongate, 1997).

Bryson, G. *Man and Society: the Scottish Inquiry of the 18th Century* (Princeton: Princeton University Press, 1945).

Burney, F. *Journals and Letters. Selected with an Introduction by Peter Sabor and Lars E. Troide* (Harmondsworth: Penguin, 2001).

Burstall, S.A. *Frances Mary Buss: An Educational Pioneer* (London: Society for the Promotion of Christian Knowledge, 1938).

Butler, J. *Gender Trouble* (London: Routledge, 1999 edn).

Caine, B. *English Feminism 1780–1980* (Oxford: Oxford University Press, 1997).

Chavannes, D.A. *Exposé de la Méthode Elémentaire de M.Pestalozzi* (Paris: Chez Levrault Schoell et Comp., 1805).

Cole, M. *Marriage Past and Present* (London: J.M. Dent and Sons, 1938).

Cole, M. *The Rate for the Job* (London: Fabian Publications, 1946).

Cole, M. *Women of Today* (London: Thomas Nelson and Sons, 1946 edn).

Cole, M. *Growing up into Revolution* (London: Longmans, Green & Company, 1949).

Cole, M. *Servant of the County* (London: Dennis Dobson, 1956).

Cole, M. *The Story of Fabian Socialism* (London: Mercury Books, 1961).

Cole, M. *The Life of G.D.H. Cole* (London: Macmillan, 1971).

Collini, S. *Public Moralists. Political Thought and Intellectual Life in Britain 1850–1950* (Oxford: Oxford University Press, 1993).

Colvin, C. (eds) *Maria Edgeworth in France and Switzerland: Selections from the Edgeworth Family Letters* (Oxford: Clarendon Press, 1979).

Connell, R.W. *Gender and Power* (Cambridge: Polity, 1987).

Connell, R.W. *Masculinity, Law and the Family* (London: Routledge, 1995).

Copelman, D. *London's Women Teachers: Gender, Class and Feminism* (London: Routledge, 1996).

Corbett, M.J. *Representing Femininity: Middle-Class Subjectivity in Victorian and Edwardian Women's Autobiographies* (Oxford: University Press, 1992).

Cosslett, T., Lury, C. and Summerfield, P. (eds) *Feminism and Autobiography* (London: Routledge, 2000).

Cousin, V. *Report on the State of Public Instruction in Prussia,* translated by S. Austin (London: Effingham Wilson, 1834), 2nd edition, 1836.

Cousin, V. *Report on the State of Public Instruction in Prussia,* translated by S. Austin (London: Effingham Wilson, 1834, American edition, ed. E.W. Knight, 1930).

Curtis, B. *True Government by Choice Men? Inspection, Education and State Formation in Canada West* (Toronto: University of Toronto Press, 1992).

Curtis, S.J. and Boultwood, M.E.A. *A Short History of Educational Ideas* (London: University Tutorial Press, 1953).

de Pange, V. *Le Plus Beau de Toutes Les Fêtes. Madame de Staël et Elisabeth Hervey, duchesse de Devonshire, d'après leur correspondance inedite 1804–1817* (Paris: Klincksieck, 1980).

de Staël, G. *Germany* [*De l'Allemagne*] translated From the French in three volumes (London: Murray, 1813).

Deane, S. *The French Revolution and Enlightenment in England, 1789–1832* (Cambridge Mass.: Harvard University Press, 1988).

Dolan, B. *Ladies of the Grand Tour* (London: Harper Collins, 2001).

Dyhouse, C. *Girls Growing Up in Victorian and Edwardian England* (London: Routledge and Kegan Paul, 1981).

Dyhouse, C. *No Distinction of Sex? Women in British Universities 1870–1939* (London: UCL Press, 1995).

Eisenstein, H. *Gender Shock: Practising Feminism on Two Continents* (Sydney: Allen and Unwin, 1991).

Finn, M. *After Chartism: Class and Nation in English Radical Politics, 1848–1874* (Cambridge: Cambridge University Press, 1993).

Frank, K. *Lucie Duff Gordon: A Passage to Egypt* (London: Hamish Hamilton, 1994).

Gautrey, T. *'Lux Mihi Laus': School Board Memories* (London: Link House n.d.).

Gleadle, K. and Richardson, S. (eds) *Women in British Politics, 1760–1860: The Power of the Petticoat* (London: Macmillan, 2000).

Gleadle, K. *British Women in the Nineteenth Century* (London: Palgrave, 2001a).

Gordon, P. and White, J. *Philosophers as Educational Reformers: the Influence of Idealism in British Educational Thought and Practice* (London: Routledge and Kegan Paul, 1979).

Green, A. *Education and State Formation. The Rise of Education Systems in England, France and the USA* (London: Macmillan, 1990).

Grewal, I. *Home and Harem: Nation, Gender, Empire and the Cultures of Travel* (Leicester: Leicester University Press, 1996).

Griffiths, M. *Feminism and the Self. The Web of Identity* (London: Routledge, 1995).

Hamburger, L. and J. *Troubled Lives: John and Sarah Austin* (Toronto: University of Toronto Press, 1985).

Hamburger, L. and J. *Contemplating Adultery: the Secret Life of a Victorian Woman* (Basingstoke: Macmillan, 1991).

Hamilton, E. *Translation of the Letters of a Hindoo Rajah: Written Previous to and During the Period of His Residence in England: to Which is Prefixed a Preliminary Dissertation on the History, Religion and Manners of the Hindoos*, 2 vols (London: G.G. & J. Robinson, 1796).

Hamilton, E. *Memoirs of Modern Philosophers*, 3 vols (Bath: R. Cruttwell, 1800).

Hamilton, E. *Letters on the Elementary Principles of Education*, 1st edn, vol. 1 (Bath: R. Cruttwell, 1801); vol. 2 (Bath: R. Cruttwell, 1802).

Hamilton, E. *Memoirs of the Life of Agrippina, the Wife of Germanicus*, 3 vols (Bath: R. Cruttwell, 1804).

Hamilton, E. *Letters Addressed to the Daughter of a Nobleman, on the Formation of Religious and Moral Principles*, 2 vols (London: R. Cadell and W. Davies, 1806).

Hamilton, E. *The Cottagers of Glenburnie: A Tale for the Farmer's Ingle-nook* (Edinburgh: Manners and Miller, and S.Cheyne; London: T. Cadell, W. Davies and William Miller, 1808).

Hamilton, E. *Exercises in Religious Knowledge; for the Instruction of Young Persons* (Edinburgh: Manners and Miller; London: T.Cadell and W.Davies, 1809).

Hamilton, E. *A Series of Popular Essays: Illustrative of Principles Connected with the Improvement of Understanding*, 2 vols (Edinburgh: Manners and Miller; London: Longman, Hurst, Rees, Orme and Brown; and T. Cadell and W. Davies, 1813).

Hamilton, E. *Hints Addressed to the Patrons and Directors of Schools* (London: Longman, 1815a).

Hamilton, E. *Examples of Questions Calculated to Excite and Exercise the Infant Mind* (London: Longman, 1815b).

Hannam, J. and Hunt, K. *Socialist Women Britain, 1880s to 1920s* (London: Routledge, 2002).

Hans, N. *Comparative Education: a Study of Educational Factors and Traditions* (London: Routledge and Kegan Paul, 1949).

Hare, A.J.C. *The Life and Letters of Maria Edgeworth*, 2 vols (London: Edward Arnold, 1894).

Harris, J. *Private Lives, Public Spirit: Britain 1870–1914* (Harmondsworth: Penguin, 1993).

Harrison, B. *Prudent Revolutionaries. Portrait of British Feminists Between the Wars* (Oxford: Clarendon Press, 1987).

Heafford, M.R. *Pestalozzi* (London: Methuen, 1967).

Heilbrun, C.G. *Writing a Woman's Life* (London: The Women's Press, 1989).

Herold, J.C. *Mistress to an Age. A Life of Madame de Stael* (London: Hamish Hamilton, 1959).

Hollis, P. *Ladies Elect. Women in English Local Government 1865–1914* (Clarendon: Oxford, 1987).

Horner, L. *On the State of Education in Holland as Regards Schools for the Working Classes and for the Poor by M. Cousin translated with Preliminary Observations on the Necessity of Legislative Measures to Extend and Improve Education among the Working Classes and the Poor in Great Britain: and on the Course most Advisable to Pursue at the Present Time* (London: Murray, 1838).

Hunt, F. *Gender and Policy in English Education, 1902–1944* (Hemel Hempstead: Harvester Wheatsheaf, 1991).

Hunter, I. *Rethinking the School. Subjectivity, Bureaucracy, Criticism* (New South Wales: Allen and Unwin, 1994).

Hutcheson, F. *A Short Introduction to Moral Philosophy in Three Books Containing the Elements of Ethics and the Law of Nature, translated from the Latin* (Glasgow: R. & A. Foulis, 1772, 4th edn).

Isbell, J.C. *The Birth of European Romanticism. Truth and Propaganda in Staël's De l'Allemagne', 1810–1813* (Cambridge: Cambridge University Press, 1994).

Jackson, M. *The Borderland of Imbecility. Medicine, Society and the Fabrication of the Feeble Mind in late Victorian and Edwardian England* (Manchester: Manchester University Press, 2000).

Jameson, A. *Sisters of Charity and the Community of Labour* (London: Longman, 1859).

Jullien, M.A. *Précis sur l'Institut d'Éducation d'Yverdon* (Milan, 1810).

Jullien, M.A. *Esprit de la Méthode d'Éducation de M.Pestalozzi* (Milan, 1812).

Kay-Shuttleworth, J. *Four Periods of Public Education as Reviewed in 1832–1839–1846–1862* (London: Longman, Green, Longman & Roberts, 1862).

Keane, A. *Women Writers and the English Nation in the 1790s: Romantic Belongings* (Cambridge: Cambridge University Press, 2000).

Kelly, A. *The Missing Half: Girls and Science and Education* (Manchester: Manchester University Press, 1981).

Kelly, G. *Women, Writing and Revolution, 1790–1827* (Oxford: Clarendon Press, 1993).

Kenney, R. *Westering* (London: Dent, 1939).

Kerckhoff, A.C., Fogelman, K., Crook, D. and Reeder, D. *Going Comprehensive in England and Wales: A Study of Uneven Change* (London: Woburn Press, 1996).

Kidd, C. *Subverting Scotland's Past: Scottish Whig Historians and the Creation of an Anglo-British Identity, 1689–1830* (Cambridge: Cambridge University Press, 1993).

Kramer, R. *Maria Montessori* (Oxford: Blackwell, 1976).

Lapage, C. *Feeble-Mindedness in Children of School-Age* (Manchester: Manchester University Press, 1910, 2nd edn, 1920).

Lawrence, E. *Friedrich Froebel and English Education* (London: Routledge and Kegan Paul, 1952).

Lerner, G. *The Creation of Patriarchy* (Oxford: Oxford University Press, 1986).

Levine, P. *Victorian Feminism 1850–1900* (London: Hutchinson, 1987).

Lewis, J. *Women and Social Action in Victorian and Edwardian England* (Aldershot: Elgar, 1991).

Liebschner, J. *Foundations of Progressive Education: the History of the National Froebel Society* (Cambridge: Lutterworth Press, 1991).

Lister, R. *Citizenship: Feminist Perspectives* (London: Macmillan, 1997).

Liu, A. *Wordsworth, The Sense of History* (Stanford: Stanford University Press, 1989).

Lovenduski, J. and Norris, P. (eds) *Women in Politics* (Oxford: Oxford University Press, 1996).

Maclure, J.S. *Educational Documents England and Wales 1816–1963* (London: Chapman & Hall, 1965).

Maclure, S.A. *History of Education in London 1870–1990* (London: Allen Lane, 1990).

Mansell, P. *Paris Between Empires 1814–1852* (London: John Murray, 2001).

Marcus, L. *Auto/biographical Discourses. Theory, Criticism, Practice* (Manchester: Manchester University Press, 1994).

Martin, J. *Women and the Politics of Schooling in Victorian and Edwardian England* (Leicester: Leicester University Press, 1999).

Martineau, H. *Household Education* (London: E. Moricon, 1848).

Martineau, H. *Autobiography*, vol. 1 (London: Smith, Elder and Co, 3rd edn, 1877; Virago reprint ed. G. Weiner, 1983).

Maynes, M.J. *Schooling in Western Europe: A Social History* (Albany: State University of New York Press, 1985).

McCann, P. and Young, F.A. *Samuel Wilderspin and the Infant School Movement* (London: Croom Helm, 1982).

McCosh, J. *The Scottish Philosophy from Hutcheson to Balfour* (New York: R. Carter & Brothers, 1975; London: MacMillan, 1975).

McKinnon, A. *Love and Freedom: Professional Women and the Reshaping of Personal Life* (Cambridge: Cambridge University Press, 1997).

McLachlan, H. *Records of a Family 1800–1933, Pioneers in Education, Social Service and Liberal Religion* (Manchester: Manchester University Press, 1935).

Miller, J. *School for Women* (London: Virago, 1986).

Miller, N. *Getting Personal. Feminist Occasions and Other Autobiographical Acts* (London: Routledge, 1991).

Miller, P. *Transformations of Patriarchy in the West, 1500–1900* (Bloomington: Indiana University Press, 1998).

Mills, C.W. *The Sociological Imagination* (Harmondsworth: Penguin, 1970).

Mitchison, M. *You May Well Ask. A Memoir 1920–1940* (London: Victor Gollancz Ltd, 1979).

Montessori, M. *The Montessori Method: Scientific Pedagogy as Applied to Child Education in 'The Children's Houses'*, trans. Anne. E. George (London: Heinemann, 1920).

More, H. *Strictures on the Modern System of Female Education: The Works of Hannah More*, vol. 111 (London: H. Fisher, R. Fisher and P. Jackson, 1838).

Mulvaney, D.J.and Calaby, J.H. *So Much that is New. Baldwin Spencer, 1860–1929, A Biography* (Melbourne: University of Melbourne Press, 1985).

Oram, A. *Women Teachers and Feminist Politics, 1900–1939* (Manchester: Manchester University Press, 1996).

Orville Taylor, J. *Digest of M. Victor Cousin's Report on the State of Public Instruction in Prussia, also the Organisation and Administration of the School System of the State of New York, Taken from the Report of the Superintendent of Common Schools of 1836* (Albany: Packard and Van Benthuysen, 1836).

Pascal, R. *Design and Truth in Autobiography* (London: Routledge and Kegan Paul, 1960).

Pestalozzi, J.H. *Leonard and Gertrude* (Boston: D.C. Heath, 1907, trans. and abridged by E. Channing, first published 1805).

Pestalozzi, J.H. *How Gertrude Teaches her Children. An Attempt to help Mothers to Teach their Own Children and an Account of the Method* (London: Quantum House Reprints, 1966, trans. L.E. Holland and F.C. Turner, ed. with introduction by E. Cooke, first published 1805).

Peterson, L.H. *Traditions of Victorian Women's Autobiography: the Poetics and Politics of Life Writing* (Virginia: University Press of Virginia, 1999).

Poovey, M. *Making a Social Body* (Chicago: Chicago University Press, 1995).

Price, M. and Glenday, N. *Reluctant Revolutionaries: a Century of Headmistresses 1874–1974* (Bath: Pitman, 1974).

Pugh, M. *The March of the Women. A Revisionist Analysis of the Campaign for Women's Suffrage, 1866–1914* (Oxford: Oxford University Press, 2000).

Pugh, P. *Women and the Women's Movement in Britain 1914–1959* (London: Macmillan, 1992).

Raikes, E. *Dorothea Beale of Cheltenham* (London: Constable, 1910 edn).

Rendall, J. *The Origins of the Scottish Enlightenment, 1707–1776* (London: Macmillan, 1978).

Rendall, J. *The Origins of Modern Feminism: Women in Britain, France and the United States, 1780–1860* (London: Macmillan, 1985).

Richter, M. *The Politics of Conscience. T.H. Green and His Age* (Cambridge, Massachusetts: Harvard University Press, 1964).

Riley, D. *'Am I That Name?' Feminism and the Category of 'Women' in History* (London: Macmillan, 1988).

Robson, J.M. and Stillinger, J. (eds) *Autobiography and Literary Essays by John Stuart Mill* (Toronto: University of Toronto Press, 1981).

Rose, M.R. *Darwin's Spectre: Evolutionary Biology in the Modern World* (Princeton: Princeton University Press, 1998).

Ross, J. *Three Generations of Englishwomen: Memoirs and Correspondence of Mrs John Taylor, Mrs Sarah Austin and Lady Duff Gordon*, 2 vols (London: Murray, 1888).

Ross, J. *The Fourth Generation: Reminiscences by Janet Ross* (London: Constable, 1912).

Rousseau, J.J. *Émile où l'Education* (London: Dent, 1911, first published 1762).

Rousseau, J.J. *Social Contract: Essays by Locke, Hume and Rousseau* (London: Oxford University Press, 1946, first published 1762).

Rousseau, J.J. *Julie, où la nouvelle Héloïse. Lettres de deux amants, habitants d'une petite ville au pied des Alpes etc.* (Paris: Gallimard, 1961, first published 1761).

Sabor and Troide (eds) *Journals and Letters by Fanny Burney* (USA: Penguin, 2001).

Sapiro, S. *A Vindication of Political Virtue: the Political Theory of Mary Wollstonecraft* (Chicago: University of Chicago Press, 1992).

Savage, M., Barlow, J., Dickens, P. and Fielding, T. *Property, Bureaucracy and Culture: Middle Class Formation in Contemporary Britain* (London: Routledge, 1992).

Scott, J. and Griff, C. *Directors of Industry* (Cambridge: Polity Press, 1984).

Selleck, D. *James Kay Shuttleworth. Journey of an Outsider* (Essex: Woburn, 1994).

Shakeshaft, C. *Women in Educational Administration* (London: Sage, 1989).

Shonfield, Z. *The Precariously Privileged* (Oxford: Oxford University Press, 1987).

Showalter, E. *A Literature of Their Own: British Women Novelists from Bronte to Lessing* (London: Virago, 1988).

Silber, K. *Pestalozzi: The Man and His Work* (London: Routledge and Kegan Paul, 1960).

Simon, B. *The Politics of Educational Reform 1920–1940* (London: Lawrence and Wishart, 1974a).

Simon, B. *The Two Nations and the Educational Structure, 1780–1870* (London: Lawrence & Wishart, 1974b).

Simon, B. *In Search of a Grandfather Henry Simon of Manchester, 1835–1899* (Leicester: The Pendene Press, 1997).

Simon, J. *Shena Simon: Feminist and Educationist. Based on the Correspondence and Writings of Lady Simon of Wythenshawe* (privately printed, 1986).

Simon, S.D. *A Century of City Government* (London: George Allen & Unwin, 1938).

Smart, R. *On Others' Shoulders: An Illustrated History of the Polhill and Lansdowne Colleges, now De Montfort University Bedford* (Bedford: Steven-Howard Press, 1994).

Squires, P. *Anti-Social Policy. Welfare, Ideology and the Disciplinary State* (London: Harvester Wheatsheaf, 1990).

Stanley, L. *The Life and Death of Emily Wilding Davison* (London: The Women's Press, 1988).

Stanley, L. 'Feminist Auto/biography and Feminist Epistemology', in Aaron, J. and Walby, S. (eds) *Out of the Margins. Women's Studies in the 90s* (Lewes: Falmer Press, 1991).

Stanley, L. *The Auto/biographical 'I': the Theory and Practice of Feminist Auto/biography* (Manchester: Manchester University Press, 1992).

Stedman Jones, G. *Outcast London: a Study in the Relationship Between Classes in Victorian Society* (Harmondsworth: Penguin, 1992 edn).

Steedman, C. *Landscape for a Good Woman: A Study of Two Lives* (London: Virago, 1986).

Steedman, C. *Childhood, Culture and Class in Britain: Margaret McMillan 1860–1931* (London: Virago, 1990).

Stewart, D. *Elements of the Philosophy of the Human Mind*, 3 vols (Edinburgh, Dublin, 1792).

Stewart, W.A.C. *Progressives and Radicals in English Education, 1750–1970* (New Jersey: Kelly, 1972).

Stocks, M. *Ernest Simon of Manchester* (Manchester: Manchester University Press, 1963).

Strachey, R. *The Cause* (London: Virago, 1988 edn).

Sutherland, G. *Ability, Merit and Measurement: Mental Testing and English Education, 1880–1940* (Oxford: Clarendon, 1984).

Talbot, M. *Edouard Seguin: A Study of an Educational Approach to the Treatment of Mentally Defective Children* (New York: Teachers College Press, 1964).

Thomson, M. *The Problem of Mental Deficiency: Eugenics, Democracy and Social Policy in Britain, c.1870–1959* (Oxford: Oxford Historical Monographs, 1998).

Tytler, A. Lord Woodhouseless, *Memoirs of the Life and Writings of the Honourable Henry Home of Kames* (Edinburgh: 1807).

van Drenth, A. and de Haan, F. *The Rise of Caring Power: Elizabeth Fry and Josephine Butler in Britain and the Netherlands* (Amsterdam: Amsterdam University Press, 1999).

Vernon, C. *Margaret Cole, 1893–1908. A Political Biography* (London: Croom Helm, 1986).

Vicinus, M. *Independent Women: Work and Community for Single Women, 1850–1920* (London: Virago, 1985).

Walkerdine, V. *Schoolgirl Fictions* (London: Verso, 1990).

Walkowitz, J. *City of Dreadful Delight: Narratives of Sexual Danger in Late-Victorian London* (London: Virago, 1996).

Watts, R. *Gender, Power and the Unitarians in England, 1760–1860* (London: Longman, 1998b).

Webb, B. *My Apprenticeship* (London: Longmans, Green and Co, 1938 edn).

Winzer, M. *The History of Special Education: From Isolation to Integration* (Washington: Gallaudet University Press, 1993).

Woolf, V. *Three Guineas* (London: Hogarth Press, 1986 edn).

Zedner, L. *Women Crime and Custody in England* (Oxford: Clarendon Press, 1991).

Unpublished Papers

Goodman, J. ' "Called to Their Patriotic Duty": English Women Educationists, Economic Humanism and Educational Authority, 1798–1805, Unpublished paper, ISCHE, San Paolo, 2003.

Harrop, S. 'Faith Above Faction: the Role of Religious Affiliation in the Foundation and Growth of Liverpool's Higher Education Institutions in the Late Nineteenth Century', Unpublished paper, ISCHE, Dublin, 1997.

Martin, J. 'The Origins and Development of Gendered Schooling in Nineteenth Century England', Unpublished M.A., University of Warwick, 1987.

Rendall, J. Gender and the Legacies of the Scottish Enlightenment. John Millar, Dugald Stewart & Elizabeth Hamilton: Adapting the Legacy, Institute of Historical Research, 2002.

Weiner, G. 'Disrupting Autobiographical Narratives: Method, Interpretation and the Role of Gender', Unpublished paper presented at the ISCHE symposium, 19th International Congress of Historical Sciences, Oslo, Norway, 2001.

Unpublished Theses

Butcher, B.W. 'Darwinism and Australia 1836–1914', Unpublished PhD, University of Melbourne, 1992.

Russell, R. 'Women of the Scottish Enlightenment: Their Importance to the History of Scottish Education', Unpublished PhD, University of Glasgow, 1988.

Weiner, G. 'Controversies and Contradictions: Approaches to the Study of Harriet Martineau, 18-2-76', Unpublished PhD, Open University, 1991.

Index

ɔ